On the Margins of Protection

ON THE MARGINS OF PROTECTION

CHALLENGING THE DISCOURSE ON THE REFUGEE CRISIS

Edited by

PAULA BANERJEE

Orient BlackSwan

ON THE MARGINS OF PROTECTION: CHALLENGING THE DISCOURSE ON THE REFUGEE CRISIS

ORIENT BLACKSWAN PRIVATE LIMITED

Registered Office
3-6-752 Himayatnagar, Hyderabad 500 029, Telangana, India
e-mail: centraloffice@orientblackswan.com

Other Offices
Bengaluru, Chennai, Guwahati, Hyderabad,
Kolkata, Mumbai, New Delhi, Noida, Patna

First published by Orient Blackswan Private Limited 2025

ISBN 978-93-5442-589-9

040884

Typeset in
Goudy Oldstyle Std 11/13
by Manmohan Kumar, Delhi

Printed in India at
Avantika Printers Private Limited, New Delhi 110020

Published by
Orient Blackswan Private Limited
3-6-752 Himayatnagar, Hyderabad 500 029, Telangana, India
e-mail: info@orientblackswan.com

This volume is dedicated to the memory of **Ilina Sen**, *a woman who lived her life with great courage and great generosity*

CONTENTS

Abbreviations

AAPSU	All Arunachal Pradesh Students' Union
AKP	Adalet ve Kalkinma Partisi (or Justice and Development Party)
C-BED	Community-Based Enterprise Development
CEAS	Common European Asylum System
CRC	Convention on the Rights of the Child
CRRF	Comprehensive Refugee Response Framework
DWEP	Domestic Workers Empowerment Programme
EC	European Commission
ECR	emigration clearance required
EU	European Union
FY	Fiscal Year
ICCPR	International Covenant on Civil and Political Rights
ICE	Immigration and Customs Enforcement (US)
ILO	International Labour Organisation
IOM	International Organisation for Migration
IDPs	Internally Displaced Persons
KE	Kasergode Embassy
LDCs	Least Developed Countries
LTTE	Liberation Tigers of Tamil Eelam
MDCs	More Developed Countries
MWEP	Migrant Women Empowerment Programme
NEFA	North East Frontier Agency
NGOs	Non-governmental Organisations
NHRC	National Human Rights Commission
OEC	Overseas Employment Certificate
OECD	Organisation of Economic Co-operation and Development
OHCHR	Office of the United Nations High Commissioner for Human Rights

OSCE	Organization for Security and Co-operation in Europe
PIL	Public Interest Litigation
PLO	Palestine Liberation Organization
POEA	Philippine Overseas Employment Administration
R2P	Responsibility to Protect
SAR	Search and rescue
TESDA	Technical Education Skills Development Authority
UDHR	Universal Declaration of Human Rights
UN	United Nations
UNHCR	United Nations High Commissioner for Refugees
UNRWA	United Nations Relief and Works Agency

Acknowledgements

This book is the product of an unlikely friendship. Ilina-di and I bonded over cups of tea while waiting for checkups at the Tata Memorial Hospital in Mumbai. In those poignant waiting moments, we spoke of everything under the sun but our illness. By that time Ilina-di was a close associate of the Calcutta Research Group (CRG), an extraordinary motley group of scholars, journalists, and lawyers that provided me and others, including Ilina-di, sustenance and respite from the Bengali's greatest passion—health. CRG and its leader, Ranabir Samaddar, created this safe space for us to come together, talk research projects, and discuss our challenges without ever discussing careers. When I was planning this volume, it was done with Ranabir-da's prodding and Ilina-di's support, and I remain so grateful for that. Ilina-di, on listening to my ramblings about the project, immediately agreed to give us a chapter for the volume, but sadly, even before we could discuss it at length, she was no longer with us.

The volume was made possible because of a CRG conference held with UNHCR support on a thorough discussion on the newly drafted Global Compact for Refugees and the Global Compact on Migration. Always known for their critical thinking, CRG members and associates took upon themselves the task of drafting a South Asian Response to the Global Compacts, and came out with the now well-known Kolkata Declaration. This book is a treatise on the thoughts and critiques that percolated from that conference. Although the chapters were written a few years ago, as the Covid-19 pandemic happened in between, most of the thinking behind this volume is not just contemporary but also perhaps perennial. Among the CRG members with whom I collaborated and discussed the project at length were Ranabir Samaddar, Sabyasachi Basu Ray Chowdhury, and Byasdev Dasgupta. When the task of publication was embarked upon, Roopa Sharma from Orient BlackSwan, who became a friend over the course of this book, stepped in energetically. But alas, Covid put a stop to all publications. We came out of it, but not unscathed. Roopa passed on the task to Asmita Choudhury and then Proteeti Banerjee stepped in. I am grateful to all of them for never losing hope that the book is needed. I can say with confidence that readers will find the job well done, and so I remain grateful to the entire team.

I am also grateful to all the authors. Their friendship was sorely tested as the project kept being delayed. But not one of them pulled their papers out from the volume. For this project, we had a series of research assistants. Preeshita Biswas helped us with the first draft and then left to pursue her Ph.D. in the United States. There were others who kept making corrections and changes to the project until Rituparna Dutta took it up in her firm hands. Polite to a fault, almost, her diligence is something that I always admired over the years. I also remain grateful to Priya Singh, who brought the work of addressing queries so ably to its much-needed conclusion. My sister Purna, always a compatriot, filled in the gaps with her comments, suggestions, and changes where required.

As this project continued for some time, I took up new jobs. As the IDRC Chair Professor at AIT, I am obliged to manage a number of things. Neither my colleagues in AIT nor those in IDRC stopped supporting when I pushed my own concerns to the forefront. I thank all of them for their unstinted support, and Edgard and Roula for their unconditional friendship. Over and above my CRG colleagues, friends and associates such as Nasreen, Samata, Sucharita, Sumona, and many others have always been sources of encouragement and camaraderie. Over and above, it is Ilina-di's friendship and the memory of this extraordinary person that I want to celebrate with zest, as she lived her life with passion and fortitude.

This work was conceived in friendship and my work continues due to it. For any omission and commission, it is despite all the help and support I got from friends, *mea culpa*.

INTRODUCTION

PAULA BANERJEE

In the summer of 2015, commonly referred to as the summer of migrations, Europe witnessed a 'troubling' phenomenon. Thousands of desperate Syrian refugees were trying to reach the borders of Europe. Coming on the heels of the spectre of African 'boat people', frantic to move to Europe, the deluge of Syrian refugees caused a sense of horror among the Atlantic countries and was internationally termed a 'crisis'. It is said that 'the number of African migrants crossing the Mediterranean had been rising since the Arab Spring and the fall of Libyan leader Muammar Gaddafi. But the scale of the 2015 influx, its intensity and the resultant media attention caught governments and policymakers off guard.'[1] This European crisis resulted in a revaluation of the refugee management paradigm and gave birth to two Global Compacts, of which one befell the refugees and the other descended on the migrants. Our collection of essays is a response to the Global Compact. This anthology is a product of year-long deliberations, driven by the United Nations High Commissioner for Refugees (UNHCR) on the Global Compact on Refugees.

Apparently, the year 2015 was so eventful and packed with so much on the 'westward'-movement-of-refugees front that the UNHCR created a special section on its website dedicated to reportage on these events.[2] A brief sample of the reports on the UNHCR website is as follows:

> 600 fleeing refugees drowned in the depths of the Mediterranean Sea when the boat that they were travelling in turned upside down shortly before midnight on April 18. The incident took place in the waters off the Libyan coast, around 180 kilometres south of Italy. An Italian cum Maltese rescue operation could only rescue 50 of

> an estimated 700 people who had been originally on the vessel. It was stated that overcrowding was the principal factor leading to the boats capsizing.[3]

These reports, however, neglected to address the fact that desperate Africans or Syrians were trying to reach Europe, and that there was no safe passage for them to do so. Grappling with the fear of being intercepted on high seas, they travelled in unsafe boats or dinghies, in the middle of the night, to somehow reach Europe. Yet, their vessels often capsized on the way. Thus, the reason for the deaths of these Africans or Syrians was not only over-crowded boats, but also the constant fear and desperation that blanketed their exile on high seas.

Such events led to what has been termed the summer of migration. There are other sources that contend that the mayhem and death were of much greater proportions during that dreaded summer. One source cites the death of 3,770 migrants trying to cross the Mediterranean in 2015.[4] These mixed and massive flows of people towards Europe had serious aftermaths. The migration of these post-colonial people—who are racially different, several practising a different religion, and all without any tangible resources—created a perception of crisis in Europe. However, this crisis completely overlooked the fact that many more refugees had been accommodated within the continents of Africa and Asia in the last decades than anywhere else in the world. Furthermore, what was also slighted was the fact that these refugees, seemingly so threatening, habitually brought along with their bare bodies a wealth of skills, decency, plurality, and a corpus of knowledge that are all required for sustainable development. It has to be noted that often, crisis happens not when thousands are displaced from the underdeveloped, post-colonial countries because of policies undertaken in the developed world, but when these same displaced individuals begin to appear on the borders of these developed countries for sheer survival.

The European refugee crisis of 2015 simply refers to a series of political events where, by the count of such institutions as the Pew Research Centre, about 1.3 million refugees sought asylum in the 28 member states of the European Union, plus Norway and Switzerland. This was double the previous record of 700,000 set in 1992 when the Iron Curtain collapsed.[5] Of course, as already acknowledged, the primary drivers for this record number of refugees were the ongoing civil war in Syria, where a number of developed countries have a stake, as well as the ongoing violence and threats from the equally ravaged regions of Afghanistan and Iraq. Apart from these so-called 'distressing nations', the problems in Eritrea and increasing poverty in Kosovo were also contributing factors, albeit minor ones. A BBC news report concludes that 1,011,700 migrants arrived by sea in 2015, and almost 34,900 by land.[6] It is perhaps ironic for students of history that Germany was the most popular place for asylum applications, with Hungary a distant second. Predictably, a large number of setbacks and problems befell the fleeing refugees in many instances. The UNHCR reflected on how the matter revealed the desperation of people seeking a protected life in Europe, and urged a close coordination between European police forces, international organisations, and security agencies to deal with the situation. However, 'the refugee and migrant crisis has been one of the most important and divisive issues in recent European politics.'[7]

All such journeys undertaken by these impoverished people were in search of a protected life for themselves and their families. However, often the situation would turn out to be the deadliest time for many of them. Most of those attempting to reach Europe from Africa would reach Italy, and those from Turkey and Syria tried for one of the islands of Kos, Chios, Lesvos, or Samos in Greece, often in rubber dinghies or small wooden boats while navigating killing waters. In September 2015, the lone figure of a young Syrian boy, Aylan Kurdi, washed up on a Turkish beach following a failed attempt to reach Greece, and caused widespread sadness and horror. Arab news reported:

> Three-year-old Aylan Kurdi, together with his older brother and his mother, died from drowning. The Kurdi family were Syrian Kurds trying to reach Europe amid the refugee crisis of 2015. Their ancestral town Kobani was devastated by battles between Kurdish

fighters and Daesh, which had set up a proto-state spanning the Syria-Iraq border.[8]

The horrific image of Aylan Kurdi's lifeless body suddenly brought the plight of refugees to the centre-stage for a time. By the time Aylan lost his life in 2015, 300,000 people had attempted to flee to Europe, with over 2,600 dying in these attempts. Even when they reached Europe, they had to face several problems. For example, in the month of September 2015, the Hungarian government suddenly decided to not provide trains to Austria or Germany, leading to 1,000 refugees marching out of Budapest towards the Austrian border in protest. As a mark of basic decency, ordinary people gave the dehydrated and starved refugees water and food. The decision to stop trains was overturned by the Hungarian government, but only for this one occasion. By and large, in September, a lot of European countries had reinstated border controls, with Hungary erecting a fence along the Serbian border. This move came after twenty years of the promise of 'open borders' within the European Union. The UNHCR warned at the time that refugees would probably find themselves wandering everywhere in 'a legal limbo', and that there was an urgent need to establish a comprehensive European response, instead of the differential border control measures that various European states were introducing.[9]

The European reaction to the influx of refugees generated a perception of a worldwide refugee 'crisis', and created a context for revisiting the global protection mechanism for refugees and migrants as enshrined in the UN Refugee Convention of 1951 and the UN Protocol of 1967. Under the aegis of the UN, two new Global Compacts were discussed. On 19 September 2016, the United Nations General Assembly adopted the New York Declaration for Refugees and Migrants. It set in motion a complex negotiation process which culminated by September 2018 in the 'Global Compact on Safe, Orderly and Regular Migration' and the 'Global Compact on Refugees'. In adopting the New York Declaration for Refugees and Migrants, the 193 UN Member States recognised the need for a comprehensive approach to human mobility and enhanced cooperation on a global level.

It was a landmark political declaration, directed at improving the way in which the international community has hitherto responded to large movements of refugees and migrants, and to protracted refugee situations. However, also noticeable is the fact that the Declaration envisaged the Global Compact being developed through an open, transparent, and inclusive process of consultations and negotiations, and the effective participation of various relevant stakeholders, including, among others, the private sector, parliaments, and the diaspora communities. The Global Compact also set out a Comprehensive Refugee Response Framework (CRRF), with specific actions needed to ease pressure on host countries, enhance refugee self-reliance, expand access to third-country solutions, and support conditions in countries of origin for return in safety and with dignity.

The Global Compact proposed a multi-stakeholder process for taking care of the refugees, which was based on partnership between civil society, governments, policymakers, faith-based organisations, media, multinationals, and intellectuals. The Global Compact is one reality, but the other reality for refugees is much starker and consists of closing the state borders, increasing protracted refugee situations, mounting number of deaths in the high seas, growing racism, cumulative environmental degradation, and decreasing healthcare or any support for average individuals, but particularly for the displaced—a reality that this pandemic brought to the fore. When posited against the construction of fences by states to prevent refugees from coming in, the closing of borders, and acts of intercepting, detaining, and returning refugees, the Global Compact seems well-intentioned but lacking in enforceability. This is because even though it speaks of multi-stakeholder solutions, in the end it still depends on convincing states to protect refugees, when it is these states that have failed to protect them in the first place.

One very significant purpose for the Global Compact was arguably to make refugees more self-reliant so that they can reap developmental dividends for the host country. According to one South Asian expert, the declaration was 'unambiguous in linking the question of protecting the migrants and refugees with a global development agenda'.[10] The Global Compact urges the fostering of 'inclusive economic growth for host communities and refugees, in support of host countries and subject to their relevant national laws and policies, States and relevant stakeholders'.[11] However, the UN bodies had to work against the widespread scare that the refugees would impose an enormous strain on the resources of the European countries, which might eventually destroy their economy. Nevertheless, the flip side of such an insistent claim that they are economic burdens on the host countries may force refugees to take up vocations that they may not want or be suited to. The refugees then become modern-day serfs, forced into joining the labour force for which they are either over-qualified or unsuited. The problem that arose then and still persists is not about the economic health of Europe. Yet, as Sebastien Dullien notes, in many European countries,

> the refugee inflow has strengthened right-wing, xenophobic, and anti-EU parties. In Germany's March 2016 elections, the anti-immigration party Alternative for Germany (AfD) entered all three regional parliaments that held a vote. In countries such as Poland and France, the mere prospect of larger refugee inflows has fuelled a growth in support for far-right parties.[12]

Another issue for consternation has to do with disparities within EU refugee-hosting states. However, that disparity seems not quite relevant when compared to the refugee-hosting countries in the Global South.

A major flaw in the Global Compact and its ancillaries is that it makes states hosting refugees responsible for their well-being. Any loan that refugee-hosting countries can expect from developed countries to provide for the refugees has to be repaid. However, this is particularly difficult as more than 80 per cent of the refugees are still located in the Global South. In fact, as one research concludes, '[m]igration from least-developed countries (LDCs) to more-developed countries (MDCs) in the Global South is growing at a rapid rate'. This contradicts the narrative that people from LDCs are all moving towards the North.[13] The research further notes that:

> [a]ccording to the UNHCR...the top refugee-hosting countries are developing countries. Turkey, for instance, hosts 2.6 million refugees, Pakistan 1.4 million, Lebanon 1 million, Iran 979,400, Uganda 940,800 (mostly South Sudanese fleeing the ongoing political turmoil), and Ethiopia 791,600. Germany was the 8th most important host country for refugees in 2016.[14]

It is a matter of concern that the roadmap for the Global Compact neglects any discussion of the issue of reparations. Further, even for the promises made by the developed states, as one social scientist would have us believe, 'no tracking mechanism exists to assess whether developed states have acted on their commitments or met their obligations (or the extent to which they have done so), undermining the burden-sharing component on which the GCR is premised.'[15]

Relevance for Asia

In present times, the Asian region is one of the most volatile in terms of population flows. The protracted wars in Afghanistan and Iraq, the tremendous hostilities in Syria, and the prolonged violence against Rohingyas in Myanmar have created massive displacements in Asia. Hundreds of thousands of people have become refugees, internally displaced, trafficked, and stateless. The Asian region has had a long history of refugee movements. The Palestinian refugees and partition refugees in South Asia numbered in millions, followed by many other refugee groups including the Tibetans, the boat people of Vietnam, the Bangladeshis, and the Sri Lankans, to name a few. The narrative of displacement is further propelled by the trajectory of migrant labour (to a great extent, illegal labour migration) that flows into Malaysia, India, Turkey, and other Asian nations like Bangladesh, Syria, or Afghanistan. It is a situation marked by tight and brutal border controls, violent borderlands, no labour rights, and below subsistence wages. It is also a situation that confirms that today's population flows are mixed and massive. The Asian context is also characterised by regional features such as the Australian policies for off-shore internment of shelter seekers from various Asian regions, the Bali Process,[16] common dimensions of labour migration in countries of the region, and growing statelessness. Thus, a study of the narrative of migration demands a holistic approach towards ensuring human rights, protection, and justice, to replace piecemeal policies dovetailed for old and redundant administrative categories like refugees, asylum seekers, illegal immigrants, trafficked women, trafficked labour, and boat refugees. Consequently, it can be argued that at the same time and in many ways, the Asian migration situation reflects the global migration scenario as a whole.

South Asia, and India in particular, have witnessed some of the most massive population flows in contemporary times. However, countries in the South Asian and Southeast Asian regions have also hosted large numbers of refugees on a scale unimagined in Europe. There are judicial decisions, legal decisions, and political movements in defence of the rights of the migrants and forced migrants. The issue of the IDPs (Internally Displaced Persons) and stateless population groups has also come to the forefront. The Rohingya refugees epitomise issues regarding refugee groups. In 2015, the trials and tribulations of the Rohingyas became known to the world when it was discovered that hundreds of them were perishing in boats while trying to escape persecution in Myanmar. None of the other countries in the region was willing to take in the Rohingyas. Not only were they being denied safe haven, but they were also denied resources essential for survival. In these boats were women, children, the maimed, and the sick, one and all trying to escape persecution and survive. Some social scientists refer to the Rohingyas as 'the world's most persecuted minority without citizenship'.[17] Today, the most critical of all refugee groups in South Asia are the Rohingyas from Myanmar, who number around 860,000 (registered and unregistered).

Any analysis of forced migration in South Asia has to inevitably begin with India, the largest country in the region. It has to be mentioned that India is not a signatory to the 1951 Refugee Convention and the 1967 Protocol. If one does not count

Afghanistan, none of the South Asian states has signed either the Convention or the Protocol. However, in the recent past these countries have ratified several other human rights instruments. All of them have ratified the four Geneva Conventions as well. Yet, South Asian states have been reluctant to accept the 1951 Convention, even though they provide no official reasons for such a decision. In India, the refugees, like all other migrants, fall under the jurisdiction of the Foreigners Act (1946) and the Passport Act (1955). These Acts are relevant to all non-citizens alike, and they make entering India without valid papers a legal offence. However, this is not to say that India has not given refugee status to any groups. The regional record of South Asia with refugees is not completely negative. Like India, Pakistan has received and hosted for nearly two decades thousands of Afghan refugees; Bangladesh has received nearly half-a-million Rohingya refugees; and Nepal about 100,000 south Bhutanese refugees, besides hosting Tibetan refugees. Most refugee groups are usually accommodated within the region. Also, refugee protection jurisprudence has helped the refugees, and Courts in the region have upheld human rights obligations.

Yet, refugee protection in recent years has been perceived as a problem. The attitude towards refugees has gradually changed all over Asia with fresh bouts of migrations. Racism has increased as well. With considerations and discourses of security on the rise, citizens now have a threat perception of footloose people, including footloose labour. This has led human rights communities to seek new protection strategies for refugees.

The question of our contemporary times, then, is: Can global conflict be a problem solvent for this region? This collection of essays addresses refugee protection against the backdrop of the Global Compact on refugees. The volume aims to unpack the multiplicities imbedded in the concept of 'protection' as it operates in different contexts in an unevenly interconnected world. The chapters are arranged around three conceptual cores: new technologies of protection aimed at governing mixed migratory flows; the fault-lines of race, religion, and gender among displaced groups in a shifting protection regime; and neoliberalism and immigrant economies.

A Post-Colonial Look at Protection

This volume intends to privilege a post-colonial view of protection. The first five chapters address the question of protection from different perspectives. Chapter 1 is predicated upon a society facing a perfect cacophonic storm of populist leaders' voices in the Americas, EU, Asia, and Africa, which continue to attribute the ills of their societies to migrants. As a result, pathways to migration of 'choice' that lead to citizenship, with access to a full range of rights, in destination countries are being reduced all around the world. Bandana Purkayastha outlines some of the ways in which nation-states are trying to govern flows of people at the present moment by stepping up their 'national security' efforts. She lays particular emphasis on the process of strategic blocking being practised by the US, UK, and EU. She explores how governance has to a large extent become about managing flows, creating bounded spaces for stopping and holding people and children, and containing them, particularly in camps and privatised prisons. Purkayastha avers that nation-states are involved in 'distancing practices' centred on changing the discourse about the rights of migrants to make such actions palatable for their political constituencies. In the cross-matrix of the discussion as it weaves around migrants, migration, and human security, Purkayastha's analysis is predicated on the fact that if we are to understand the structures shaping the lives of migrants and refugees in our contemporary times, we need to avoid the conceptual trap of having clear and rigid boundaries between types of migrants. Purkayastha focuses on certain case studies of the US, the EU, and Australia, but a particular highlight of her chapter is also on the exploration of how the nexus of the UNHCR itself with state interests adds further 'distance' to the ability of refugees to politically advocate for themselves.

The present scenario of the 'crisis' of refugees, asylum seekers, and migrants affecting the European space has prompted Frederico Rahola to read the phenomenon through the image of a 'borderland' in Chapter 2. Rahola defines a borderland as a fragmented and uneven space, one crisscrossed by a relentless movement and by new and old border devices harnessing it, that contains as it detains, disperses as it concentrates, and exploits as it excludes. This is vis-à-vis a 'fortress', an increasing selective area which is typified by an almost complete non-permeability, as particularly evinced in the case of the European Union. For the EU, as Rahola delineates, seems to have become something that demarcates a new 'topology' of Europe—merging together a landscape shot through by 'fences', 'hotspots', 'detention/reception centers', 'informal encampments', and diverse corridors and routes—that seems to no longer correspond to any sort of a linear map. To investigate the issue, Rahola uses the image of a 'leash'. Literally, for Rahola, a leash is that which governs mobility through mobility, by the process of imposing a narrow gauge, limited in time and space. Under its mortgage, every movement becomes 'secondary'. However, as Rahola notes, it is only very rarely that those who are led on a leash accept the regime of forced mobility. Therefore, at the ends of the leash, a particular tension is established, which strives to seek out as many 'rips' as it can—rips being expressions of the will to conduct oneself in a different way. By reading those attempts as peculiar forms of Foucauldian 'counter-conducts', producing many of the 'counter-spaces' of Henri Lefebvre, the chapter ends by suggesting a sort of 'Underground Europe', in an analogy with the historical Black experience of the Underground Railroad in the decades before the US Civil War.

Shibashis Chatterjee, in Chapter 3, discusses three interrelated arguments. The first is the fact that over the past few years, global refugee flows have been increasing and have increasingly been deteriorating. As a result, the international refugee crisis appears much more expansive and worse than ever before. Each continent in the world, barring Antarctica, abounds with enormous displacement issues, while international efforts are meagre, inconsistent, and without teeth. The chapter puts forward a call to action to international actors and agents to prioritise their duties to human and humanitarian assistance. For most of the major powers of the world, predicated by the twin factors of realist geopolitics (a sort of geo-realpolitik) and neoliberal policies, humanitarian assistance is a very small footnote in their global 'efforts'. Second, the chapter reflects on liberal, communitarian, radical, and political tracts in order to question why it is that the refugee has remained perennially a marginal figure, despite years of effort to place them at the centre. Third, the chapter investigates the 'Responsibility to Protect' in a trajectory spanning the astounding burst of its origin to the equally astounding burst of its spectacular unravelling. It makes the point that in a world guided by the notion of sovereignty of the state, the 'responsibility' to protect itself becomes but a mere function and exercise of state power.

The European migration question is in essence an Asian migration question and that is the argument that Anita Sengupta makes in Chapter 4. Sengupta investigates how this relationship between European and Asian migrations can be understood in terms of geopolitical significance—as she puts it—particularly how it is constructed and by whom, and the ways in which it is challenged and subverted. To this end, Sengupta explores the questions of 'durable solutions', resettlement, repatriation, and local integration and the 'right to return', with mixed associated results and responses in the context of the broad region of Asia vis-à-vis Europe. In the course of her analysis, she particularly highlights certain factors such as state-building processes across the region, which leave people—like the Uzbek brides of Kyrgyzstan—bereft and stateless because they fall outside the official and legally sanctioned definition of citizens. Sengupta then brings in the idea of the Global Compact in her argument and illustrates the problems inherent in this. Foremost, she highlights how even within the European Union, with its common refugee and asylum law, questions of interpretation regarding states persist, and that despite the enforcement of legal instruments and the fact that most states in the Union are signatories to common refugee and human rights instruments, protection levels vary. The mind then positively boggles at the question as to what can happen in regions without such aids. However, at a broader level, Sengupta further argues that the Global Compact, in its claim for 'assistance' but not 'protection', is in essence a ploy of the European states through which Europe, with a promise of functional assistance, can buy itself 'safety', as it were, from the threat of being overrun by the refugees, who would present a risk to its Christian character and values. As such, Sengupta contends that Europe in the present context refuses to look at a durable solution to the refugee crisis.

The European refugee crisis is touted to have broken out within and outside Europe because of waves of refugee movements. This has given rise to a dilemma which is at once humanitarian and political, and requires elaboration within the context of the policies and practices pursued by different European governments and by the European Union particularly. Since 2015, there have been several attempts to frame the crisis that took place within the prismatic viewpoints of different kinds of constructs, and also to shine a spotlight upon the narratives of movements, solidarities, and resistances, which are intertwined with the actions of various governments and regional and global organisations. Such is the context within which Priya Singh writes Chapter 5. The chapter provides an overview of all that surrounds the question of the migration to Europe. It then analyses the EU-Turkey refugee pact, with particular attention paid to the fact of its operation within a very mutable context, and the consequences of that for the refugees. Singh studies the actions that Turkey took following its conference with Europe to meet its commitments towards assisting Syrian refugees within the country, and the reasons and rationale behind Turkey's concurring on a compact with Europe to assume the status of 'safe third country of resistance': briefly put, Turkey was eyeing a closer relationship, in some ways an integration, with the European Union, in exchange for these actions. In conclusion, the chapter is critical of the exceptionality of this particular 'crisis'.

The five chapters discussed above question the notion of crisis. The authors argue that even though the Global Compact was meant to protect the refugees, the states that have a duty to protect often reneged on their responsibilities. All the chapters point to the integral connection between geopolitics in the Global North, their asylum policies, and protracted dislocations in the Global South. They address innovative technologies of migration governance operating in the context of mixed and massive population flows and point to the uneven geography of protection. One of the primary areas of focus is the newly emerging and technologically advanced bordering strategies, such as offshore detention techniques and hotspots often located outside the state where refugees seek asylum. Some of the chapters also raise the important question of migrant resistance to the imbalances in the protection regime. They point out that the current migratory movements and practices of the displaced groups often exceed the regulatory capacities of governance. Migrants create their own 'underground cartographies' of counter-conducts that attempt to challenge the exclusionary protection regimes.

A central theme of the volume is the emerging fissures in the protection regime along the fault-lines of race, religion, and gender. In Chapter 6, Sabyasachi Basu Ray Chaudhury points to the increasing statelessness resulting from skewed protection policies. In delineating global imbalances in the acts of responsibility sharing between powerful Western nations and their post-colonial counterparts, the volume raises an ethical question: Should protection regimes be premised on principles of humanitarianism with implicit assumptions of care and hospitality, or should it ultimately be a question of rights? Basu Ray Chaudhury contends that in the light of this aforementioned fact, existing legal mechanisms at the international level—and in certain cases, even ones prevailing at a more microcosmic register at the regional level—are not only sometimes partially redundant, but also on the whole insufficient, largely ineffective, and in a word toothless, in the face of the evolving system of capitalist globalisation throughout the world.

Women constitute about 49 per cent of the world's refugee population. However, the existing protection regime for migrants as well as refugees often glosses over the gendered and racialised nature of migration. Paula Banerjee, in Chapter 7, highlights the differential experiences of migrants of colour and religious minorities, and further critiques the hierarchised citizenship regimes pertaining to migrants across the world. Her chapter foregrounds the role of gender as an unspoken fourth axis of differentiation in the protection regime. Banerjee argues that modern nation-states, built upon a fundamental predication on gender differences, develop precariously tense relationships with their women. In this context, she looks at South Asia. In order to do so, she investigates how work done on the forced displacement of women often goes against a state-sanctioned narrative about refugee women being victims. She looks particularly at the ways in which value judgements can occur in order to minimise the importance of crimes committed against women, marginalise them, and reduce them to the state of political non-subjects.

In Chapter 8, Ilina Sen highlights the conditions of Asian female migrants who work as domestic workers in the Gulf region, and the gendered nature of the violence routinely experienced by them. Most migrant women work on the bottom rung of the occupational hierarchy, and as a result they are exceedingly vulnerable because principally, they work as housemaids, entertainers, nurses, and factory workers. They face a battery of problems, including sexual harassment, rape, non-payment or underpayment of wages, verbal abuse, and physical abuse. In fact, Sen contends that although the movement of the women could be seen as proof of their comparatively greater 'agency', as in the Philippines and Sri Lanka, in effect it can be viewed as a response to the desperate circumstances into which the variables of loss of rural livelihoods, poverty, and conflict have pushed these women.

Finally, the volume delineates how conditions of protracted forced displacements are entwined with the technologies of neoliberal capitalism. Chapter 9 by Byasdeb Dasgupta focuses on the cheap labour of refugees and migrants, which fuels neoliberal global capitalism. Dasgupta notes that refugee protection has become an affair of technocratic management, oriented towards the necessities of the market and development goals. As refugees have been reframed from 'subjects of protection' to 'subjects of neoliberal development', they are valued on the basis of their economic viability to fuel neoliberal growth. Therefore, a refugee has no other option but to get absorbed in the informal space—and this, most of the time, at a monetary return value which is significantly lower compared to a citizen in the host economy. Furthermore, as Dasgupta enunciates, such absorption is not without violence at multiple levels, for it involves contestation with the local working force as well as within the ranks of the refugees themselves. The chapter thus asserts that the productive labour of a refugee is devalued, which facilitates the cheapening of labour as variable capital. Moreover, since refugees lack most of the basic rights of a citizen in a modern nation–state, the capacity of the working population of the refugee community to represent themselves remains rather weak. This is the crucial determining factor, Dasgupta notes, that enables the productive capitalist to control labour much more easily.

PANDEMIC, AND A CRITICAL LOOK AT PROTECTION

The volume offers a post-colonial critique of the global protection regime and its contribution lies in adding a critical perspective to the issue of 'protection'. It provides insights into the various fault-lines of forced migration like gender and race, which are often not given due consideration in the existing literatures on the subject. Furthermore, the chapters draw out the connection between the protracted refugee-like situation in the Global South and geopolitics in the Global North, and point out how it all functions to serve the requirements of late capitalism. The chapters are interwoven with a constant critique of how protection regimes often move in circles and fall short of providing long-term solutions to conditions of protected displacements because the machinery of late capitalism essentially depends on the low-paid informal labour provided by refugees and migrants.

The precariousness of the regime of protection as delineated by the Global Compact was proven beyond doubt during the Covid-19 pandemic. All protection of refugees was abrogated, with refugee camps facing heightened threats. As one report concludes, people in 'refugee camps in Syria, Greece and Bangladesh face a heightened risk of COVID-19 due to more densely populated conditions than even the Diamond Princess—the cruise ship where transmission of the virus was four times faster than in Wuhan.'[18] In June 2020, Covid-19 hit the Kutupalong Camp in southern Bangladesh. A report on this camp pointed out that: '[t]he refugees are entirely reliant upon aid for their day-to-day survival. And living conditions are dire. Homes are cramped and often built from flimsy materials while toilets and washing facilities are shared.'[19] That the pandemic will hit such places is not surprising. As for refugees and migrants in Europe, another report states that:

> Greek authorities imposed a 14-day quarantine on an overcrowded migrant camp on the island of Lesbos on Wednesday, after one man who had been living outside the official camp tested positive for the coronavirus. The 40-year-old Somali man is the first confirmed coronavirus case at the Moria camp, which as of August 31, housed 12,714 people, well over its capacity of 2,757.[20]

These reports suggest that whether in South Asia or in Europe, refugees exist in a perpetually precarious state.

This anthology interrogates the issue of protection promoted by the Global Compact. It takes a critical look at the states and the international regime of protection and concludes that, as a report argues:

> With global refugee flows manifestly worsening in the last decade and the perceived global migrant crisis appearing deeper and more expansive than ever, international efforts at various levels towards human rights and humanitarian protection remain paltry and inconsistent. The refugee and the migrant remain at the same time a marginal category despite years of efforts to reverse this marginalization. In this situation, the principle of global responsibility as a function of power, framed for instance as the 'Responsibility to Protect', seems to have reached an equally striking but inglorious end. Meanwhile, local, regional, customary, bilateral, and other multilateral efforts to provide humanitarian protection and the protection of the rights of the refugees and migrants have continued as ignored but valuable instances of human dignity.[21]

The chapters call for a change in refugee policies that will be region-specific, but will also respect the dignity of people on the move. The authors argue that categories such as refugees, migrants, and the stateless are all progressively being challenged by critical theorists. They also argue that any mandate on protection should contain in it the concerns and voices of the forced migrants themselves. They are not bare bodies to be tossed around, but people with rights. As one expert says, the Global Compact chose humanitarianism over human rights, and as a result of this the 'refugee and the migrant was ... up against two realities—the reality of sovereignty and the reality of a global economy, which could think of the refugee only as cheap labour employed in informal economies and supply chains.'[22] This volume therefore challenges the notions of protection as formulated by the Global Compact as the authors bring back notions of rights, ethics, and justice amidst the cacophony of development and technology.

That the established mode of protection for refugees and migrants is not working has become clear to many. Aleinikoff and Zamore, in their recently published book, *The Arc of Protection*, discuss how the system is broken and cannot provide protection for the swelling numbers of the displaced that is the reality of our current times. They also elucidate how better protection can be delivered to these persecuted people.[23] In our volume, the authors delineate why, in post-colonial times, we can only talk about moments of protection: because protection should be viewed as dynamic and needs to be constantly evolving. Protection, as we argue, is in the moment. Even if we approximate protection needs for the future, a time will come when those same needs will change. And thus arises a need to arrive at a new moment of protection. This work, spearheaded by the Calcutta Research Group's analysis of the protection needs of displaced people, is also meant to be evolving and dynamic. Therefore, this volume is for our moment. In future, there will be other moments and other volumes following.

NOTES

1. 'The Situation in Libya: Prospects and Role of the Council of Europe'. Report, DOC 14519, 29 March 2018, Council of Europe.

Available at https://assembly.coe.int/nw/xml/XRef/Xref-XML2HTML-en.asp?fileid=24533&lang=en (accessed May 2024).

2. '2015: The Year of Europe's Refugee Crisis', 8 December 2015, UN High Commission for Refugees. Available at https://www.unhcr.org/news/stories/2015/12/56ec1ebde/2015-year-europes-refugee-crisis.html accessed on 3 September 2020 (accessed January 2025).

3. Ibid.

4. 'Migrant Crisis: Migration to Europe Explained in Seven Charts'. *BBC News*, 4 March 2016. Available at https://www.bbc.com/news/world-europe-34131911 (accessed May 2024).

5. 'Number of Refugees to Europe Surges to Record 1.3 Million in 2015', Pew Research Center, 2 August 2016. Available at https://www.pewresearch.org/global/2016/08/02/number-of-refugees-to-europe-surges-to-record-1-3-million-in-2015/ (accessed January 2025).

6. 'Migrant Crisis', *BBC News*, 4 March 2016.

7. Ireneusz Pawel Karolewski and Roland Benedikter, 'Europe's refugee and migrant crisis'. *Politique europeenne* 60, 2018, p. 99.

8. Emina Osmandzikovic, 'The drowning of Aylan Kurdi'. *Arab News* 45, 18 April 2020. Available at https://www.arabnews.com/node/1660926 (accessed January 2025).

9. '2015: The year of Europe's refugee crisis', 8 December 2015, UN High Commission for Refugees.

10. Ranabir Samaddar, 'The Global Gaze of Protection, Care, and Power', *Refuge* 35 (1), p. 76.

11. 'Global Compact on Refugees'. Report of the United Nations High Commissioner for Refugees, A/73/12 (Part II), Article 70, 2018, p. 13, General Assembly Official Records, Seventy-third Session, Supplement No. 12 (A/73/12 [Part II]).

12. Sebastian Dullien, 'Paying the Price: The Cost of Europe's Refugee Policy'. Policy Brief, European Council on Foreign Relations, 2016. Available at http://www.jstor.com/stable/resrep21576 (accessed May 2024).

13. Asmita Parshotam, 'The UN Global Compacts on Migration and Refugees: A New Solution to Migration Management or More of the Same?' Occasional Paper 273, South African Institute of International Affairs, 2017, p. 6.

14. Ibid. p. 8. Also refer to World Economic Forum, '84% of refugees live in developing countries'. Available at https://www.weforum.org/agenda/2017/06/eighty-four-percent-of-refugees-live-in-developing-countries/ (accessed May 2024).

15. Kate Mlauzi and Michelle Small, 'Is the Global Compact on Refugees Fit for Africa's Purposes?' Occasional Paper 302, South African Institute of International Affairs, 2019, p. 15. Available at https://www.jstor.org/stable/resrep25889 (accessed May 2024).

16. The Bali Process on People Smuggling, Trafficking in Persons and Related Transnational Crime was established in 2002 to deal with issues of human trafficking, people smuggling, and irregular migrations. It is an international forum for collaboration, information sharing, and policy discussions on these issues.

17. Md. Razidur Rahaman, 'Rohingya: The Community of No Human Rights', *The Daily Observer*, 13 April 2017.

18. 'New IRC analysis reveals risk that coronavirus transmission rates in Moria, Al Hol and Cox's Bazar refugee camps could outpace those seen on the Diamond Princess cruise ship'. Press Release, International Rescue Committee, 1 April 2020. Available at https://www.rescue.org/press-release/new-irc-analysis-reveals-risk-coronavirus-transmission-rates-moria-al-hol-and-coxs (accessed May 2024).

19. Robert Leslie, 'COVID-19 is hitting Rohingya Muslims in the world's biggest refugee camp, and humanitarian groups are fearing mass infection', *Business Insider India*, 23 July 2020. Available at https://www.businessinsider.in/international/news/covid-19-is-hitting-rohingya-muslims-in-the-worlds-biggest-refugee-camp-and-humanitarian-groups-are-fearing-mass-infection/articleshow/77117526.cms (accessed May 2024).

20. 'Coronavirus: Crowded Greek refugee camp quarantined after COVID-19 case', *Euro News*, 2 September 2020. Available at https://www.euronews.com/2020/09/02/coronavirus-crowded-greek-refugee-camp-quarantined-after-covid-19-case (accessed May 2024).

21. 'Kolkata Declaration 2018', Mahanirban Calcutta Research Group, 30 November 2018, p. 2. Available at http://www.mcrg.ac.in/RLS_Migration/Kolkata_Declaration_2018.pdf (accessed May 2024).

22. Samaddar, 'The Global Gaze of Protection, Care, and Power', p. 81.

23. T. Alexander Aleinikoff and Leah Zamore, *The Arc of Protection: Reforming the International Refugee Regime*. Stanford: Stanford Briefs, Stanford University Press, 2019.

1

Distancing as Governance

Reflections on Migrants and Contemporary (in)Securities

Bandana Purkayastha

Over the past few years, headline news and social media around the world have featured men, women, and children who were fleeing large-scale violence, disasters, and loss of prospects of livelihood. Their search for safer havens has been interrupted by expanding terrains of state security initiatives on land and sea, which prevent migrants from reaching the state's territories through their incarceration in detention camps within and across nation-states. Furthermore, attempts by migrants to cross borders between nation-states are also thwarted by the dangers associated with the growth of human smuggling rings, which profit from a failure to deliver on promises to move people safely. According to United Nations High Commissioner of Refugees (UNHCR), by the end of June 2024, 122.6 million people worldwide had been forcibly displaced as a result of persecution, conflict, violence, human rights violations, or events seriously disturbing public order. As a result, deserts and seas are littered with the bodies of those who have perished trying to reach safe havens in recent years.[1] This chapter outlines some of the ways in which nation-states are governing the flows of migration by reinforcing their 'national security' efforts to block the migrants from the US, UK, EU, and other countries.

Some observers, such as Michael Flynn,[2] point out that privatised detention centres and their rapid global expansion are both features of contemporary immigration. Whether these are referred to as 'facilities', 'guesthouses' (Turkey), 'guarded shelters' (Hungary), 'welcome centres' (Italy), or 'detention centres' (US), their presence raises questions about the culpability of Western liberal democracies, which often claim a palpable discomfort when locking people up outside criminal processes, especially people protected by additional norms such as those contained in the UN Refugee Convention. Euro-American countries selectively apply only those human rights norms that do not call into question the 'sovereign right' to detain and deport. There is a progressive criminalisation of migrants, which leads to the subversion of the norm-based responsibilities of states concerning the granting of asylum. Moreover, their endeavour is to characterise many of those subjected to this form of detention in such a way as to provoke public fears, and thereby justify locking up migrants. These detention centres not only create spaces where normal rules are suspended, but they are also often located in spaces, including countries, that had few detention centres through most of the twentieth century.

Distancing as governance is broadly about the ways in which the governance of migrants, asylum seekers, and refugees is changing spatially, structurally, and temporally. Despite 142 nation-states having signed the 1951 Refugee Convention and 1967 Protocol, governments—especially, though not exclusively, many in the Global North—are actively involved in rebuffing migrants, refugees, and asylum seekers, and in many cases, holding them in distant places. Governance has thus primarily become about managing flows, creating bounded spaces for stopping and containing men, women, and children—including in camps and privatised prisons. Powerful nation-states are also involved in distancing practices that involve changing the discourse about the rights of migrants in order to make these state-sanctioned acts of incarceration palatable to their political constituencies. These practices are part of the contemporary structures that migrants encounter in their quest for more secure lives.

Two broad facets of this issue are discussed in this chapter. First, I discuss the (re)conceptualisation of refugees and migrants, not as separate categories, but as arrayed on a continuum of migrants who search for more secure lives through migration. As part of their distancing practices, many governments have begun to elide—

through rhetoric and practice—the difference between migrants who cross national boundaries without 'proper' documents and those seeking refuge, even though they also maintain separate bureaucracies to manage different types of migrants. Without a scrutiny of the discrete migrant categories that continue to be at the heart of most scholarly discussions, it is difficult to understand the extent of the current shifts and changes taking place through distancing practices. The second part of the discussion focuses on the structuring of distance, including the use of force and violence as part of the managerial tools used to govern migrants. The concluding section examines the implications of these practices.

The discussion is embedded in scholarship on migration, violence, and migrants' human rights and human security. The cases discussed here are derived from scholarly and media accounts. The term 'migrant' is used broadly, unless specified otherwise, and encompasses all varieties of migrants, including refugees, asylum seekers, and stateless persons. The rationale for the use of this broad term is discussed in the next section. Violence is also conceptualised holistically to emphasise the structures and the purveyors of violence at transnational, national, and local levels. The idea of human rights in this discussion is drawn from earlier works on human rights enterprise.[3] This perspective focuses less on legal edifices and more on people wresting rights from governments. The idea of human security is linked to the human rights enterprise.[4] It focuses on building lives which have some modicum of dignity, lives that are free from the constant threat of violence, that is, lives that are secure from threats 'derived from economic, food, health or environmental security, and threats to personal, community, and political security'.[5]

Migrants, Refugees, and Structural Violence

In an earlier discussion on migrants, migration, and human security, I had argued that if we want to understand the structures shaping the lives of migrants and refugees today, we need to avoid the conceptual trap of upholding clear and rigid boundaries between types of migrants, for example, between internal and international migrants, and between migrations of choice and forced migration.[6] On one level, governments and transnational actors maintain bureaucracies to manage migrants separately according to these categories. However, on another level, recent trends also indicate both the maintenance of bureaucratic boundaries *and* an elision of these categories in order to expand the terrain of control over migrants. Earlier works—for example, Samaddar (2015) and Glenn (2015)[7]—have pointed out the need to look at histories and *cycles* of forced migration and displacements, some of which occur within the boundaries of nation-states, and others across these boundaries. However, political boundaries are also dynamic, redefined to uphold the interests of state security (or of dominant groups that define the security of 'the state')—classifications that distinguish between internal and international migrants, or migrants and refugees, reflect state interests.

Conceptually, if we draw upon critical scholarship from different parts of the world and on the documented experiences of a variety of migrants, we are better able to trace the multiple levels of the socio-political-economic-cultural-environmental processes and events that shape migration. We should conceptualise migrants, and the dynamic structures and processes in which they are enmeshed, as though they are arrayed on a continuum: from international migrants at one end, through internal migrants, refugees, internally displaced persons (IDPs), to trafficked persons at the other end.[8] While there are very definite differences between the groups at either end of the array, the groups in proximity to each other are not as sharply defined. Equally importantly, these positions on the array are dynamic—as a consequence, with a change in structural circumstances, migrants might end up in different 'categories' during their lifetime. The line between people who choose to move, those who are sufficiently desperate to choose temporary labour migration—frequently indentured terms of labour migration—and those who are forced to move are often blurred. This array also recentres the need to understand the conditions of migrants prior to, during, and after migration. Without losing sight of the worlds of formal policies and laws that govern migrants' moves across borders, their ability to settle, and their access to resources critical to their survival and well-being, we should examine the changing terrain of migration. Which actors are involved in shaping migration terrains, and what is the scope of their actions? These questions recentre discussions of power and hierarchy. As Ranabir Samaddar has argued, the terrain of internal to international migration does not exist as a benign continuum; instead:

> [s]tudies of hunger in the 19th century, of itinerant movements, transportations of coolies, spread of famines, shipping of children, adult girls, trafficking in sex, labour, and human organs, and welfare legislations to cope with this great infamy tell us how actually we have arrived at our own time of subject formation under the conditions of empire. This is certainly different from the tradition of nation-centred histories.[9]

Such a historical perspective on migrant flows and structures of control is needed to understand the similarities and differences in migrant governance in the nineteenth, twentieth, and twenty-first centuries. The current trend in neoliberal states is to construct migrants as threats to state security. As a rising crescendo of populist leaders' voices in the Americas, EU, Asia, and Africa continue to attribute the ills of society to migrants, pathways to migration (of 'choice') that lead to citizenship (with access to a full range of rights) in destination countries are rapidly shrinking in many parts of the world. At the same time, it is not easy to get a 'refugee' designation that, theoretically, offers some modicum of rights.[10] Since the end of the twentieth century, managing migrants' flows has become big business: both the trade in human beings[11] and the detention of human beings in privatised prisons are part of contemporary global, legal, and illicit commerce. For such commerce to be profitable, the contributions of migrant labour are being delinked from access to rights so that states can benefit from their labour while paying few of the social costs that are essential to the migrants seeking to rebuild their lives.[12] The continual growth in the number of stateless citizens indicates another pathway through which many states have acted to prevent people from accessing rights. The cases of the Rohingyas (see Mahanirban Calcutta Research Group[13]) or the Japanese Peruvians in the United States[14] are examples of histories of force and political violence within regimes of migrant governance.[15] The recent massive migration from the Middle East and North Africa—of people fleeing large-scale conflict—to Europe has created conditions for successful smuggling and trafficking, both of which are predicated upon force and violence. Stories of migrants in sealed trucks have been in the news in Austria,[16] the US,[17] and other countries. At the same time, there are examples of refugees, as described by Antje Missbach and Frieda Sinanu,[18] who are tired of waiting in camps for the rest of their families to join them and are willing to pay smugglers to bring their wives and/or children to wherever they are located. In their report on migrant smuggling to Europe, Rick Lyman and Eddy Smale[19] point out that EU law officials have stated that smuggling human beings is now bigger business than illicit trade in drugs and weapons.

Violence and force are a part of distancing practices, but in order to understand the role of the violence to which migrants are subject, it is important to consider holistic definitions, such as those being used by international entities like the Special Rapporteur on Violence Against Women.[20] Such holistic definitions cover issues from gendered interpersonal violence within families, including migrant families,[21] to structural violence at intercommunity, intra-state, and inter-state levels.[22] Discussions of migrants, refugees, and trafficked persons typically recognise that violence plays a part in forced migration, and also when migrants attempt to settle in their destinations. However, the holistic definition—with its emphasis on transnational, national, and local violence linked to the commerce in wars (and the arms trade), technologies of force and surveillance, and the development of tools to mobilise hatred—points to other forms of violence that have not been documented by migration scholars. At the least, it reminds us to include, in the definition of forced migration, all those who are forcibly detained and/or evicted from 'receiving' countries. At its broadest, this perspective offers a glimpse of a terrain of violence that migrants experience, including through governance structures, prior to and during their migration and after they settle. The questions shift from what happens within nation-states to the broad zones in which migrants are managed, often with force and violence. In other words, violence and force occur in the countries of origin, countries where people might halt (or be forced to halt), as well as in the destination countries. These patterns reflect the contemporary processes of distancing as governance.

Managing Flows through Distancing

According to UN data, the total number of migrants—which includes migrants, refugees, and asylum seekers—has reached 281 million, which includes 117 million internationally and internally displaced people.[23] These figures indicate the growing numbers of people who are on the move, but it is important to note some of the altered political-economic-social structures that make it difficult to trace what is happening to people classified within these categories. Nation-states control the flow of international migrants, that is, those assumed to move primarily in search of economic opportunities, through a variety of border controls and visa restrictions enforced at points of departure; many affluent countries are now controlling the flows of international migrants by granting them temporary residence, often on terms reminiscent of indenture. The vastly expanded reach of modern-day warfare and conflicts has significantly increased the number of people who are affected. At the same time, repeated climate disasters related to human acceleration of climatic changes add to the number of people who are displaced. Many move in search of human security.

Nation-states are engaged in a variety of practices to control (and profit from) the management of these flows; force, as mentioned above, is central to these endeavours. Other actors such as humanitarian aid providers are also part of the terrain of managing migrants. Three overlapping processes are particularly important to note: the practices of repelling migrants before they reach their intended destination; the practices of holding them in camps and detention centres, including those situated at a distance from the nation-state managing the migrant flows; and the ceding of the tasks of governance to third parties, which further distance migrants from the path leading towards a substantive claiming of rights, which is a key issue in building more secure lives.

REPELLING MIGRANTS ON LAND AND SEA[24]

Over the last few decades, nation-states have been engaging in sustained efforts to repel migrants, refugees, and asylum seekers, so that they find themselves unable to reach the borders of their intended destination. These distancing practices extend to a variety of migrants. For those seeking employment via employment visas, the rapid expansion of temporary and contingent visa categories—which allow migrants to contribute labour, but with very few political rights—have instituted avenues of control to prevent migrants from long-term residence and access to rights.[25] Those seeking refuge are intercepted before they reach land and sea borders; many are turned back and others are diverted to third countries. The US, the EU, and Australia, among other countries, provide examples of contemporary repelling practices used against refuge seekers.

The US case illustrates long-standing practices to repel migrants from a distance. While the country's involvement in various Central American countries has created humanitarian disasters that initiated migrant flows towards it, its policies and practices repel migrants from these regions. Discussing the case of Central American refugees and asylum seekers to the US, Karen Musalo and Eunice Lee[26] point out that between 2016 and 2017, the US raised the total number of refugees the country would receive from 85,000 to 110,000. With a regime change, this number was reduced to 50,000 in 2017. Tom Cohen[27] notes that the Obama administration requested $3.7 billion to address the women and children who were moving out of Central America. The funding included heightened enforcement at the border and monetary reimbursement for 6,300 new beds to detain families.[28] The budget also included money for State Department officials, so they could deter people in Central American countries from thinking they might be allowed to enter the US. Bill Frelick, et al.[29] point out that the US government also funded and encouraged the Governments of Mexico, Guatemala, and Honduras to turn around Central American asylum seekers before they could ever reach the US border. Repelling practices include the recent calls to build another wall as well as to expand detention centres. As headline news in the US document, these distancing practices are accompanied by apolitical rhetoric that equates asylum seekers to migrants who attempt to enter the country without proper documents, thus ascribing criminality to all migrants, which in turn is used to justify their harsh incarceration.[30] Practices of repelling migrants have included firing tear gas on the Mexican side of the border in the name of state security, as well as prosecuting all migrants—in the so-called migrant caravan—as criminals, and separating adults from children through this process.

Another instance of repelling migrants is underway in the European Union. As conflicts have escalated or dragged on over decades in North Africa and the Middle East, migrants have sought alternate routes to reach countries as formal channels shut down. By 2015, migrants and refugees were streaming into Turkey, Greece, and other parts of the EU.[31] Photographs of migrants trying to reach EU shores on boats now abound in the media, along with accounts of drownings and deaths. The EU countries have been stringent about enforcing their maritime boundaries, repelling migrants at the three (maritime)-mile boundary to ensure they never reach land. In addition, they have diverted migrant flows and created holding spaces in bordering countries. In an article, Kemal Kirişci[32] discusses EU's negotiation with Turkey over membership in the EU, where Turkish leaders expressed concern that the country would be liable for upholding EU policies while acting as the place of detention for migrants attempting to reach other EU countries. BBC media action[33] reports that:

> [U]ntil March 2016 refugees could pass through the Western Balkans and receive humanitarian assistance at key points along

> the route from the United Nations High Commissioner for Refugees (UNHCR) and other agencies. Since 2015 more than a million people have attempted to reach northern European countries using unofficial migration routes. According to UNHCR, 70% of these displaced people come from Syria, Iraq or Afghanistan. Governments started to impose border restrictions from August 2015, culminating in the Western Balkans route being declared shut by early March 2016 and leaving more than 46,000 people stranded in camps in Greece.

More recently, and parallel to the US–Mexico deal, EU leaders approved a controversial deal with Turkey in March 2016, promising billions of euros, visa liberalisation, and other incentives for a halt to migrant flows into Greece and other parts of Europe.[34]

Australia's use of its maritime boundaries is another example of repelling migrants. Mary Crock[35] discusses how a Norwegian ship, which rescued Afghan and Iraqi refugees from a sinking Indonesian ship and then sailed to the nearest territory—Australian Christmas Island—was ordered to turn back to Indonesia. She notes the legal liminality that affected the victims; as victims rescued from a sinking ship, they should have been accorded victim status according to maritime law. However, according to Australian lawmakers, since they had not reached the zone of Australian domestic laws, they could be ascribed the status of migrants who were illegally attempting to enter Australia. The latter view prevailed. Following this incident in 2000, a wave of policies was put in place to ensure that refugees attempting to reach Australia would be diverted to a number of Pacific Islands, where they would be processed without being provided any legal help. According to Katrina Stats,[36] Australia used similar strategies against South-East Asian refugees between 1975 and 1983. More recently, Amnesty International charged Australian officials with violating international law by paying smugglers to turn back to their point of embarkment.[37] Thus, Australia has used a variety of strategies to repel migrants at the maritime boundaries, irrespective of whether they are refugees, asylum seekers, or migrants who might be bureaucratically classified as illegal migrants.

These three cases illustrate practices of distancing by repelling migrants. Nation-states are active both at formal political borders and on political-borders-through-practice as part of their strategy to forcibly repel migrants. Agreements between states to turn away migrants or hold them, as well as states' use of their islands to enforce jurisdiction over wider maritime territory, have become key to understanding the context in which these distancing practices exist. These boundaries-of-practice effectively cut off migrants' access to legal remedies, while keeping some of these distancing efforts away from the knowledge of a nation-state's publics. Instead of being episodic practices tied to occasional crises, these cases reveal more sustained patterns of methods of distancing. The use of force and violence are normalised in these practices, which in turn become a normal part of managing migrant flows. Repelling migrants works with two other related practices—outsourcing governance and migrant detention—as profit-making enterprises.

Distancing through Outsourcing Governance: Non-state Actors in Camps

Historically, governments have rarely been wholly responsible for the human security of migrants. However, increasingly from the twentieth century, with a rapid rise in refugees and asylum seekers, two patterns have been evident. Refugees are mostly placed, initially or for the long term, in camps in the Global South,[38] and many of the tasks of providing relief and rehabilitation for these migrants are given over to non-state actors, especially non-governmental organisations (NGOs) and international entities, through humanitarian action. One stated rationale for this shift is that civil society organisations, rather than governments, are most effective (and efficient) in providing solutions to people in conditions of distress. In 2022, the humanitarian funding gap grew; US$ 52.4 billion was requested through the UN, while the unmet needs grew to US 22.1 billion. At the same time, the additional layers of civil society actors further distance migrants from governance structures based in nation-states.

According to Antonio Donini, humanitarianism consists of a vast edifice of ideologies, movements, and professions that are supposed to provide assistance and protection to people in distress, but in order to sustain the enterprise, modern humanitarianism has expanded into areas of advocacy, development, human rights, and peacekeeping.[39] Silke Roth adds disaster management and preparedness to the list of humanitarian actions.[40] Thus, humanitarianism now consists of a set of 'institutions, business and an industry that employs hundreds and thousands of people… an outcome of diminished inhibitions about waging wars and privatization of social services…it has become central and salient to North-South discourse and practice'.[41] The UNHCR reports show that it employs nearly 17,000 people worldwide, so the humanitarian budgets include the salary and allowances of these employees.[42] Samaddar describes the endeavour as 'gigantic humanitarian machines which would liken to the transnational corporations (TNCs)…managing societies, which produce the obdurate refugees and migrants to stop them from leaving the shores, to keep them within the national territorial confines'.[43]

On one level, powerful nation-states continue to drive the agendas on managing migrants, and the humanitarian enterprise contributes to the employment of people from these same nation-states. The structural causes that force people to move, the very wars and conflicts that are profitable to some countries, are rarely addressed in the humanitarian relief and rehabilitation efforts. Roth[44] points to another, interrelated issue: less visible practices of humanitarianism, its managerialism and audit cultures, are centrally complicit in distancing practices. She argues that the rise of the big humanitarian NGOs, which pursue their brand identities to secure donations from individuals as well as government support, entails a corporatisation of activism that results in constraining the advocacy of groups concerned with global social justice.

The shifts within the UNHCR, the leading agency which determines the status of refugees, showcases a facet of the incomplete efforts at providing relief. The UNHCR *attempts* to ensure that refugees are able to access protection and assistance wherever they are living. However, a perusal of UNHCR's documents historically shows that the earlier objectives of relief, rehabilitation, and return are increasingly interspersed with justification for local government surveillance, as well as the need for refugees to become *self-sufficient economically*.[45] In these documents, while camps continue to be recognised, at least theoretically, as spaces where refugees are to be accorded rights and protections, by 2009 there are also statements about

> some degree of limitation on the rights and freedoms of refugees and their ability to make meaningful choices about their lives.... Host governments may insist upon the establishment of camps for reasons of public order or security. Camps may be seen as providing better control over the presence and movement of refugees.[46]

By 2014, in reports on alternatives to camps policies, UNHCR documents were pointing to camps as the exception[47] in refugee resettlement.[48] These shifts show how, in the interaction of UNHCR with the security agendas of states, these agendas begin to frame initiatives that started, at least historically, with the security of refugees as a focus of practice. This nexus of UNHCR and state interests adds further distance to the refugees' ability to politically advocate for themselves. Thus, their lives remain insecure.

This point about eroding migrants' human security is at the heart of a critique by Sari Hanafi,[49] who affirms, on the basis of his research on Palestinian refugees in Lebanon, that the bio-power exercised by the humanitarian organisations has the effect of depoliticising refugees. Refugees are transformed into bodies to be fed and sheltered, without political existence. He further emphasises that humanitarian law is used to talk about 'protected people', but current humanitarian practices focus mainly on 'victims'. By classifying people as victims, the basis of humanitarian action has shifted from rights to welfare. In disaster areas, the emphasis on values of generosity and pragmatism obscures any references to the rights and responsibilities of the concerned people.

Since Palestinian refugees are the largest single group of refugees today, their case is instructive. The interviews that Hanafi conducted in 2008 in different camps show that Palestinian refugees have lived in a state of political disarray. On the one hand, international actors could not provide adequate food and shelter, nor did they engage in any sustained efforts to negotiate jobs for refugees locally. On the other hand, as the presence of international actors waxed and waned, there was a corresponding ebb and flow of resources. This was particularly critical in the closed camps—those from which refugees could not exit—where a series of groups filled the political void over time as the intense interest in Palestinian refugees faded.[50] Camps came to be governed by a web of complex power structures comprising two popular committees (one pro-Syrian and one pro-Palestine Liberation Organization [PLO]), the security committee, committee of the camp notables, a local committee, political factions, Islamist non-Palestinian groups, imams of mosques, PLO popular organisations (workers, women, engineers, etc.), NGOs, and the United Nations Relief and Works Agency (UNRWA) director. These camp leaders imposed measures which kept changing the balance of power between these different groups. For refugees, there was no clear path to political advocacy.

In her analysis of NGOs in the Czech Republic, Alice Szczepanikova[51] reaches a similar conclusion. She probes the modes of governance employed by NGOs in the settlement of refugees and concludes that they have become 'subcontractors' of governments or of the United Nations in the Czech Republic. Infantilisation of refugee newcomers by well-meaning settlement agency staff emphasises how refugee-ness is a reflection of the link between power and performance. Szczepanikova argues that NGOs play a unique role in constructing and maintaining refugee identities, and these performances reveal a regulatory context of scripts to be followed by refugees.[52]

Similar patterns are evident among IDPs, the group that makes up the vast majority of forcibly displaced persons (40 million out of 68.5 million displaced). Roseanne Njiru's study of the camp life of IDPs in Kenya provides a picture of regulation, disarray, scarcity of resources, and enhanced vulnerability to gendered violence.[53]

Njiru points out that the objective of working with IDPs seems to include containing them within countries so they do not become refugees. There are no international covenants on IDPs, although there are guiding principles based on various human rights conventions. In some regions, including via the Organisation of African States, these principles are formally adopted. However, in practice, not enough attention has been paid to ensure the dignity of the internally displaced people living in camps. Consequently, IDPs in every region face a range of risks, including threats to their physical security and integrity, gender violence, discrimination, lack of access to basic necessities (such as food, clothing, health, shelter) and means of livelihood, and the violation of their rights relating to land and property. As in refugee camps, bodily security is an issue because of overcrowding and a lack of private spaces. Sexual violence is widespread. Non-state actors are unable to make a positive difference, even in IDP camps, where presumably people have some kind of claim to rights as citizens, because they were displaced within their own country.

The cases of non-governmental management of camps, as discussed above, illustrate other facets of distancing. These camps act as containers for migrants in places distant from their intended destination. Conditions in camps reflect chronic shortages and continuing human insecurities. While a few scholars have argued that the presence of international actors allows refugees to advocate for themselves using international conventions,[54] most scholars agree that outsourcing governance to the UN and/or NGOs, in the absence of mechanisms through which migrants can access rights, reduce them to a state of liminality. In other words, the NGOs, through their selective interactions with local governments, contribute to distancing practices at the expense of refugees' rights. While some relief and rehabilitation is available in camps, the gaps in processes on the ground, especially over a longer term, contribute to the control and management of migrants in ways that are inconsistent with the charters and conventions that are supposed to address the human insecurities of migrants—even where UN agencies are involved. Furthermore, the holding of refugees in camps—the cases described here—has to be understood as part of the deals that powerful political actors are able to set up in order to hold migrants in other countries. The case of the camps in Turkey as part of the deal with the EU, noted in the previous section, is an example of such containment and distancing. Thus, the camps emerge as one more repelling project for some countries. The confinement of refugees to camps and the restriction of their ability to advocate for themselves or live according to the terms set out by migrant and refugee conventions are mechanisms of governance through distancing.

PROFITING FROM MIGRANT DETENTION

While camps are places where migrants are housed, in theory temporarily, till they can move to other locations, the non-governmental governance structures that manage camps showcase how humanitarian actors benefit from these enterprises. However, the other facet of this type of management, that is, the holding of migrants in detention centres, illustrates a starker reality—profiteering from holding migrants in conditions where they have very few rights. Much of the detention takes place in private prisons so that asylum seekers, *like trafficked persons*, are treated as commodities for profit-making. According to UNHCR's 2012 guidelines, seeking asylum is not an unlawful act, and asylum seekers and refugees are supposed to be protected by a series of rights. Edwards[55] points out that governments flagrantly violate these guidelines, which are supposed to protect migrants. Migrants are increasingly detained and interned around the world, suffering not only the deprivation of liberty, but also other forms of abuse of human rights. Governments have begun to elide the differences between migrants (with and without documents), refugees, asylum seekers, and trafficked persons, both rhetorically and through distancing practices. Furthermore, the ascriptions of criminality attributed to migrants rationalise practices of holding them in detention centres.

Accounts of migrant detention centres are now growing. The US is one of the leaders in incubating businesses that profit from detention, partly from the lower costs associated with the privatisation of prisons. Countries such as Australia and New Zealand are using these institutions as well.[56] As the immigrant population in the US has increased from the late twentieth century onwards, immigration policy has shifted away from regulation and towards enforcement, punishment, and deterrence, making immigration enforcement goals more aligned with those of the criminal justice system. The merging of these systems—now referred to as 'crimmigration'—has a significant impact on the functioning of both immigration and detention, and the state and federal prison systems. Violations related to migration are now deemed crimes, which results in an increase in the number of immigrants who are deportable and are held in immigration detention centres. The US Supreme Court has upheld a law that requires mandatory detention until removal for any noncitizen who has been convicted of an aggravated felony and served their sentence, without requiring an individualised due process hearing. Simultaneously, the government has outsourced the task of holding 'these criminals' to private prisons.

Not surprisingly, then, the last few decades have witnessed the rising involvement and influence of the private prison industry in US immigration enforcement, alongside the expansion of the immigration detention system. During the fiscal year (FY) 2016, approximately 353,000 immigrants identified for detention or removal by the US Immigration and Customs Enforcement (ICE) passed through one of more than 200 immigration detention facilities, up from 209,000 in 2001. By August 2016, nearly three-quarters of the average daily immigrant detainee population was held in facilities operated by private prison companies—a sharp contrast from a decade ago, when the majority were held in immigration-contracted bed space in local jails and state prisons.[57] US immigration services paid GEO—the largest private prison company—$32 million a year to house, feed, and provide medical care for 1,000 detainees. In a further blurring of boundaries, so-called charities, such as SouthWest Key, have received millions of dollars from the US government to house the children of migrants in 'shelters'. These shelters have subsequently been sharply criticised for the harsh, inhumane conditions to which children were subject, while the management profited through greatly enhanced salaries.[58]

These detention centres hold men, women, and children in a state of rightlessness, distancing them from systems of redress. At the same time, the business of migrants is highly profitable. According to John Burnett,[59] forced labour is a constant at these privatised detention centres. Two lawsuits alleged that people were forced to work for a dollar a day, which the GEO group does not deny, pointing instead to ICE as setting its rates, while it holds no political position for or against any immigration policy itself. Similarly, Victoria Lopez and Sandra Park[60] report that neither the US immigration service nor private prison managements are proactive in stopping sexual assault in these centres. With the US's current practice of separating children from their parents, the situation has been further exacerbated.

This industry is transnational in character. For instance, since 1997, the Australian immigration detention apparatus has been privately operated,[61] but from 1997 until 2004, Australia's mainland detention centres were run by Australian Correctional Management in partnership with an Australian corporation, Thiess Constructions, and a US-based security company, Wackenhut Corporation. After charges of detainee abuse, Australian Correction Management was replaced. Between 2004 and 2009, combinations of the British Global Solutions Limited and other transnational corporations received the contract, which was financed by venture capitalist funds. These corporations attract such funds on the basis of the idea that the detention industry is growing rapidly.

Drawing on the case of Canada, Janet Cleveland[62] has argued that immigration detention centres are prisons in all but name. Detainees are under constant surveillance by cameras and uniformed guards, subject to repeated searches, in a facility with centrally controlled locked doors surrounded by fences topped with razor wire. Men and women are held in separate wings, with a special section for children detained with their mothers. There is no family section, so fathers are separated from their children, although they can see them daily. Personal effects are confiscated. Movement from one area to another within the centre is prohibited, unless escorted by a guard.

DETAINED CHILD ASYLUM SEEKERS

Detained asylum seekers are deprived of liberty and agency, not only through confinement but also through rigid rules, constant surveillance, and the use of restraints. The rules for children—including unaccompanied migrant children, children in families (including young infants), asylum-seeking and refugee children, and children whose parents are seeking asylum or are refugees—are similarly draconian. According to *The Independent*, children in US detention centres are expected to follow strict rules about sleeping, eating, sitting, using nicknames, and crying, but are also expected to make their beds, and mop, scrub, and clean bathrooms. Alice Farmer[63] points out that Greece is one of the major gateways for migrants entering the EU, but it has particularly bad practices for migrant children. Unaccompanied children can spend months in detention centres—often in the same cells as unrelated adults—in conditions that the European Committee for the Prevention of Torture has called 'unacceptable'. Once released from detention in Greece, unaccompanied migrant children are typically served an order to leave the country. If they do not leave the country, they may find themselves back in detention, no matter how vulnerable they are or whether they have a claim to asylum.

Flynn[64] points to the case of Mauritania, which in 2006 opened its first dedicated detention centre for irregular migrants in the port city of Nouadhibou, with assistance from the Spanish Agency for International Development Cooperation. Spain's involvement in establishing the detention centre has raised questions over which authority controls the facility and who guarantees the rights of the detainees. He notes, '[A]s the Mauritania case demonstrates, efforts by core countries to deflect migratory pressures are leading to the externalisation of controls to states that are not considered main destinations of migrants and where the rule of law is often weak.'

Many scholars have begun to note that the growth of the prison complex has become a highly profitable business. They act as nodes of local economic growth.[65] The detention of immigrants in privatised detention centres is part of this economic trend. Discussing Australia, Welch has pointed out that the steady rise of asylum seekers detained on that Australian outpost has led to an influx of immigration officials, guards, interpreters, and other personnel. Scholars have also recognised the social force of privatisation. 'Such corporate interest in detention underscored both its potential profitability and the way commercialisation of immigration detention has contributed to a reinvention of the carceral relationship between the state and the detainee.'[66]

DISTANCING AS GOVERNANCE: CONCLUDING THOUGHTS

Historically, migrants, who provide free and unfree labour, have contributed significantly to economies around the world. States have also devised many practices to govern migrants so that the costs of having migrants—potentially new residents and citizens with claims to resources—are minimised in comparison to their significant labour contributions. Moreover, through centuries, the control of migrants resided in a combination of governments and intermediaries, and in some ways the current scenario is no different. Given this history, it is important to reflect on what is newly significant about these distancing practices.

A key issue is that as nation-states have become independent of colonial powers—which was complicit in many forms of human exploitation (including that of migrants and forced migrants)—there has been an international effort to develop human rights norms and standards, in part to protect people from the might of governments. From the middle of the twentieth century, these conventions and standards were extended to protect migrants; for a short period, it appeared as though the migration terrain was better poised to support migrants' security. However, states have developed an arsenal of 'soft' governance practices to control and reduce the costs of migrants to nation-states while profiting from them. Along with other practices such as using points systems to determine the value of migrants to nation-states,[67] distancing practices sort and sift the value of asylum seekers, refugees, and other migrants. Distancing is part of this arsenal and involves repelling migrants and holding them in camps and detention centres under conditions that offer them little access to rights. These distancing practices are, on one level, a flouting of the many agreements to which most states are signatories. On another level, these practices are devised to keep these violations somewhat invisible. Nation-states detain migrants and force them to return, just as they hold them in distant camps to curtail their ability to seek justice as migrants. In the process, nation-states profit from migrant detention and their labour. Apart from the implications concerning access to rights substantively, distancing projects show that nation-states are simultaneously guarding their established boundaries and operating flexible boundaries-of-practice to manage flows of migrants. While global security regimes and the expansion of surveillance and control have been discussed by migration scholars,[68] these distancing practices are not often marked as a consistent part of contemporary governance practices.

Furthermore, outsourcing governance—in camps and privatised detention centres—is an important part of distancing, since it reduces the direct involvement of nation-states even as their national security agendas remain intact. The use of force and violence are normalised through these projects, whether it is through leaving governance voids so that vigilante groups can flourish, or through direct and institutionalised violence against migrants in detention centres.

It is also important to pay attention to the economic dimensions of distancing practices. Historically, the use of indentured labour and slaves was profitable for many states. We also recognise a brisk trade in human beings for sexual, labour, and organ exploitation.[69]

Distancing introduces legal actors in the profit-making chain. With the rise of crimmigration within countries and the rapid growth of detention centres and camps, private corporations and governments profit from these forms of migrant management. In other words, if temporary labour regimes introduce conditions that are close to indentured labour, then the migrant detention and profit-making from human beings as commodities required for detention complexes appear to be similar in some regards to the conditions of trafficking. Distancing governance creates the scaffold for such profit-making.

In sum, we are in a period where nation-states are interested in both maintaining distinctive migrant categories and blurring the boundaries between them so that established bureaucracies and outsourced governance structures can both be deployed to uphold the security agendas of states. Distancing practices protect states from being charged with human rights violations, since the relative invisibility of such practices makes them appear as disjointed, episodic actions instead of normalised practices. Yet, these distancing practices are key to understanding migrant governance, and indeed, all governance today.

NOTES

1. See UNHCR, 'Figures at a Glance: 122.6 Million People Worldwide Were Forcibly Displaced'. Available at https://www.unhcr.org/us/about-unhcr/who-we-are/figures-glance (accessed March 2025); Rick Lyman and Eddy Smale, 'Migrant Smuggling in Europe is now Worth Billions'. *The New York Times*, 3 September 2015.

2. Michael Flynn, 'Be careful what you wish for'. *Forced Migration Review* 44, 2013, pp. 22–23.

3. William Armaline et al. (eds), *Human Rights in Our Backyard: Injustice and Resistance in the US*. Philadelphia: University of Pennsylvania Press, 2011; Bandana Purkayastha, 'Humanitarianism and Human Rights', in Silke Roth, Bandana Purkayastha, and Tobias Denskus (eds), *Handbook of Humanitarianism and Inequality*, pp. 92–107. Cheltenham, UK: Edward Elgar, 2024.

4. Bandana Purkayastha, 'Migration, Migrants, and Human Security'. *Current Sociology Monograph* 66(2), 2018.

5. Aili Marie Tripp et al. (eds), *Gender, Violence and Human Security: Critical Feminist Perspectives*. New York: New York University Press, 2013, p. 6.

6. Purkayastha, 'Migration, Migrants, and Human Security'.

7. Evelyn Nakano Glenn, 'Settler Colonialism as Structure: A Framework for Comparative Studies of US Race and Gender Formation'. *Sociology of Race and Ethnicity* 1, 2015; Ranabir Samaddar, 'Returning to the Histories of the Late 19th and Early 20th Century Immigration'. *Economic and Political Weekly* 50(2), 2015, pp. 49–55.

8. Purkayastha, 'Migration, Migrants, and Human Security'.

9. Ranabir Samaddar, 'Returning to the Histories of the Late 19th and Early 20th Century Immigration'. *Economic and Political Weekly* 50(2), 2015, p. 16.

10. See 'What is a Refugee', UNHCR, 2018 (available at http://www.unrefugees.org/what-is-a-refugee [accessed February 2025]), for the definition of a refugee vs. an internally dispersed person. According to UNHCR, a refugee is someone who has been forced to flee their country because of persecution, war, or violence. A refugee has a well-founded fear of persecution for reasons of race, religion, nationality, political opinion, or membership in a particular social group. Getting the status of a refugee means the UNHCR has to recognise the migrant as a refugee. For more, see 'Refugee Status Determination', UNHCR, 2019. Available at http://www.unhcr.org/en-us/refugee-status-determination.html (accessed February 2025).

11. Bandana Purkayastha and Farhan Navid Yousaf, *Human Trafficking: Trade in Sex, Labour, and Organs*. London: Polity Press, 2019.

12. Yen Le Espiritu, *Asian American Women and Men: Labour, Laws, and Love*. Walnut Creek, Lanham, New York, Toronto, Oxford: Rowman and Littlefield Publishers, 2003.

13. See the discourses created by the Mahanirban Calcutta Research Group. Refer to Sabyasachi Basu Ray Chaudhury and Ranabir Samaddar (eds), *Rohingyas in South Asia: People Without a State*. New Delhi: Routledge, 2018.

14. Ana Paulina Lee, 'Memory and Non-place: Visual Testimonies of Japanese Latin American Internment During WWII'. *Journal of Latin American Cultural Studies* 28(1), 2019; US House Hearing, 19 March 2009. Available at https://www.govinfo.gov/content/pkg/CHRG-111hhrg48322/html/CHRG-111hhrg48322.htm (accessed June 2024).

15. Lee, 'Memory and Non-place'.

16. Lyman and Smale, 'Migrant Smuggling in Europe is now Worth Billions'; Alison Smale and Melissa Eddy, 'Grisly Discovery in Migrant Crisis Shocks Europe'. *The New York Times*, 27 August 2015. Available at https://www.nytimes.com/2015/08/28/world/europe/bodies-austria-truck-migrant-crisis.html (accessed June 2024).

17. David Montgomery, Manny Fernandez, and Yonette Joseph, 'Journey fatal for migrants found in a San Antonio Parking Lot'. *The New York Times*, 23 July 2017. Available at https://www.nytimes.com/2017/07/23/us/san-antonio-truck-walmart-trafficking.html (accessed June 2024).

18. Antje Missbach and Frieda Sinanu, 'People Smuggling in Indonesia: Dependency, Exploitation and Other Vulnerabilities', in Sallie Yea (ed.), *Human Trafficking in Asia: Forcing Issues*. London: Routledge, 2014.

19. Lyman and Smale, 'Migrant Smuggling in Europe is now Worth Billions'.

20. Yakin Erturk and Bandana Purkayastha, 'Linking research, policy and action: A look at the work of the special rapporteur on violence against women'. *Current Sociology* 60(2), 2012.

21. See, for example, Margaret Abraham, *Speaking the Unspeakable: Marital Violence Among South Asians in the U.S.* New Brunswick, New Jersey: Rutgers University Press, 2000; Sundari Anitha, 'Understanding Economic Abuse Through an Intersectional Lens: Financial Abuse, Control, and Exploitation of Women's Productive and Reproductive Labour'. *Violence Against Women*, 25(15), 2019, pp. 1854–1877; Roseanne Njiru and Bandana Purkayastha, *Voices of Internally Displaced Persons in Kenya: A Human Rights Perspective*. Kolkata and London: Frontpage Publications, 2015.

22. For example, Margaret Abraham and Evangelia Tastsoglou, 'Interrogating Gender, Violence and the State in National and Transnational Contexts'. *Current Sociology* 64(4), 2016; K. Lalitha and Deepa Dhanraj, *Rupture, Loss and Living: Minority Women Speak about Post Conflict Life*. Hyderabad: Orient BlackSwan, 2016; Anja Parish, 'Gender based Violence Against Women: Both Cause for Migration and Risk Along the Journey', Migration Policy Institute, 7 September 2017. Available at http://www.migrationpolicy.org/article/gender-based-violence-against-women-both-cause-migration-and-risk-along-journey (accessed June 2024); Ram Puniyani, *Communalism: India's Struggle for Democracy and Pluralism*. Kolkata and London: Frontpage Publications, 2018; Bandana Purkayastha and Kathryn

Ratcliff, 'Routine Violence: Intersectionality at the Interstices.' *Gendered Perspectives on Conflict and Violence* 18(B), 2014.

23. UN, 'World Migration Report', 2018. Available at https://worldmigrationreport.iom.int/what-we-do/foreword/foreword (accessed January 2025); UNHCR, 'UNHCR Global Trends: Forced Displacement in 2018, 2018'. Available at https://www.unhcr.org/en-us/statistics/unhcrstats/5d08d7ee7/unhcr-global-trends-2018.html (accessed June 2024).

24. In the World Development Report 2023, the category of refugees, migrants, and asylum seekers are clubbed together because the state practices are, more often than not, similar in all three categories. A case in point is the US southern borders of 2021. Many social scientists discuss it as the 'mixed and massive flows'. See Christoph Tometten, 'Juridical Response to Mixed and Massive Population Flows'. *Refugee Watch* 39 & 40 (June and December), 2021.

25. Sallie Yea, 'Trafficked Enough? Missing Bodies, Migrant Labour Exploitation, and the Classification of Trafficking Victims in Singapore'. *Antipode* 47(4), 2015, pp. 1080–1100.

26. Karen Musalo and Eunice Lee, 'Seeking a Rational Approach to a Regional Refugee Crisis: Lessons from the Summer 2014 "Surge" of Central American Women and Children at the US-Mexico Border'. *Journal on Migration and Human Security* 5(1), 2017.

27. Tom Cohen, 'Obama Seeks Emergency Immigration Funds'. CNN, 9 July 2014. Available at http://www.cnn.com/2014/07/08/politics/immigration/ (accessed June 2024).

28. Lutheran Immigration and Refugee Service (LIRS) and Women's Refugee Commission (WRC), *Locking Up Family Values, Again*. Baltimore: LIRS and WRC, 2014, p. 5. Also see, on US President Donald Trump's preferred policy on immigrants, Alayna Treene and Kristen Holmes, 'Trump plots mass detention and deportation of undocumented immigrants should he regain power'. *CNN Politics*, 11 November 2023. Available at https://www.cnn.com/2023/11/11/politics/trump-stephen-miller-immigration-detention-deportation/index.html (accessed March 2025).

29. Bill Frelick, Ian Kysel, and Jennifer Podkul, 'The Impact of Externalization of Migrant Controls on the Rights of Asylum Seekers and Other Migrants'. *Journal on Migration and Human Security* 4(4), 2016.

30. Alan Yuhas, 'US Agents Fire Tear Gas Across Mexican Border'. *The New York Times*, 1 January 2019.

31. Lyman and Smale, 'Migrant Smuggling in Europe is now Worth Billions'; Matthew Brunwasser, 'A 21st-Century Migrant's Essentials: Food,

Shelter, Smartphone'. *The New York Times*, 25 August 2015. Available at https://www.nytimes.com/2015/08/26/world/europe/a-21st-century-migrants-checklist-water-shelter-smartphone.html (accessed February 2025); Alison Smale and Melissa Eddy, 'Grisly Discovery in Migrant Crisis Shocks Europe'. *The New York Times*, 27 August 2015. Available at https://www.nytimes.com/2015/08/28/world/europe/bodies-austria-truck-migrant-crisis.html (accessed June 2024).

32. Kemal Kirişci, 'The Question of Asylum and Illegal Migration in European Union-Turkish Relations'. *Turkish Studies* 4(1), 2003.

33. BBC Media Action, 'Voices of Refugees: Information and Communications Needs of Refugees in Greece and Germany'. Research Report, July 2016. Available at http://downloads.bbc.co.uk/mediaaction/pdf/research/voices-of-refugees-research-report.pdf (accessed June 2024).

34. 'Migrant Crisis: EU-Turkey Deal Comes into Effect'. *BBC News*, 20 March 2016. Available at https://www.bbc.com/news/world-europe-35854413 (accessed June 2024).

35. Mary Crock, 'In the Wake of the Tampa: Conflicting Visions of International Refugee Law in the Management of Refugee Flows'. *Pacific Rim Journal of Law and Policy* 12(1), 2003.

36. Katrina Stats, 'Welcome to Australia? A Reappraisal of the Fraser Government's Approach to Refugees, 1975–83'. *Australian Journal of International Affairs* 69(1), 2015.

37. Matthew Doran and Jane Norman, 'Amnesty says Australian officials who paid people smugglers to turn boats back committed transnational crimes'. *ABC News*, 29 October 2015. Available at https://www.abc.net.au/news/2015-10-29/paying-people-smugglers-to-turn-around-is-transnational-crime/6894610 (accessed June 2024).

38. According to the latest figures, the top refugee-hosting countries are Turkey, Uganda, Pakistan, Lebanon, and Iran.

39. Antonio Donini, 'The Far Side: The Meta Functions of Humanitarianism in a Globalised World'. *Disasters* 34(S2), 2010, p. 5221.

40. Silke Roth, *The Paradoxes of Aidwork—Passionate Professionals*. Oxon and New York: Routledge, 2015.

41. Donini, 'The Far Side, p. 5221.

42. UNHCR, 'UNHCR's Strategic Directions 2017–2021', 2017. Available at https://www.unhcr.org/5894558d4.pdf (accessed June 2024).

43. Ranabir Samaddar, 'Returning to the Histories of the Late 19th and Early 20th Century Immigration'.

44. Roth, *The Paradoxes of Aidwork—Passionate Professionals*.

45. UNHCR, 'UNHCR's Strategic Directions 2017–2021'.

46. UNHCR, 'UNHCR Policy on Alternatives to Camps', 2009, p. 4. Available at https://cms.emergency.unhcr.org/documents/11982/45535/UNHCR+-+Policy+on+alternatives+to+camps/005c0217-7d1e-47c9-865a-c0098cfdda62 (accessed June 2024).

47. This is so because settling people in camps is not a permanent solution. Camps cannot be taken as modes of rehabilitation, and so this is an exceptional measure.

48. 'UNHCR Alternative to Camp Policy, 2009'. UNHCR, 2009. Available at https://cms.emergency.unhcr.org/documents/ 11982/45535/UNHCR+-+Policy+on+alternatives+to+camps/005c0217-7d1e-47c9-865a-c0098cfdda62 (accessed June 2024).

UNHCR 2014a. Available at https://www.unhcr.org/alternatives-to-camps.html (accessed June 2024).

UNHCR 2014b. Available at https://cms.emergency.unhcr.org/documents/ 11982/53652/Camp+Security+Guidelines/e96b31e5-7344-4137-9b84-ba23f49e5ac6 (accessed June 2024).

49. Sari Hanafi, 'Palestinian Refugee Camps in Lebanon: Laboratories of State-in-the-Making, Discipline and Islamist Radicalism', in Ronit Lentin (ed.), *Thinking Palestine*. London: Zed Books, 2008.

50. In the recent past, there has been a resurgence of this interest due to the genocidal acts that are being committed on Palestinian refugees by the Isreali army.

51. Alice Szczepanikova, 'Performing Refugeeness in the Czech Republic: Gendered Depoliticisation through NGO Assistance'. *Gender, Place & Culture* 17(4), 2010.

52. These refugees were largely from Belarus, Chechnya, and Armenia. The conflicts that led to their being displaced began in 2006.

53. Njiru and Purkayastha, *Voices of Internally Displaced Persons in Kenya*.

54. See, for example, Elizabeth Holzer, 'What Happens to Law in a Refugee Camp?' *Law and Society Review* 47(4), 2013.

55. Alice Edwards, 'Detention Under Scrutiny'. *Forced Migration Review* 44, 2013, pp. 4–6.

56. Wayne Calabrese, 'Privatised Corrections:-United States, Australia and New Zealand'. Canberra: Australian Institute of Criminology, 2017.

57. Livia Luan, 'Profiting from Enforcement: The Role of Private Prisons in U.S.'. Immigration Policy Institute, 2 May 2018. Available at https://www.migrationpolicy.org/article/profiting-enforcement-role-private-prisons-us-immigration-detention (accessed June 2024).

58. Lim Barker, Nicholas Kulish, and Rebecca Ruiz, 'He's Built an Empire, With Detained Migrant Children as the Bricks'. *The New York Times*, 2 December 2018.

59. John Burnett, 'Big Money as Private Immigrant Jails Boom'. *National Public Radio*, 21 November 2017. Available at https://www.npr.org/2017/11/21/565318778/big-money-as-private-immigrant-jails-boom (accessed June 2024).

60. Victoria López and Sandra Park, 'ICE Detention Center Says It's Not Responsible for Staff's Sexual Abuse of Detainees'. *American Civil Liberties Union*, 6 November 2018. Available at https://www.aclu.org/blog/immigrants-rights/immigrants-rights-and-detention/ice-detention-center-says-its-not-responsible (accessed June 2024).

61. Calabrese, 'Privatised Corrections:-United States, Australia and New Zealand'; Binoy Kampmark, 'Securitization, Refugees, and Australia's Turn Back the Boats Policy, 2013–2015'. *Antipodes* 31(1), 2017; Michael Welch, 'Economic Man and Diffused Sovereignty: A Critique of Australia's Asylum Regime'. *Crime, Law and Social Change* 61(1), 2014.

62. Janet Cleveland, 'Psychological Harm and the Case for Alternativesm'. *Forced Migration Review* 44, 2013, pp. 7–8.

63. Alice Farmer, 'The impact of immigration detention on children'. *Forced Migration Review* 44, 2013, pp. 14–16.

64. Flynn, 'Be careful what you wish for'.

65. William Armaline et al. (eds), *Human Rights in Our Backyard: Injustice and Resistance in the US*. Philadelphia: University of Pennsylvania Press, 2011; Burnett, 'Big Money As Private Immigrant Jails Boom'.

66. Welch, 'Economic Man and Diffused Sovereignty: A Critique of Australia's Asylum Regime', p. 88.

67. James Walsh, 'From Nations of Immigrants to States of Transience: Temporary Migration in Canada and Australia'. *International Sociology* 29(6), 2014, pp. 584–606, and 'Quantifying Citizens: Neoliberal Restructuring and Immigrant Selection in Canada and Australia'. *Citizenship Studies* 15(6–7), 2011, pp. 861–879.

68. See, for example, the review in Purkayastha, 'Migration, Migrants, and Human Security'.

69. Purkayastha and Yousaf, *Human Trafficking*.

2

The Leash and the Rip

Struggles and Conflicts Beneath Migrants' and Asylum Seekers' 'Secondary Movements'

Federico Rahola

Fortress/Borderland

The so-called 'EU crisis'—of refugees, asylum, migration, and borders—leaves behind, as a material trace, its own specific geography. It is a new 'topology' of Europe—one connecting fences, (hot)spots, detention/reception centres, informal encampments, corridors, and routes—that seems to no longer correspond to any possible linear map. Such a peculiar, stirred, and selected surface is produced by the movements of both migrants and asylum seekers—their forced, chosen, or sought routes—and by the superimposition of a renewed EU and EU states' border regime that, under the seal of the crisis, has been implemented to govern and control those very movements.

Accordingly, the first impression is that of a battleground within and outside the EU borders, one translating itself into a shifting and moving sequence of signs, names, and localities: Idomeni, Lesvos, Kios, Lampedusa, Ceuta, and Melilla; but also Calais, Ventimiglia, the Brennero passage at Italy, and Austria borders, up to the border zone crisscrossing the so-called 'Balkan route' (the towns of Bihac and Velika Kladusa between Bosnia and Croatia, that of Šid, between Serbia and Croatia, the Austro-Hungarian border pass of Nickelsdorf, or the one of Spielfeld between Austria and Slovenia). This apparently impossible map, actually an assemblage of scattered points, may coalesce into a unified narrative of closure, which nonetheless seems to reflect a broader fragmentation, a series of rips, scars, or frictions.[1]

From the standpoint of external borders, this map suggests and fosters the image of a fortress, of an increasingly selective area characterised by a growing impermeability. The idea of a 'spectacle of border',[2] in this regard, must be assumed almost literally as the theatre of barbed-wire, nocturnal visors, navy vessels, shipwrecking, and search and rescue operations (SAR), as well as of identification, detention, and expulsion centres, and of special police forces for border patrol. It is a spectacle where the (otherwise frequently made invisible) bodies of migrants and asylum seekers are over-exposed, becoming almost transparent to the technologies of surveillance through biometric data mining and scanned fingerprinting archives. However, it is also the staging of a spectacle of 'invasion' and, above all, it is a spectacle of race: one where race is relentlessly produced through the management of bodies that are marked, identified, confined, and illegalised as clandestine, or represented as deprived and demanding subjects. Finally, it is a murderous spectacle of death, with over 34,000 men, women, and children, whose death 'in and for' migration, from 1998 to May 2018, has been documented by a survey promoted by the militant and activist network UNITED.[3]

From this specific angle, the renewed EU borderscape reveals itself to be primarily a necropolitical space.[4] Further, death seems to work as the other complementary and possible aspect in the life of an exceeding (rather than national, as suggested by the Foucauldian notion of a thanatopolitics)[5] population. There is a kind of sovereign power in such a spectacle, in the deflected sense of an act blurring the distinction between life and death, of a decision that may act at a distance, upon a grey zone, in terms of a 'let-to-die'. This, at the same time, seems to produce sovereign effects in defining a rescuable yet detainable and deportable humanity, exceeding any binary code or dialectical opposition between exclusion and inclusion.[6]

There exist, in many respects, analogies with the European situation of the 1930s, when a massive and growing number of stateless people wandered around the hyper-striated national geography of post-World War I Europe, were rejected by every single state,[7] and ended up finding space in a detention centre or an internment camp, which were the only possible places to territorialise their 'nothing but human' rights.[8] The recent blockade of the Italian ports, in the last weeks of the summer of 2018, where NGO vessels operating in the SAR area were forced to wander around without finding a safe harbour, appears in this regard a further step in the ongoing militarisation and sovereign-isation of external borders. In other words, it is the projection outwards of a 'spectacle' that oversteps the land and ends up investing the overall Mediterranean, transforming it into a hyper-striated and nationalised area. Additionally, it is a step that resonates with the ongoing militarisation of both external (as in the case of the fences and walls in Ceuta/Melilla, the Spaniard enclaves in Morocco) and internal EU borders (as testified by the Austrian project of a wall on the Italian frontier, and by the actual electrified one protecting the border between Hungary and Serbia), further improving the image of a fortress, as the sum of a whole range of fortified national territories.

Besides, the image of an impenetrable space surrounded by peremptory frontiers is reinforced by the adoption of two further border apparatuses. The first is the implementation of the 'hotspot approach', that is, of allegedly temporary centres and accelerated procedures to identify and filter migrants and asylum seekers, which operate already on the fringe of EU external borders (as in the case of southern Italy, in Lampedusa, Trapani, Pozzallo, Taranto, and of the Greek islands, or again in Ceuta and Melilla). The second is the adoption of a series of renewed *refoulement* agreements, signed both at national and European levels with 'safe' third countries such as Turkey, Libya, or Niger, where to possibly and directly 're-patriate', that is, expel, those people on the move (the so-called '"bogus" refugees'), whose application for asylum or humanitarian protection has been denied or not taken into account. This is in accordance with a process of externalisation and outsourcing of EU borders, the origins of which go back to the late 1990s. From this angle, we can actually argue that the European geography produced by the crisis and its governance reveals itself as an overall militarised (and 'sovereignised') one, reflecting the impression of a homogeneous and almost sealed space.

Yet there exists another immediate (governmental) dimension related to the spectacle of the border, as well as another geography produced by the EU crisis of refugees, migrants, and borders, one which may arguably seem less spectacular if compared to the aforementioned 'sovereign' momentum, but that nonetheless reveals itself to be deeper, or at least as effective, in its capacity to reshape the European space. It deals with the massive proliferation of internal borders, and the uneven and hierarchised quality of the space thus produced. In order to address such a hyper-striated dimension, which corresponds to the material ground that migrants and asylum seekers actually experience while moving and dwelling within European territories, it is worth recalling the image of an overall '*borderland*'[9]—a highly fragmented and racialised territory, crisscrossed by a proliferation of borders and border apparatuses. Such a dimension ends up revealing itself to be as far from the original idea of EU integration, enlargement, and unification as it is from the image of a fortress, if only because it has definitely splintered and fallen apart.

It is in the contradictory and mutual interplay—as well as interference and tension—between the projection of the image of a fortress and the actual production of a 'borderland' that we must situate the reshaping of the European political space enacted by the governing of the EU 'refugee crisis', which conceives it as the outcome of a specific sovereign-governmental machine, or a 'sovereign machine of governmentality'.[10] While the former term indicates a harshening in the logics of closure and expulsion,[11] the latter suggests a relentless implementation of less spectacular, yet equally impressive and powerful, racialised processes of bordering as well as of the subaltern, differential, and 'obscene' inclusion (or reclusion/containment) of the migrant presence within EU-rope. It thus mainly points to the reshaping of the material conditions of life and the dwelling of migrants, refugees, and asylum seekers within and amidst European territories.

Further, while the former refers to the peremptory staging of fences and walls, the latter stands for a technique by which the movement and presence of migrants is governed, by controlling, directing, containing, isolating, and imposing a pace and forced paths to it. At first glance, we would argue that walls and fences alike pertain to an array of devices and objects that harks back to a specific and rather conventional notion of nation-state sovereign power. Wendy Brown suggests conceiving them also as implicit symptoms of a certain lack or a weakness of sovereignty,[12] revealing its incapacity to control and govern its own borders and territory. Yet, if something similar to a sovereign act has to be detected in the very gesture of producing a certain dimension of space (and time as well), and of imposing, through borders, differential regimes of inhabiting and circulating within such a space, we could envisage a whole series of actual sovereign effects in the governmental production of the current European borderscape, and view them as the most tangible outcome of the specific sovereign-governmental machine corresponding to the EU governance of the refugee crisis.

It is such a specific dimension of 'borderland', conceived as an overall uneven, striated, racialised, and controlled, yet conflicting and contested, political space, that will be questioned and focussed on in this chapter, foremost by asking what it reacts or responds to. In the wake of different critical studies on contemporary migrations, which emphasise their autonomy,[13] I start from the assumption that current migrant movements and practices always, in some way, exceed the regulative capability of state powers, and that they also direct those assemblages of power towards an updated response ('movement first' could sound in this case as a translation of the Deleuzian 'resistance first' in the specific framework of border politics). This is particularly true in the case of the current refugee and border crisis, insofar as it has been triggered by a relentless 'drive', a path or a direction materialising as a concrete 'right to escape',[14] and filled with thousands of practices and spectacular acts or events of border-crossing (like the long march from the Keleti station in Budapest towards the German border in the summer of 2015) that openly defied and forced the EU government towards a renewed borderscape. In other words, 'to make sense of what otherwise presents itself as a "crisis" of border control for the various sovereign powers implicated in the heterogeneous superintendence of the European border regime, the primacy of the autonomy and subjectivity of human mobility is paramount.'[15] To assume the European borderland as primarily an answer or a reaction to the 'primacy' of such autonomous internal movements means therefore to detect the way those movements are governed and 'translated' by EU border apparatuses and logics.

THE PROSE OF COUNTER-MIGRATION

There is a certain lack of imagination in the way the 'prose' of EU migration governance (which refers to the whole production of reports, briefings, and benchmarks drafted by a heterogeneous and often conflicting set of actors involved, on different levels, in governing the presence of migrants and asylum seekers at the borders of or within and amidst EU territories[16]) tends to represent its own 'objects' of attention. Within such an objectifying and 'positive' discourse, behind the persistent adoption of scientific, physical, or hydraulic metaphors (flows, push and pull factors, quota), a peculiar definition has resurfaced, whose adoption, although dating back some fifteen or twenty years ago, has increased significantly since 2014–2015. This re-emergence signals a growing emergency, or a threat to a technique of government that results in synchronised, selected, and governed flows. It is therefore a definition that translates, by being its immediate signifier, a whole array of unpredictable or less predictable phenomena and behaviour. The proper formula, in EU governance jargon, is 'secondary movements', but what kinds of movement does it designate while defining them as secondary? Here is the official definition of 'secondary movements', as given in a EU Parliamentary Briefing in November 2017: '[T]he phenomenon of migrants, including refugees and asylum-seekers, who for various reasons move from the country in which they first arrived, to seek protection or permanent resettlement elsewhere.'[17]

This is a very synthetic and apparently anodyne formula, one which nonetheless demands further explanation, starting from the notion of 'country of first arrival'. The reference here is to the

Dublin Regulation/Convention and the obligation it imposes on the first EU country 'touched' by a newcomer migrant to identify them, collect their personal data (biographical and/or biometric, the filing of which coalesces into centralised big-data archives like SiS-EuroDac), register their possible asylum application, and bind their presence and stay within its own territory. It must be added that the strict adoption of the Convention provoked huge opposition, even at the institutional level, given the effects of congestion and overcrowding it leads to in the countries of first arrival (such as Italy, Greece, and Spain).[18]

Leaving aside the evident contradictions and imbalances in European policies of reception, and upon a mere reading of the text, it is worth focussing here on a significant shift. Indeed, the use of the term 'secondary movements' seems to allude to an unforeseen or less predictable phenomenon, which exceeds and transgresses the restrictions on mobility and displacement imposed by the Convention. Further, this shift is registered even in language. On the one hand, to define the routes or the uncertain journeys that lead to the EU external borders, the most conventional term 'flows' is preferred. On the other hand, by using this term to refer to a series of disordered yet substantially unidirectional and defined or pre-established routes, the encounter with a European territory and a EU border device translates those flows into something less linear and predictable. It is as if, by breaking on the first solid obstacle intercepted, these flows reorganise themselves into a multiplicity of scattered possible branches. Here, then, appears the more heteroclite, disordered, and plural 'movements'. In other words, after intercepting the first border signal or device, the flows that confer predictability and unidirectionality to primary mobility rearticulate themselves in the scattered and multifarious dimension, induced or otherwise, of 'secondary movements', and thereby become symptoms of a (further and different) problem of government. The briefing obviously does not limit itself to unconsciously recording such an evolution; instead, aiming to intervene in it, it proceeds with a first recognition and interpretation of the phenomenon, alluding to its immediate consequences in terms of a progressive sequence of possible infractions:

> While most asylum-seekers seek protection in countries close to their countries of origin, some are compelled or choose to move onwards from or through countries in which they had, or could have sought, international protection, to other countries where they may request such protection. Such secondary or onward movements are often done in an irregular manner, that is, without the prior consent of the national authorities or without an entry visa, or with no or insufficient documentation normally required for travel purposes, or with false or fraudulent documentation.[19]

Here, it is possible to catch at work something like an axiom, the imposition of a 'rule' that defines or fixes an abstract principle—the idea that the majority of asylum seekers look for protection in countries close to their own—on the basis of which it is possible to build up a gradation of exceptions or discrepancies. Nothing but the obvious truism, that every exit or escape from one's own country (unless it is surrounded by water) necessarily has to pass through neighbouring countries, can support such a statement. Nonetheless, starting from a similar truism, the text establishes a norm according to which can be set 'rational' behavioural standards—a direction, some ordered flows. In other words, it translates the mobility into ideally linear, intelligible, predictable, regulated, and regular terms, and in so doing it implicitly designates the existence of a transgression to such a logic of legibility and regularity, which is nothing but the effect imposed by the logic adopted to govern such movements.[20]

However, the starting assumption notwithstanding, it is hypothetically admitted that asylum seekers are either compelled (without specifying, at least at this level, by whom or what) or (and this is different) choose to 'move onward', and that this choice, induced or not, is at various levels in conflict with the forms of mobility defined as a norm, namely the criteria established as legitimate by the Convention (a formal authorisation of internal mobility, a permit or a visa to a third country, etc.). There is no need to investigate what, barring the application of this 'abstract norm', makes such mobility practices increasingly 'irregular', since such a consequence is inscribed in the tautological circularity imposed by the initial assumption. Rather, it is worth questioning the significance of the adjective 'compelled', with which those unusual practices are associated, emphasising how, in the case of secondary movements, the word takes on a meaning that sensibly differs from the conventional and mainstream one adopted to indicate some of the most recurrent corollaries (the 'trafficking', the 'human trade') of 'primary movements' when read as forced migrations.

It is as if, between the lines, behind the (trafficked, traded) victim and the (legitimate or not) potential refugee, an incomprehensible route (and not just the escape), as expression of a simple survival instinct, was hidden a will to migrate—desires and aspirations that exceed the bounded or 'harnessed' institutional reception of European states, becoming synonymous, in the prose of the EU counter-migration, of as many transgressions or irregularities. The following statement, and the specific 'will to knowledge' animating the prose of the briefing, partly contribute to clarifying this (not completely unconscious) mechanism, the foreclosure of the 'desiring' character, and the implicitly political aspirations driving the specific migrants and asylum seekers' movements registered as 'secondary': 'There has been growing interest among academics and stakeholders in the reasons why asylum-seekers prefer to make an application for asylum in one country over another, both in Europe and beyond.'[21]

The implications of a survey on the reasons for unpredictable behaviour that appeals to academic knowledge—or to a 'science of migrations', with its relative stakeholders—should be further investigated. The reference to a constellation of knowledge (and powers) to make sense of 'abnormal' patterns of conduct that belie the axiom of the 'first country' (safe or not), produces a list of realistic, plausible, and understandable reasons (translated, in the jargon of migration studies, in terms of push and pull factors, through the profile of a rational collective actor, on whose behalf every apparent infraction is read along the complementary polarities of a victimised or an irregular subject). The report therefore motivates such a 'push onward' on the basis of the need for effective forms of protection, family reunification, better living and working conditions, etc. Yet, we can add something about these 'comprehensive' interpretations. For instance, we can underline the fictional assumption on whose basis the unitary subject enunciating them is positioned. Starting from an obvious fact: that Portugal, Italy, Greece, or Spain (hence the infamous acronym PIGS), and arguably even more so Hungary, Poland, the Czech Republic, and Slovakia, are not exactly the same thing as France or Belgium, which in turn are not Germany, Denmark, and Sweden, which are probably not the United Kingdom, the United States, or Canada. In other words, if the secondary 'onward' movements are harnessed and bound within a space, a Convention, a set of norms, and a discourse that bind them to fixed points within such a space, the existence of these movements calls into question the very space of enunciation presupposed by the briefing, the hologram of a unitary space, federated and conceived as homogeneous. Their routes materially denounce the uneven geography of Europe, and as it has been suggested, they 'vote with their feet' against the effects of any sovereign debt restructuring or memoranda imposed by European governance.[22]

The report fails to explicitly state or admit all this. The knowledge it relies upon can at least induce it to recognise how these onward routes may be determined by 'objectively different' material opportunities as well as by the weight of 'colonial legacy', and not strictly because of 'family' reunifications and so on. Yet, despite such a mix of 'comprehensive' knowledge, it does not read the routes and places chosen or inhabited by the subjects of the 'secondary movements' as alternatives to the geography it presupposes and to the specific model of protection or reception it envisages and supports. More precisely, the report and 'its' knowledges fail to admit that the routes of those identified as the subjects of secondary movements may be constituted 'along the way', and their rules and directions decided as they go along, against any attempt to govern and know them from above. In other words, these movements are 'forced' by government interventions and border devices that they themselves contribute to trigger (according to an old rule, movements first), and against which they often react in terms of opposition, not resignation, but as 'insurrection'. Finally, the movements and behaviour cumulatively recorded as 'secondary' are expressions of an idea and a map of Europe that are radically opposed to those implicitly assumed and explicitly reproduced by EU migration governance.

Such an implicitly opposed alternative and contesting dimension—as it emerges from the tenacious building up of new border passages or informal encampments after their systematic closure, patrolling, or dismantling—operates as the subtext that covertly moves and animates the governmental prose of the report, representing secondary movements as a 'problem' and encouraging the irregularisation and criminalisation of their subjects. In the final part of the report, by leaving aside any 'justifiable' causes or reasons and focussing specifically on the implications and immediate effects of these secondary movements, the prose changes its tone: it alludes to the alleged risks of exploitation and trafficking that asylum seekers are exposed to (even within European territories and without identifying causes and responsibilities); denounces the pressures placed on the reception capacities of some single countries; evokes probable hostile reactions from the public; configures possible abuses or 'misuses' of the protection system (multiple asylum applications and asylum shopping); underlines how such movements may produce tensions and frictions among the different member-states, resulting in the tightening of control measures, extension of detention, and an increase in recourse to deportations. In the end, it outlines a process of criminalisation, culminating in a list of punitive measures to counter those internal movements—all this after reiterating the quest for harmonious protection policies within the framework of the Common European Asylum System (CEAS), in order to inhibit and limit the phenomenon:

> Whereas the main objective of CEAS instruments is to provide a common level of protection, their preambles also state that harmonisation 'should help to limit the secondary movements of applicants for international protection between Member States'. For this purpose, some of the instruments provide for:
>
> – the possibility to withdraw reception conditions from asylum-seekers (Article 20, Reception Conditions Directive),
> – the detention of applicants (Article 8, Reception Conditions Directive), and

- the reduction of procedural guarantees under certain circumstances (Articles 31, 32, 33 and 43, Asylum Procedures Directive).[23]

In addition to the implicit will to separate 'the wheat from the chaff', the legitimate refugees from the 'bogus' ones—that is, the economic migrants—and besides the immediate effect of using asylum as a tool for criminalising migrations,[24] it is worth focusing here on the apparent disjunctures characterising the prose of the report. A 'comprehensible' phenomenon, yet one recorded as an 'exception' to abstract criteria taken as a standard, reveals itself to be at the same time a security problem and an 'irregular' behaviour to be inhibited, opposed, governed, and repressed; what does a similar ambivalence—the oscillation and deviation that the aseptic prose of the text registers between the lines—stand for?

My point, as has already been made clear, is that what has been cumulatively defined as 'secondary movements' does actually represent a heterogeneous and differentiated set of practices, movements, and conducts that, from any angle and beyond the many different reasons and conditions they may reflect, always exceed, contest, and try to subvert the European government's strategies and the violent and harsh legal and material border apparatuses they come equipped with. The subjects of those movements always embody an excess and enact an overt and explicit form of resistance that does not coincide with or reflect the material map and borderland that the EU 'sovereign machine of migration government' draws up and imposes.

The next several pages will focus on this latent form of 'insurgency', denied and 'foreclosed' by the EU prose of counter-migration. The aim is to bring out the war implicit in the pacified language of 'secondary movements', and to read it through the lens of what, paraphrasing the title of an outstanding book by Partha Chatterjee,[25] could be defined as the 'politics of the confined'. This, however, after noticing a final slip, almost a Freudian *lapsus*, in the prose of the report: in the last lines, the subjects of secondary movements are suddenly referred to as 'absconded',[26] literally hidden, fugitive, clandestine, as were the fugitive slaves, the *cimarrones* fleeing the sugarcane plantation systems of the Caribbean and West Indian colonial companies. 'Absconded' refers to the one who flees, runs away and hides in the bush, but who also acts in the shadows and thus becomes invisible within the folds of a territory and a discourse, whereby their presence directly contributes to animate and subvert.

Within (and Against) Borderland

The term 'absconded' should be further explored. As we have seen, it can be traced to the emotional and almost ontological condition of the fugitive slaves, the *marrones* who, running away from the plantations system, broke the material chains they were tied to, often gathering together in clandestine settlements or encampments where they organised themselves in a temporary yet radically different society.[27] It is arguably little more than an evocative analogy, but even the contemporary European borderland is full of temporary, 'informal' encampments that are built and dwelled in by many of the actors of the secondary movements. Sometimes these places grow to a considerable size, near official and overcrowded emergency reception or containment centres (as in the case of Moria, on Lesvos island). However, they also emerge within or close to several cities and towns localised on the margins of EU territory (Bihac, Thessaloniki, Sofia). It is as if they were spread out through a kind of meiosis, working most of the time as a harsh and gloomy parallel or surplus—a side effect, the 'out of shot' or 'off-screen'—of what elsewhere I have referred to as a 'camp-form'.[28] Yet they can also spring up and rise in the urban public spaces of European core cities (Paris, Brussels, Milano, Athens), amidst parks or squares, near railway stations, or in vacant lots. More frequently, they are assembled near a border or directly on a border zone, as gatherings and crossroad places or waiting rooms, dwelled in by a heterogeneous, temporary, and shifting population of subjects in transit.[29]

In the first case, the impression is that those (more or less) temporary encampments work mainly as an emergency, deprived, half-relinquished, and improvised way to get by, as a gloomy and shadowy supplement paralleling and accompanying the overcrowded institutional reception or containment centres. But on the contrary, they actually seem to trigger or prompt the existence of an official relocation/detention centre, which in turn reveals itself as a means to govern an otherwise ungovernable space, and irregular forms of inhabiting and moving within it. Indeed, though frequently hidden, these specific encampments are overexposed to police control and stigmatised in terms of social perception and public opinion. Debated and contested, they are always represented as a security threat, a scandal, a way of dwelling embodying dangerous, unhealthy, unsafe, and uncivilised practices, and thus labelled as jungles, ghettos, or habitats for an (un)urban outcast. An overt or silent, yet always violent, process of racialisation invests these places and the people inhabiting them, the myth of a proper space to be found in a camp, as a legitimate place producing its own 'race'. Not surprisingly, then, they are constantly under siege and systematically dismantled, their dwellers evicted and relocated to institutional reception/detention centres through spectacular and often mediatised police operations of cleansing, which are justified under health and security reasons. Seldom, and particularly when placed at the margins—as in the case of Idomeni or Moria—they are merely forgotten, as if they had been deleted or repressed once their echo had died away.

Yet, these camps also work as a kind of crossroads and meeting spots where different biographies, routes, and languages encounter each other and share experiences through hidden passwords and maps. Though highly segregated and frequently internally splintered along national or ethnic divisions and conflicts, they may produce their inner idioms, a common jargon, which is a form of tactical mimicry of EU governance prose. Such a relational dimension could be further amplified by their being a peculiar contact zone, since their actual existence, in terms of production and material reproduction, is the outcome of a cooperation between migrants or asylum seekers and some NGOs, or militant and activist groups. The most outstanding instance of such cooperation—an exception in this scenario, insofar as it radically reverses the perception of precariousness characterising these places—is probably represented by the City Plaza Hotel in Athens, where a group of activists and dwellers occupied and still manage together an abandoned four-star hotel located in the city centre, near the Archeological Museum, transforming it into a second 'safe' step where to decompress and reorganise projects and routes for many actors of the secondary movements who have passed through the Greek islands' encampments or official centres.

Much more can be said about those variegated, informal occupied places, more figures to be provided and, above all, direct stories and experiences to be told. Indeed, a series of ethnographic accounts have tried to describe, give back, or denounce the usually harsh conditions of life, the specific functioning and the political significance characterising those encampments.[30] Here, however, I would like to briefly move on a different cartographic path by questioning what, more specifically and even directly—in a way geographically—those places suggest and materially enact. I start from the assumption that they may embody a kind of 'counter-field' or 'reverse-shot' of what I have elsewhere assumed as a 'camp-form' (in French, it sounds better, something like '*contre-champ de la form camp*'). Such an explicit dimension stands for a geographical and political gesture, one that reflects a direction and stance that is radically opposed to the EU border regime.

In other words, taken together, and amidst those (highly) different forms and practices of dwelling (a kind of 'encampment-form), it is possible (and necessary) to detect a drive, an intentional or desired route, made up of a series of possible passages and steps. More precisely, they represent temporary stations along specific, inner (and forbidden) directions, thus suggesting a kind of *underground geography* cutting and crisscrossing the European borderland. At stake, therefore, between such underground 'spaces of representation' (made up of informal settlements and by the routes and directions they directly signal) and the actual 'representation of space' defined by the idea of a borderland (made up of official reception/detention/identification centres and by the borders those material apparatuses directly embody) is a kind of mimetic or isomorphic relation, one which could in turn be read as a specific concatenation (*enchaînement*), that is, through the theoretical framework of the axiomatic set of what Deleuze and Guattari refer to as a nomadic or 'war machine' and the state and capital's 'apparatus of capture', respectively.[31] Within such a framework, the impression is thus of a loop without any possible last word (just a first one, movement), locked in a relentless and ongoing mimetic game. The space, thus produced, according to a Lefebvrian perspective,[32] seems to be defined by the unstable and shifting relation between the actual 'spatial practices' of migrants' and asylum seekers' movements—their 'representational spaces'—and the shifting and violent 'representations of space' materialising in the European borderland.

Much more can be said even about such an isomorphic relation, for instance, exploring the specific 'logistic reason' (made up of corridors, platforms, and special zones, where different yet synchronised flows, operations, and exchanges run along specific directions and selective geographies)[33] driving the EU apparatus of capture and the governance prose, and the relation it entails with a possible logistic 'counter-reason' enacted by migrants' and asylum seekers' movements and spatial practices. Here, however, and always through the lens of corridors and 'mobility infrastructures', I want to focus on a different analogy, one that brings us back to the original meaning of 'absconded'.

Indeed, even the absconding and fugitive slaves, the rebels of the southern US states' plantation system, defied and fled from an apparatus of capture—one whose material translation was epitomised by a chain, as a sign of constriction, captivity, and chattel, and whose blackmail, *le prix à payer*, lay in a lynching, a hangman's noose. In their running away, they build up a series of secret escape routes, at times organised into regular pathways, imaginatively defined as an 'underground railroad'. It was a matter of secret passages, through hidden shelter stations and steps, made possible by the active (yet often over-emphasised) support of white abolitionists, whose extraordinary significance goes well beyond the actual figures and numbers of those who passed through them, insofar as they materially enacted a renewed and reversed geography by confusing and reconfiguring the trajectory of the 'color line'.[34]

Although contained and bounded, the majority of the asylum seekers and migrants inhabiting current temporary zones or encampments do always perceive themselves as on the move. Over them looms a 'chain' that works differently (though not radically) from the material ones that captured and subsumed labouring slaves in the plantation regime. More precisely, they are harnessed within the controlled, delimited, differential, and flexible regime of movement defined through material and juridical border apparatuses such as the Dublin Convention, and to the specific and striated space corresponding to the EU borderland. In the very act of dismantling an informal encampment and relocating and dispersing the dwellers into a myriad scattered and faraway official centres, as well as in the deterritorialised archives of biometric data built up to counter 'asylum shopping', or in the alternate adoption of measures and tools to either block, contain, or force subjects to a Brownian movement of sorts, it is possible to detect a peculiarly flexible and mobile strategy that seems to reproduce and parallel the tactics employed in migrants' movements.

In other words, closer to the image of a 'concatenation' suggested by Deleuze and Guattari, to the nomadic machine enacted by those defined as the subjects of the secondary movements it indicates an apparatus of capture that tends towards a mobile constellation of materials. This in turn suggests that migrants and asylum seekers who are captured within the EU internal borders actively prompt those apparatuses to rearticulate themselves into a border regime apt to 'govern mobility through mobility',[35] by materially defying them through their internal movements and by spatially and temporally containing, delimiting, or addressing it.

Accordingly, if the present is still a time of slavery and chains, instead of permanently blocking and capturing a body in terms of both property and immobility, the current chains impose an indirect mark of captivity by imposing a regime of forced mobility. It should therefore be a matter of representing the isomorphic struggle hidden at the core of the notion of 'secondary movements', as the one between the 'autonomous drive' pushing forward migrants' and asylum seekers' harnessed yet nomadic movements, and the reterritorialising effects enacted by a border regime that becomes in turn increasingly flexible and, above all, mobile. It should also be a matter of locating a word to represent the overall effects of such a relation, thus synthesising the selective transition from a fortress to a borderland—that is, the violent encounters through which, in the prose of EU migration governance, primary movements rearticulate themselves into secondary ones.

In the attempt to locate such a word and indicate a tool capable of governing mobility by imposing a forced regime of (im)mobility, the most immediate association is with a 'leash'. Indeed, a leash circumscribes and reduces the radius of movement around it; it contains rather than confining or blocking, by imposing an inevitably and literally 'secondary' regime of movement. However, it is also a sign of property, of chattel, as well as of control and surveillance. Capture and captivity seem to be the terms that better embody its immediate effects. Besides, a leash becomes visible and its action perceived only when it is stressed and in tension. Moreover, tension occurs when the movement reaches the limit of its range, as a border not to be trespassed.

Rarely, indeed, do those tied to a leash accept its consequences and limitations: a special pressure is thus established at its limits. It is possible to detect such a pressure or tension both on the internal national borders of the EU, signalling and underlining the fractures and frictions affecting an uneven overall space, and within and amidst the national and urban spaces of European territories every time the leash is visible, and its action triggered and actualised. However, what exactly do those tensions and pressures stand for?

In a hotel squatted in and self-managed by a coalition of migrants and activists; in the harsh conditions of life that characterise an encampment systematically dismantled and relentlessly rebuilt near Ventimiglia or Calais; in the more discreet yet deliberate act of running and getting away from an official reception centre; in an attempt to get a ride and pass a bordered national frontier: in all these different and scattered acts and situations, it is possible to detect a specific search for a 'rip', for routes and passages that materially configure and ideally trace a different geography—one which counters the very dimension of a borderland. In short, those recurrent rips can be seen as attempts to directly conduct oneself, and refusing to be captured and brought on a leash.

At a lecture held in March 1978, during the course he conducted at the Collège de France, entitled 'Security, Territory and Population',[36] Michel Foucault offered *en passant* a brief definition of what, in his opinion, could be conceived as an alternative and opposing attitude to the pastoral power of the Christian Church. In order to suggest a word to indicate specific acts and behaviour that are idiosyncratic and resistant to the pervasive economy of power, which aims at both governing individual souls and leading the Christian herd (*omnes et singulatim*), he eventually opted for the (rather unattractive, as he himself admitted) term 'counter-conducts'. Literally—though Foucault does not explicitly state this—a counter-conduct can be conceived as an attempt to conduct oneself differently from the imposed way, and it is mainly addressed to some forms and collective practices that produce an idea of the subject, a dimension of space, and a specific temporality that are radically different from and implicitly opposed to those imposed by the pastoral power, in an attempt to loosen its hold on the subjects.[37]

Although difficult, it is not impossible to envisage counter-conducts among the spatial practices of migrants and asylum seekers neutralised within the category of secondary movements and forced within the European border regime: as rips against a leash, acts and tactics of a specific 'politics of the confined', signs of a possible 'underground Europe', and of a counter-space radically different from and opposed to the current borderland.

NOTES

1. Anna Lowenhaupt Tsing, *Friction: An Ethnography of Global Connection*. Princeton: Princeton University Press, 2004.

2. Nicholas De Genova, Sandro Mezzadra, and John Pickles, 'New Keywords: Migration and Borders: Introduction,' in Maribel Casas-Cortes, Sebastian Cobarrubias, Nicholas De Genova, Glenda Garelli, et al., 'New Keywords: Migration and Borders'. *Cultural Studies* 29(1), 2015, p. 55–87.

3. Achille Mbembe, 'Necropolitics', Libby Meintjes (trans.). *Public Culture* 15(1), 2003, p. 11–40. Available at chrome-extension://efaidnbmnnnibpcajpcglclefindmkaj/https://mirror.explodie.org/Public%20Culture-2003-Mbembe-11-40.pdf (accessed February 2025).

4. Michel Foucault, *Security, Territory, Population: Lectures at the Collége de France, 1977–1978*. New York: Palgrave Macmillan, 2007.

5. Nicholas De Genova and Nathalie Peutz (eds), *The Deportation Regime: Sovereignty, Space, and the Freedom of Movement*. Durham: Duke University Press, 2010; Federico Rahola, 'The Detention Machine', in Salvatore Palidda (ed.), *Racial Criminalization of Migrants in the 21st Century*, London: Routledge, 2011, pp. 77–86.

6. Gerard Noiriel, *Réfugés et sans papiers: La Republique et le droit d'asile*. Paris: Hachette, 1998.

7. Hannah Arendt, *The Origins of Totalitarianism*. New York: Harcourt Brace, 1958, 3rd edition.

8. Étienne Balibar, 'Europe as Borderland'. *Environment and Planning D: Society and Space* 27(2), 2009, pp. 190–205; Sandro Mezzadra, 'The Proliferation of Borders and the Right to Escape', in Yolande Jansen, Robin Celikates, and Joost de Bloois (eds), *The Irregularization of Migration in Contemporary Europe: Detention, Deportation, Drowning*. London: Rowman & Littlefield Publishers, 2015, pp. 121–136.

9. Sandro Mezzadra and Brett Neilson, *Border as Method, or, The Multiplication of Labor*. Durham: Duke University Press, 2013.

10. Saskia Sassen, *Expulsions: Brutality and Complexity in the Global Economy*. Cambridge, Massachusetts: Harvard University Press, 2014.

11. Wendy Brown, *Walled States, Waning Sovereignty*. New York: Zone Books, 2010.

12. Nikos Papastergiadis, *The Turbulence of Migration: Globalization, Deterritorialization und Hybridity*. Cambridge: Polity Press, 2000; Sandro Mezzadra, *Diritto di fuga. Migrazioni, cittadinanza, globalizzazione*. Verona:

Ombre Corte, 2006; and 'The Gaze of Autonomy: Capitalism, Migration and Social Struggles', in Vicki Squire (ed.), *The Contested Politics of Mobility: Borderzones and Irregularity*. London: Routledge, 2011, pp. 121–143; Dimitris Papadopoulos, Niamh Stephenson, and Vassilis Tsianos, *Escape Routes: Control and Subversion in the 21st Century*. London, Ann Arbor, MI: Pluto Press, 2008; Nicholas De Genova, *The Borders of 'Europe': Autonomy of Migration, Tactics of Bordering*. Durham: Duke University Press, 2017.

13. Mezzadra, *Diritto di fuga*.

14. Nicholas De Genova and Martina Tazzioli, 'Europe/Crisis: New Keywords of "the Crisis" in and of "Europe"', in Nicholas De Genova and Martina Tazzioli (eds), *Europe at a Crossroads: Managed Hospitality, Near Futures Online*. Zone Books, March 2016. Available at http://nearfuturesonline.org/europecrisis-new-keywords-of-crisis-in-and-of-europe/ (accessed June 2024).

15. Just to mention the most relevant: the EU Parliament and Commission, European and international agencies of border and migration control such as Frontex and Europol, international orsovranational institutions such as the International Organisation for Migration (IOM) or the UNHCR, several NGOs, as well as the foreign and defence Cabinets and Departments of the member-states.

16. European Parliamentary Research Service, *Secondary Movements of Asylum-seekers in the EU Asylum System*. European Parliamentary Research Service, 1, 2017. Available at http://www.europarl.europa.eu/RegData/etudes/BRIE/2017/608728/EPRS_BRI(2017)608728_EN.pdf (accessed June 2024).

17. In order to introduce redistribution criteria, in June 2016 an EU Commission directive imposed a quota system that has been rejected or silently betrayed by several EU member-states.

18. European Parliamentary Research Service, *Secondary Movements of Asylum-seekers in the EU Asylum System*, 2.

19. All this belongs to the more general abstraction characterising the language of flows, assumed essentially (and in the Marxian sense) as an operation that transfigures a series of behaviour and relationships in the abstract sign of a form, a ratio, ending up defining the reality it indicates.

20. European Parliamentary Research Service, *Secondary Movements of Asylum-seekers in the EU Asylum System*, 2.

21. De Genova and Tazzioli, 'Europe/Crisis'.

22. European Parliamentary Research Service, *Secondary Movements of Asylum-seekers in the EU Asylum System*, 8.

23. De Genova and Tazzioli, 'Europe/Crisis'.

24. Partha Chatterjee, *The Politics of the Governed: Reflections on Popular Politics in Most of the World*. New York: Columbia University Press, 2004.

25. 'An applicant who has absconded, or is *likely to abscond*, would have residence restrictions in the Member State imposed, or be detained, and would not be entitled to material reception conditions (save for emergency health care) when present irregularly in a Member State other than the one in which they are required to be present [...].' European Parliamentary Research Service, *Secondary Movements of Asylum-seekers in the EU Asylum System*, 9.

26. John Hope Franklin and Loren Schweninger, *Runaway Slaves: Rebels on the Plantation*. New York: Oxford University Press, 2000.

27. To put it briefly, the idea of a 'camp-form' refers to a specific border(ed) apparatus where subjects that, for various reasons, exceed a political geography, being thus defined as 'out of place', and whose origins go back to the colonial realm, are to be detained and territorialised, seeking in the colonial subjects the first ones to be administratively deported and detained. Federico Rahola, *Zone Definitivamente Temporanee. I luoghi dell'umanità in eccesso*. Verona: Ombre Corte, 2003; 'The Space of Camps: Towards a Genealogy of Places of Internment in the Present', in Alessandro Dal Lago and Salvatore Palidda (eds), *Conflict, Security and the Reshaping of Society: The Civilization of War*. London: Routledge, 2010, pp. 186–199; and 'The Detention Machine', pp. 77–86.

28. It is the case of Calais, Ventimiglia, Bolzano, Trieste, and Gorizia, as well as of some Slovenian border towns, or in the immediate external fringe of EU territories like Bihac, Velika Kladusa, Sid, or in Beograd, Sarajevo, and in the Gurubù forest surrounding Melilla, in Morocco.

29. Michel Agier et al., *The Jungle: Calais's Camps and Migrants*. Cambridge: Polity Press, 2018; Luca Queirolo Palmas, 'Trale macerie della Jungla di Calais: Reperti di una battaglia'. *Etnografia e Ricerca Qualitativa* 3, Bologna: Il Mulino, 2017.

30. Gilles Deleuze and Félix Guattari, *A Thousand Plateaus: Capitalism and Schizophrenia*. Minneapolis: University of Minnesota Press, 1980.

31. Henri Lefebvre, *The Production of Space*, Donald Nicholson-Smith (trans.). Oxford: Blackwell, 1991.

32. Sandro Mezzadra and Brett Neilson, 'Operations of Capital'. *The South Atlantic Quarterly* 114(1), 2015, pp. 1–9.

33. Henry Louis Gates, Jr., 'Who Really Ran the Underground Railroad?'. *Guyanese Online*, 26 October 2013. Available at https://

guyaneseonline.wordpress.com/2013/10/26/who-really-ran-the-underground-railroad-by-henry-louis-gates-jr/ (accessed February 2025); Richard J. M. Blackett, *Making Freedom: The Underground Railroad and the Politics of Slavery*. Chapel Hill: University of North Carolina Press, 2013.

34. Martina Tazzioli and Glenda Garelli, 'Containment beyond detention: The hotspot system and disrupted migration movements across Europe'. *Environment and Planning D: Society and Space* 1(19), 2018.

35. Foucault, *Security, Territory, Population*.

36. Federico Rahola, 'As we go along: Spazi, tempi e soggetti delle contro-condotte'. *Materiali Foucaultiani* IV(7/8), 2015, pp. 275–294.

3

Population Flows, Refugees, and the Responsibility to Protect in the Global Protection System

Shibashis Chatterjee

Population flows are as old as human history; there is evidence of the *Homo erectus* migrating out of Africa some two million years ago. Although human civilisation brought about a certain sedentary quality of life, population movements continued unabated. Whether people resided within empires or other political forms, political persecution, acute natural calamities, overriding scarcity of resources, and imperial expansion moved considerable masses of humanity to far-flung places, while technological backwardness made these flows slow and cumbersome. When people moved, they interacted with others, and these interactions were not necessarily friendly, as population flows involving considerable numbers were usually combustible and violent. However, the relatively open political frontiers were useful. Whether in search of food or for survival, people had to move a great deal in the past, and population flows were considered unavoidable across many parts of the globe.

The colonial system saw massive population transfers. Not only did the white men move a great deal across the old continents, but they also displaced countless persons in the service of slavery and indentured labour, and settled them in places thousands of miles away from their homes. This forced relocation also unsettled the indigenous or local populations in the colonies where plantation economies emerged, uprooting older patterns of agriculture and causing unprecedented economic hardship to the poor. At the same time, imperial economic needs brought subsequent migrations to a halt. The foisting of the Westphalian order on the colonies created a new gaze that subjected population movements to new governmentalised structures of rule. The birth of the territorial state with unitary sovereign structures transformed fluid frontiers into fixed borders, which posed unparalleled difficulties for population movements across the globe. The universalisation of the state and a gradual socialisation into governmentalised rules legalised demographics under exclusionary citizenship, which made it increasingly necessary to divide people along imaginary national lines. Modernity, geopolitics, and capitalism produced the current conditions of precarity and migration.

In this chapter, I discuss three issues related to population flows and their regulation. The first deals with our understanding of the refugee and the migrant. I look at select tracts of political theory across positions to situate the actor. The second section reflects on the idea of the Responsibility to Protect (R2P), but I conclude that the R2P is neither the best solution we have on hand, nor is it ideologically acceptable in totality. However, in the absence of a better alternative, the R2P is the best humanitarian solution we have for victims trapped in tragic circumstances, violated and brutalised either by their own state or by majority communities. Finally, I briefly discuss population flows in Asia, Latin America, and Africa, and comment on the mechanisms available to meet this challenge.

The three segments are not independent parts, though they appear fragmentary. There is, however, a logical nexus between the fragments. The chapter travels from the abstract to the more concrete, from the general to the specific, and from categories to problems. The chief argument is that the precarity refugees experience results from our conceptual impoverishment, which limits a definition of the key categories in a politically responsible and humane manner, the inevitable shallowness of humanitarian imaginations of global powers and civil societies, and the manifest limitations of existing practices that are predicated on refugee-producing dynamics. These are all part of the problem and cannot, therefore, serve as meaningful solutions. The refugee predicament is both material (social) and subjective. It cannot be reduced either to the mechanical effects of state policies or to the norms that subjectively summon categories like the refugee, the displaced, the stateless, and the homeless. Both the theory and practice of refugees would tend to bear this out.

I

In order to make sense of the present predicaments and challenges faced by refugees, stateless persons, and migrants, it is necessary to situate these ideas in theoretical terms and reflect on debates that cannot be separated from the issues bedevilling contemporary practices around them. In this section, I discuss four broad positions on understanding the refugee and the immigrant. The claim is not that these positions are in any way exhaustive. However, they are representative of the broad arguments involved, and will help in understanding the problems better before we look more closely at the empirical reality. These four positions are the communitarian, the liberal, the post-colonial, and the radical. The last may seem odd as it is not a recognised nomenclature for classifying philosophical positions on the subject. However, I find no better term of description for the positions of Hannah Arendt and Giorgio Agamben. Moreover, I will not proceed by addressing specific thinkers; rather, I intend to position the thematics and read their implications. Of the four positions noted, the first is a position of closure. It is also, in many ways, the dominant perspective, although states espousing arguments of regulation may not subscribe to communitarian arguments in other spheres of life. Similarly, the liberal-nationalist take on immigration is surprisingly close to the communitarian. I will, therefore, take these together.

The communitarian arguments on immigration and refugees are primarily centred on claims of cultural distinctiveness, the right to national self-determination, political membership, and economic sustenance. Consider Michael Walzer, the most influential spokesperson of this viewpoint. In his words:

> Admission and exclusion are at the core of communal independence. They suggest the deepest meaning of self-determination. Without them, there could not be communities of character, historically stable, ongoing associations of men and women with some special commitment to one another and some special sense of their common life.[1]

Yet, Walzer himself points to several exceptions to this vein of thinking. Thus, it foregrounds an obligation to admit outsiders if their economic survival is imperilled; immigrants who have resided in the community for an extended period cannot be excluded, as this would violate the idea of justice based on the equitable sharing of resources and responsibilities; and finally, original inhabitants who may be unacceptable to the majority cannot be expelled from political membership.[2] Hence, the right to deny entry is not as robust as it seems.

Nevertheless, Walzer's ethical position is clear. He builds a case for limiting and closure at gates, and uses a number of arguments in his support. The first of these likens the political community to a close-knit neighbourhood, where abiding ties and sentimental attachments make collective life possible. This is a problematic argument on several counts. First, comparative scales are dubious—no state is like a neighbourhood. Second, states normally have no arguments to limit internal migration. Peculiar circumstances can, however, limit movement in some cases. The reasons may be security, public order, or cultural vulnerability. However, these are aberrations and are usually temporary measures in liberal states. Hence, if the self-determining nature of a political community can withstand the individual freedom of mobility within a state, it is arbitrary to deny people this right across states.

Walzer has a second reason to offer. He draws a parallel between states and clubs. Clubs, in this view, decide rules of membership and thus may regulate entry to them. Again, the parallel is unconvincing. First, clubs decide to admit on certain attributes. Anyone who possesses the attribute in question cannot be denied membership. What would be the analogous attributes for a state to frame its immigration policy? Certainly, some outsiders may appear more qualified than many existing members. Can the state deny membership to those living within who do not seem worthy enough? Second, as Joseph Carens argues, the distinction between the state and the club is based on the dichotomy between the public and the private. The norms deciding the rules of membership in private associations and those of a public body can hardly be the same.[3]

However, there is a stronger communitarian argument that is also endorsed by the liberal nationalists. As David Miller explains:

> The public culture of their country is something that people have an interest in controlling: they want to be able to shape the way their nation develops, including the values that are contained in the public culture. They may not, of course, succeed: valued cultural features can be eroded by economic and other forces that evade political control. But they may certainly have good reasons to try, and in particular to try to maintain cultural continuity over time, so that they can see themselves as the bearers of an identifiable cultural tradition that stretches backward historically.[4]

While the appeal of cultural self-determination and perpetuity is apparently attractive, it also has obvious limitations. First of all, this argument seldom withstands empirical scrutiny—not all outsiders have radically different cultures. Further, it is impossible to suggest that cultures do not mutate and evolve normally. Again, cultures are not free-standing; there are material and transactional externalities that affect culture. It is impossible to show which culture is changing and how.[5] Surely, immigrants and refugees are not the sole authors of cultural change. Globalisation has wrought more changes to cultural forms through images and electronic communication than conscious human agents have in the last three decades. Moreover, the argument that whatever is culturally distinct is also of value is a specious one. Finally, the whole basis of this argument of cultures neatly reinforcing the borders of political self-determination is unconvincing. It flies in the face of reality and is particularly hostile to the logic of Westphalia that has engendered the contemporary state system.

There is a further variety of the communitarian argument, popular in International Relations, that comes from the realists.

While the realist argument is still enormously influential among the policy-making elite across major powers and powerful states, the argument is a complex one and is often caricatured unfairly by its detractors. Realists have certainly upheld the claims of the state to everything in life over other collective bodies, but it is wrong to argue that this makes realists statists. Realists are more committed to insisting on a group organisation vis-à-vis life. A political organisation, in short, is a mode of group living that will create pressures for integration within and demand some insulation without. Realists are also Hobbesian in claiming that contracts require the seal of authority. As there is no world government, there cannot be any overriding legal/political commitment on the part of states and the states' people to international organisations or conventions. Realists, however, have a nuanced reading of sovereignty. As Stephen Krasner had famously outlined, sovereignty has four meanings, namely Westphalian, international legal, interdependence, and domestic.[6] In the words of Edward Luck:

> ...Westphalian sovereignty and international legal sovereignty are all about authority, whether to exclude external actors or to make international agreements with them. Interdependence sovereignty... relates to the control of movements across borders, something that is especially challenging in an era of the internet, persistent migration, and globalisation. Domestic sovereignty... requires both authority and control.[7]

More critically, realists are agnostic on culture. In fact, the argument of cultural membership does not feature in their understanding at all. Realists tend to argue that the opening or closing of borders for the admission or prevention of outsiders is entirely predicated on the gains and losses of states. In brief, it is difficult to make strong anti-immigration claims from realist arguments unless these are supplemented, often indirectly, by a number of auxiliary claims. Realists are certainly no friends of refugees and migrants, but their arguments hold nothing inherently negative about these categories either.[8]

Liberals, on balance, have argued for open borders. However, this does not mean that the political elite taking recourse to liberal justifications have welcomed refugees consistently. This is all the more reason to scrutinise the liberal case carefully. In other words, when liberal societies close off borders to refugees and immigrants, they violate the political ideas they subscribe to. This is not the place to undertake a meticulous deconstruction of liberal strands of thought on the theme of openness and closure. It is therefore sufficient to identify the basic formulations without going into details. Among the many variants of liberalism, two contrasting models stand out. The first is the more comprehensive liberalism that is positively committed to autonomy as a political principle. The other is the *modus vivendi* variety, also known as political liberalism, which makes more modest claims.

I take all liberalism as a doctrine that allows individuals to pursue their life projects in society on terms agreed upon by them, which may or may not be endorsed by the majority. Most liberals agree that the individual has a moral capacity to form a conception of the good and of reflection that is independent of it. For liberals, life projects must be decided by individuals from within and may be revised, if required, over the course of life.[9] Liberals do not agree on the role of collective bodies in general and that of the state in particular. However, they mostly endorse the idea that a state must grant associational and contractual freedom to individuals to enable them to pursue their chosen ideas of a good life. The state will neither define a good life nor facilitate or constrain one.[10] Liberals debate on the virtues of procedural neutrality and value pluralism, but all tend to agree that it is individuals who will decide what is good for them. In theory, boundaries are irrelevant to liberalism. While liberals may endorse the role of communities, they cannot agree on settled authoritarian accounts that decide the contents of those identities, nor can they take these collective identities as given, glaciated, and immutable. Hence, no argument of cultural difference can be legitimately claimed to have emerged from or been built upon liberalism.[11]

Neither free-market liberalism nor the social welfare account, thus, has an intrinsic case for border closing. The libertarians will make a judgement on immigration on the basis of the efficacy of market arguments. Immigration cannot be opposed if it increases the freedom of entrepreneurs, enlarges consumer choices, and creates more job opportunities. Stopping migrants will mean the deprivation of these positive payoffs from life. However, if immigration complicates such trade-offs, libertarians will have no moral scruples in opposing open borders. Rawlsian liberals present a more complicated case. Rawls does treat justice in closed systems, and authority is required to operationalise redistributive welfare transfers. However, as many commentators like Charles Beitz and Thomas Pogge have shown, this stipulation is neither necessary nor desirable for a theory of fair shares.[12] The veil of ignorance cannot discriminate on borders and to refuse justice to people just because they do not 'belong' is morally unacceptable. Rawls builds his case largely on the argument for a theory of justice that stands clear of all forms of moral arbitrariness. It does not stand to reason to claim that a refugee is morally inferior as a person to a citizen. Neither can one make the argument that the capacity for rational reflection and a sense of justice are only possessed by citizens and not by outsiders. Redistribution cannot be limited to artificial political containers and the worst-off cannot be defined from a purely national perspective. If unfair inequalities demand resource transfer in line with the two principles that Rawls suggests, this cannot be artificially limited to domestic societies. In brief, Rawls may have closed off the political boundary for welfare considerations, but this closure violates the deeper moral commitments of his theory.[13] Neither the libertarian nor the welfare variants of liberalism can make a theoretically consistent case against opening borders to refugees and migrants.[14]

The post-colonial case for refugees is an interesting one. However, the post-colonial elites do not necessarily buy into it. The history of the post-colonial state is largely responsible for this paradox. After all, the post-colonial has come into being on the Westpahalian cartography and is socialised though the norms of sovereignty, non-intervention, and fixed borders. We are aware of the manifold challenges afflicting such societies vis-à-vis nation-building, economic frailties, demographic liabilities, and perennial political uncertainties. These are states that have generated the bulk of refugees and migrants through internecine domestic conflicts, enormous natural calamities, economic collapse, and ethnic feuds. The universalisation of the norms of sovereign equality of states, which gathered real momentum through the decolonisation process after 1945, created a strange paradox for many of these states. They became states almost by accident, lacking either political substance or cartographic certainties. They were Westphalian constructs without the necessary credentials.[15] Guarantees of sovereignty made the elite, mostly a rent-seeking parasitic class, utterly cavalier, with scant regard for the needs of domestic legitimacy and minimum performance. As a result, their histories are frequently marred by violent internal strife that routinely displaced hapless nationals, both within and across borders. Hard sovereignty protected these self-seeking elite against international action throughout the Cold War era.[16] The post-Cold War reality did not change matters fundamentally; neo-liberal penetration expanded to new heights and virtually all experiments of reform through structural adjustment, democratisation, and civil society movements only brought back existing trends in new forms.[17]

The post-colonial refugee narrative is therefore not one created out of the post-colonial experience. It builds rather on Western predilections and ambiguities that have waxed and waned on the refugee issue, dependent almost entirely on convenience. In the words of Gurminder K. Bhambra:

> Attempts to address the current crisis often seek to make distinctions between 'refugees' and 'migrants' and between refugees / migrants and citizens. But, I suggest, these distinctions are part of the problem. Part of the solution is to rethink our histories of 'national states'—and the rights and claims they enable—through a 'connected sociologies' approach that acknowledges the shared histories that bring states and colonies together.[18]

This is a perspective that argues that the West cannot deny its obligations towards refugees and stateless asylum seekers, no matter who they are and what cultural attributes they allegedly carry. The argument insists on the fact that these refugees are hapless victims of violence and not criminals or terrorists as they are alleged to be by the ultra-right political forces active in the West. Moreover, the West is integral to the refugee generation process, over periods both long and short, directly or otherwise. The West can hardly claim cultural separation in its history from the people of Africa and West Asia. Western colonialism was the cause of the economic underdevelopment of these societies; American and European geopolitical interests have routinely ravaged these states, and their misguided political engineering has often led to the exodus of innocent people seeking safety and shelter. The refugee, the internally displaced, and the migrant, among others, are therefore categories that demand a global historical consciousness. The West's refusal to accept refugees is thus morally bankrupt, politically indefensible, and historically naïve. As Ranabir Samaddar argues:

> What is the nature of this power and influence at the margins? This question is important because, unlike the Kantian world, the world we live in is characterised by a great dissociation of power and responsibility. Wars may be launched on countries by great powers, but the burdens of refugee flows that wars create are shouldered by countries that had little to do with them.[19]

However, the notion of responsibility is not only relevant to the West, but is also a pertinent question for post-colonial regimes. The fact is that the global categories fly in the face of both post-colonial realities and sensibilities. The global refugee framework, as defined by the UNHCR, deploys notions legalistically. Law is about definitiveness. The post-colonial categories, however, escape legal definitions as their realities are distinctive and always in the making. The idiom of legal certitude thus hardly measures up to them. The post-colonial predicament is immensely complicated by the absence of responsibility emanating from the non-recognition of people. When a community has to be divided and shared across hard borders of the state and mind, some will bear the costs of being perennially intermediate. No one owns them, names them, or claims them fully. The states may evolve temporary mechanisms for negotiating situations when numbers tend to rise above acceptable thresholds, but these are not legal guarantees of normalisation. Citizenship is the most contested precarity of a post-colonial existence. Unless the global frameworks on refugees, stateless persons, and IDPs, among others, negotiate this complexity, compulsive legal formulations will falter at post-colonial borders.

This brings me to two relatively brief discourses, one by Hannah Arendt and the other by Giorgio Agamben, which radically alter the way we understand the refugee and the asylum seeker. In one of the twentieth century's classics on political philosophy, *The Origins of Totalitarianism* (1951), Arendt spoke of a time of catastrophe that engendered 'homelessness on an unprecedented scale, rootlessness to an unprecedented depth'. For the victims of such a mass upheaval, 'powerlessness has become the major experience of their lives'. In the Preface to the first edition, Arendt writes:

> ...one after the other, one more brutally than the other, have demonstrated that human dignity needs a new guarantee which can be found only in a new political principle, in a new law on earth, whose validity this time must comprehend the whole of humanity while its power must remain strictly limited, rooted in and controlled by newly defined territorial entities.[20]

The principle that Arendt calls the 'Right to Have Rights' is about the need for a home or a locale as an anchor for rights. This required a passage from citizen's rights to human rights, but states do not recognise either the rights of or their responsibilities to people who are not within their territory. Sovereign territoriality has thus become the baseline for rights. The citizen/alien distinction was upended by the inside/outside dichotomy. States therefore became obsessed with their right to grant entry. The asylum seeker emerged as the new 'other' who had to be denied territorial access, so that the state could recognise post-citizen human rights and derecognise it at the same time. Explaining this paradox, Agamben writes that the refugee is such a 'disquieting element' because '... by breaking up the identity between man and citizen, between nativity and nationality, the refugee throws into crisis the original fiction of sovereignty'.[21]

The dilemmas confronting the refugee can be extended to the stateless persons. Their failure to satisfy both the home and the host, no matter how sincerely they try, is the supreme tragedy of their failings as truly 'human'. The asylum seeker remains a legal black hole, which explains their perennially perilous existence. The right to non-refoulement within the Refugee Convention cannot protect them as they have no state. Lacking the protection of a national jurisdiction, they have no claim to security or dignity. They are therefore human, but scarcely so. Agamben emphasises the symbols that were integral to the Nazi extermination of the stateless—the prison camps and the extermination camps—that completely stripped the person of their political affiliation before they could be killed as a being devoid of identity. In Agamben's words, 'When the rights of man are no longer the rights of the citizen, then he is truly sacred, in the sense that this term had in archaic Roman law: destined to die.'[22]

Agamben builds further on this line of thinking. Reflecting on rights and citizenship, he writes, '[r]ights, that is, are attributable to *man* only in the degree to which he is the immediately vanishing presupposition (indeed, he must never appear simply as a man) of the citizen.'[23] He likens the situation of the refugee to that of the *Homo sacer*, a human life that Roman law considered dispensable without attracting the opprobrium of murder. The refugee is likewise a human, but without the rights and dignity of the citizen. Human rights are thus incapable of uniting these two forms of life. These rights are not universal as they remain the entitlement of citizens and not of the refugee, for whom it is hardly meaningful to lead a biological life. Modern life continuously reduces humans to political categories; from birth to death, they are slotted by the state. This biopolitical reading of the refugee predicament is closer to Arendt than it is to Foucault. What stands out here is the twist in the idea of the refugee as someone both inside and outside society at the same time, simultaneously assimilated and separated, modelled on the outcast, whose unacceptability is only in the presence of the sacred and not outside it.[24]

In a remarkably perceptive essay, Omri Boehm, commenting on Angela Merkel's take on the refugee crisis in Europe in 2017, tells us what was wrong with our thinking about the refugees: 'We simply lack a vocabulary to address refugees and others without reducing them to citizens.' As Boehm puts it, 'Universal citizen rights... have so far been closely connected with Europe and its history', and have failed to answer to the refugees. She continued, 'and this close connection with universal citizen rights will be destroyed.' In 2015, in her press statement, Merkel made it clear that Germany was not accepting the idea of unconditional asylum.[25] If the Chancellor wanted to address the refugees, she should probably have said human, not citizen, rights. What she did say was all that she could politically vouch for, but it was not relevant to the refugees whose standing is precisely that of non-citizens.[26]

II

The setting up of a robust global framework for the protection of refugees and stateless persons and the development of associated structures has certainly been prevented by the political conundrum and our moral dilemmas surrounding them. However, this does not mean that there are no instrumentalities available to them. The UNHCR has done commendable work in refugee protection and the international community has laboured to put in place a series of regimes towards this aim. The final section of the chapter will briefly look at these frameworks to assess the plight of homeless persons in contemporary times. In this section, I focus on the R2P, which is widely claimed as the most significant conceptual development for the protection of people against genocide, mass violence, destruction of life and habitat, and massive violations of human rights. The idea is that refugees and stateless persons are generated broadly in two ways. First, and overwhelmingly, they are the results of domestic violence and the deliberate targeting of groups. Second, refugees are also created in vast numbers in times of war and international conflict, when people flee from indiscriminate violence that collapses the combatant/

non-combatant distinction in international law. Often, these two circumstances are inseparably linked.

The contemporary refugee crises emanating from Syria and Iraq are the worst examples of such integral conflicts. Refugee flows in Africa have varied over the decades, but the overall displacement records continue to be appalling. These population flows are mostly related to civil war, where external actors, both state and non-state, often get involved. The refugee flows from Ukraine and the Rohingya crisis are contrasting cases, inasmuch as the former resulted from a unilateral Russian military campaign, while the latter stemmed from the making of the state of Myanmar. Once these cases resulted in populations flows, however, they immediately assumed an international character. When it comes to issues of human flows across borders, the distinction between the international and the domestic is simply irrelevant.

The R2P is a compromise deal. It has a fairly long institutional history and the final product was, in many ways, different from the original formulation. Institutional history cannot be entirely sidestepped if we are to put the idea into proper perspective. The international community has long debated the diverse meanings and implications of rights. With the coming into being of the modern state systems, states are recognised under the UN Charter as containers of legal personality—states sign treaties and conventions and enter into economic and defence arrangements; states enjoy sovereign equality and a measure of immunity against intervention.[27] For a long time, international law tended to take the view that this right was inviolable and even now, the state's right to non-interference is widely regarded as one of its pillars. Several UN General Assembly resolutions also reaffirmed the rights of states against intervention in their domestic jurisdiction.[28]

However, alongside this commitment to national sovereignty, there are domestic and international obligations of states,[29] and, perhaps even more vitally, claims of individuals wronged by their states that cannot be settled fairly within the framework of domestic law. With the gradual strengthening of human rights and the realisation that states have been unable to resist all forms of interference across borders in a highly globalised world order, there was a need to revisit the absolutist right of non-intervention as claimed by many authoritarian states. It was also realised that formal structures of democratic political participation within states did not automatically create a bulwark of rights for nationals and others living within them. Sovereignty and non-intervention routinely trumped calls for more humane treatment of individuals and groups either discriminated against or orphaned by the state. Unless states recognised their responsibilities and took human rights more seriously, the predicament of vulnerable communities would remain unchanged. States were loath to accept obligations that apparently inconvenienced ruling regimes, and sovereignty was the protective shield that was invariably used to deflect the international scrutiny of human rights.[30]

However, this situation started changing once the Cold War was over and ethnic violence erupted in Africa, eastern and central Europe, and Asia. The Rwandan genocide was an eye-opener. It revealed how little great powers cared about protecting non-White human lives if vital geopolitical interests were not involved. In contrast to the meekness of UN responses in Africa, the crisis in Croatia, Kosovo, and Bosnia saw more effective and bold participation by NATO and the European Union, sovereignty-based counter-claims by Serbia and Russia notwithstanding. The then Secretary-General, Kofi Annan, regretted the inefficacy the UN had demonstrated in responding to the Rwandan crisis, which had led to the loss of uncountable lives. The practice of sovereignty and the collateral doctrine of non-intervention were out of sync with reality, and states could not hide behind these relics to cover up their failures. In his words:

> State sovereignty, in its most basic sense, is being redefined—not least by the forces of globalisation and international co-operation. States are now widely understood to be instruments at the service of their peoples, and not vice versa. At the same time individual sovereignty—by which I mean the fundamental freedom of each individual, enshrined in the charter of the UN and subsequent

> international treaties—has been enhanced by a renewed and spreading consciousness of individual rights. When we read the charter today, we are more than ever conscious that its aim is to protect individual human beings, not to protect those who abuse them.[31]

It was clear, however, that these changes would not be forthcoming unless a way was found to steer clear of the sterile binary of humanitarian intervention and human rights that had long stalemated international law and regimes devoted to ameliorating the conditions of refugees, stateless persons, asylum seekers, and internally displaced people uncared for by the state. The chequered history of R2P is a natural corollary to this. Roberta Cohen and Francis M. Deng inscribed two vital works, titled *Masses in Flight: The Global Crisis of Internal Displacement* and *The Forsaken People: Case Studies of the Internally Displaced*, published by the Brookings Institute in the US in 1998. These were benchmark publications that paved the way to the report of the International Commission on Intervention and State Sovereignty that fashioned the R2P in its December 2001 Report. The Report was an ambitious attempt to propose a comprehensive agenda concerning the various catastrophes that might befall humankind, and its principles had a commensurably large scope. These included 'overwhelming natural or environmental catastrophes, where the state concerned is either unwilling or unable to cope, or call for assistance, and significant loss of life is occurring or threatened.'[32] However, such a broad mandate was politically impossible and, therefore, at the Heads of State and Government at the 2005 World Summit, a much trimmed version survived, which limited R2P to the four crimes mentioned in paragraphs 138 and 139, commonly referred to as the 'atrocity crimes'.[33] According to the 2014 *Framework of Analysis for Atrocity Crimes* published by the UN,

> In this context, the term 'atrocity crimes' has been extended to include ethnic cleansing which, while not defined as an independent crime under international law, includes acts that are serious violations of international human rights and humanitarian law that

> may themselves amount to one of the recognised atrocity crimes, in particular crimes against humanity.[34]

The inclusion of ethnic cleansing has apparently broadened the ambit of the R2P. As most contemporary disputes have an ethnic dimension, this inclusion is both timely and relevant.

R2P consists of three pillars: pillar one concerns the protection responsibilities of the state (Sect. II), pillar two is to do with international assistance and capacity-building (Sect. III), and pillar three discusses timely and decisive response (Sect. IV). It is not necessary to catalogue here the mechanism in its entirety. Fundamentally, the R2P evolved out of a realisation that the term 'humanitarian intervention' was politically incorrect and deeply divisive as it led to the suspicion that Western states in the post-Cold War era would use this as a pretext to interfere unduly in the domestic matters of non-Western states. This scepticism was widely shared by various states: post-colonial powers like India,[35] non-democratic revisionist states like Russia and China, and a number of Islamic states, which feared cultural imperialism and the imposition of democracy. Questions were also raised on the ideational sub-text of the doctrine. Most commentators saw it as a new inflection of the democratic peace argument that was intrusive and interventionist on the flimsiest of pretexts. The ideological baggage of R2P is an important issue, but not because of the common objections hurled by state elites. It neatly dovetails with the silence of vocabulary argument that bedevils all refugee discourses emanating from the West. I will end this section by looking at the silences of the R2P that are inevitable due to its structural constitution.

R2P is fundamentally an attempt to recast sovereignty. The central idea is to remind states of their unalienable responsibility towards the safety and wellbeing of their citizens.

> State sovereignty implies responsibility, and the primary responsibility for the protection of its people lies with the state itself. Where a population is suffering serious harm, as a result of internal war, insurgency, repression or state failure, and the state in question

> is unwilling or unable to halt or avert it, the principle of non-intervention yields to the international responsibility to protect.[36]

Further, states have an international responsibility that is now mostly institutionalised through the UN and other international and regional treaties and conventions that they sign. It also meant that subtle shifts were necessary in human rights advocacy arguments and civil society narratives. Rather than damning sovereignty, responsibility called for firming it up. Concrete services cannot be performed by a fragile state. A state aware of its responsibility towards its constituencies requires threshold capacities to deliver on its promises.

Second, the concept emphasised the need to concentrate on the plight, vulnerabilities, and necessities of the people suffering in crisis situations rather than debate on the rights of external powers to intervene.[37] As Weiss puts it,

> The ICISS identified two threshold cases: large-scale loss of life and ethnic cleansing, underway or anticipated. Humanitarian intervention also should be subject to four precautionary conditions: right intention, last resort, proportional means, and reasonable prospects of success. And finally, the Security Council is the preferred decision maker.[38]

To sum up, R2P was an evolving idea that sought to steer clear of morally loaded concepts by finessing their meanings rather than creating new ideas. Primarily, R2P redefined sovereignty as territorial control plus the responsibility to protect citizens. In the process, it also viewed sovereignty and intervention as complementary rather than contradictory ideas. Sovereignty as responsibility was a commitment to protect citizens and their human rights. Where the state either failed to accomplish this task or itself perpetrated tyranny, intervention was necessary to restore the lost objective of responsible citizens' protection.[39]

Until 2004, R2P was making good progress as an ideal. It created a common denominator amongst international bureaucrats, civil society activists, peace-keeping agencies, and leaders of a number of states. While different groups saw R2P from their own vantage points, the idea that sovereignty cannot be divorced from legitimacy on the one hand, and that the state was still the last hope of the weak and the vulnerable, on the other, caught their imagination. According to Thakur and Weiss:

> The language contains a clear, unambiguous acceptance by all UN members of individual state responsibility to protect populations from genocide, war crimes, ethnic cleansing, and crimes against humanity. Member states further declared that they 'are prepared to take collective action, in timely and decisive manner, through the Security Council ... and in cooperation with relevant regional organizations as appropriate, should peaceful means be inadequate and national authorities are manifestly failing to protect their populations'. Leaders stressed 'the need for the General Assembly to continue consideration of the responsibility to protect populations from genocide, war crimes, ethnic cleansing, and crimes against humanity'.[40]

However, the momentum was lost due to a number of reasons.

First, the complications arising out of 9/11 and the Iraq War of 2004 brought back old notions of sovereignty and interventionist fears with renewed vigour. The Afghan military intervention could be separated from R2P by underscoring the differences in the situational dynamics.[41] However, Iraq was certainly different. It clearly showed that great powers could trample the sovereignty of others with impunity and without any credible evidence of ulterior motive on the part of the accused state. George W. Bush, Jr. and Tony Blair not only inaugurated a new politics of military unilateralism, but they also ensured that troops would not be available for humanitarian missions any longer. The bleeding of Darfur and the devastation of the Democratic Republic of Congo highlighted Western hypocrisy to its fullest extent. The tragedies of Rwanda, Kosovo, and Srebrenica returned with a vengeance. The 2005 Summit doctrine watered down the provisions considerably. In the words of Alex Bellamy:

> In the latter form, R2P no longer proposed criteria to guide decision-making about when to intervene; there is no code of conduct for

> the use of the veto; and there is no opening for coercive measures not authorized by the Security Council. The threshold on when R2P is transferred from the host state to international society was raised from the point at which the host state proved itself 'unable and unwilling' to protect its own citizens to that at which the state was 'manifestly failing' in its responsibility to do so. Finally, the idea that R2P implied responsibilities, even obligations, on the part of international society and especially the Security Council was all but removed, with the Council committed only to 'standing ready' to act when necessary.[42]

The second issue was more complicated. David Chandler has drawn attention to a central paradox that goes to the heart of the R2P. In his words, 'The problem with the doctrine of R2P is not the military intervention aspect per se (obviously full of unintended consequences and inherent dilemmas) but the imbrications of military actions within a discourse of external humanitarian/ Western responsibility for outcomes.'[43] He contrasts the success of the intervention in Libya with the failures in Bosnia, Kosovo, Afghanistan, and Iraq on the ground that, while the West has not assumed any responsibility for the outcomes in the former, their attempts to dictate the nature of sovereignty in the latter cases rob them of moral and political capital, which is independent of the nature of the military outcome in these cases. This is a powerful argument that draws attention to the original bargain. R2P had gained traction because it did not wish to take away the sovereignty of the state, but to help rescue people who had been failed by a given sovereign.

R2P, in other words, has been a liberal solution to a global problem. It speaks largely in the language of democratic peace. Most crucially, it talks in the familiar language of citizenship, nationality, self-determination, and sovereignty. People indeed suffer atrocities at the hands of misguided Leviathans, but millions are distressed through unacknowledged (harmful) practices. Where a state is unable to protect its own citizens, if the international community succeeds against all odds, the citizens may return to their homes, and some at least may stay back in more protected and humane environments. However, if the state refuses to recognise human beings as their citizens, and others decline admission to these collective orphans, there is hardly anything in the liberal utopia of the R2P to afford protection and restore to them a life of dignity and rights.

III

There has been an unprecedented increase in population flows across the world, with Asia, South America, and Africa being the worst affected continents.[44] The gradual hardening of the Western states on the refugee question and the rise of right-wing populism have complicated matters enormously. There are problems of both refugee acceptance and repatriation, and the existing international and national bodies are manifestly wilting under pressure. In Asia, the Rohingya crisis of the past few years has assumed deadly proportions and the fact that neither Bangladesh nor India is a signatory to the Refugee Convention of 1951 complicates matters even further. The plight of the Afghan refugees has worsened since the Taliban regained control of Afghanistan in 2021, further destabilising the region, including neighbouring provinces in Pakistan. The battles among various actors in ISIS-infested Syria and Iraq have led to a human catastrophe that exposed the fragility of the existing protection regimes yet again, in addition to causing serious backlashes in many European states.

According to UNHCR, the number of uprooted people arriving in Europe by sea swelled to around 390,432 in 2019, with nearly 53,780 arriving that year alone. In comparison, approximately 370,000 people had arrived in Europe by sea in 2016, as per IOM data According to the UNHCR:

> More than 3 million Iraqis have been displaced across the country since the start of 2014 and over 260,000 are refugees in other countries. Mass executions, systematic rape and horrendous acts of violence are widespread, and human rights and rule of law are

> under constant attack. It is estimated that over 11 million Iraqis are currently in need of humanitarian assistance. More than 1.5 million people have taken refuge in the Kurdistan Region of Iraq, where one in every four is either a refugee or an internally displaced person....[45]

This unprecedented refugee outflow was triggered by the Syrian civil war, which saw incessant fighting between Western powers, Russia, and the Islamic State. Reliable sources revealed that the civil war forced over 6.7 million Syrians into refugee camps in neighbouring states, and UNHCR states that about 6.2 million were displaced internally. Lebanon, Turkey, and Jordan had hosted the refugees since 2011. In 2013, thousands took refuge in Iraq, despite the shattered economy and the worsening conditions of internal displacement there. The war in 2015–2016 broke the backs of the ordinary Syrian and the intensity of the violence forced them to flee as far as they could. In 2013, 16 Western countries, including the USA, finally woke up to the situation and pledged resettlement opportunities for asylum seekers. The UK also pledged to shelter vulnerable Syrian refugees.

Unfortunately, the big push came thereafter. With ISIS on the offensive in Mosul, over 500,000 Syrians escaped and a large part of this population arrived in Europe. This period also saw the hardening of European attitudes as sporadic ISIS terrorist strikes began to claim innocent lives in France and Belgium. National security trumped humanitarian responsibility. The brief window that had opened in 2013 was now virtually shut across Europe. States like Greece and Hungary began to repel the refugees from entering their jurisdictions by land and sea. The desperate refugees, who were dying as boats capsized in the turbulent seas, began to violate these restrictions and took enormous risks to find shelter. Germany's decision to accept refugees on principle further increased the number of new arrivals. By 2016, millions were on European soil and this, among others, was a primary trigger in the gradual ascension of rightist populist political forces across Europe.[46]

The Rohingya crisis added to the refugee flows in Asia. According to the UNHCR:

> The latest exodus began on 25 August 2017, when violence broke out in Myanmar's Rakhine State, driving more than 742,23,000 to seek refuge in Bangladesh. Most arrived in the first three months of the crisis. An estimated 12,000 reached Bangladesh during the first half of 2018. The vast majority reaching Bangladesh are women and children, and more than 40 per cent are under age 12.[47]

The details of the crisis need not detain us here. Like all humanitarian crises, this one too has multiple narratives and it is not easy to arrive at an economy of moral agreement. There is a clear understanding that the Rohingya is a political construct and there exists a well-recorded history of their presence in the Rakhine state. However, political constructs of ethnic identity are meant to create differences and justify these through mythical imaginations of the past. The clear religious trigger for the crisis was reinforced by the proclaimed Bengali-ness of the Rohingyas, which provided an added axis of othering. Dhaka has done a commendable job so far to mitigate the plight of the refugees, who have mostly taken refuge in Bangladesh. The UNHCR, of course, has tried to stand by the displaced people and restore to them a life of dignity and provide them with basic material needs. Yet, the nature of the responses betrays a clear difference. As the UNHCR's 2018 *Joint Response Plan for Rohingya Humanitarian Crisis* notes,

> In keeping with its policies, the Government of Bangladesh refers to the Rohingya as 'Forcibly Displaced Myanmar Nationals', in the present context. The UN system refers to this population as refugees, in line with the applicable international framework for protection and solutions, and the resulting accountabilities for the country of origin and asylum as well as the international community as a whole.[48]

Since none of the South Asian states have signed the 1951 Convention, no South Asian state legally recognises having refugees. They have sought to deal with the challenges of population displacement through national legal frameworks and there is very little regional coordination in such matters. Hence, national interest decides state responses. While Pakistan, Bangladesh, and

India have a good record of hosting displaced populations, the absence of regional mechanisms seriously handicaps efforts at rehabilitation, burden sharing, and repatriation efforts. This stands in contrast to Southeast Asia, Africa, and Latin America where the international organisations, regional bodies, and national agencies work more closely. As Zahid Shahab Ahmed puts it:

> In terms of North-South endeavours, there are examples of UNHCR-led initiatives, such as in Africa, Latin America and Southeast Asia (Betts, 2008), and other initiatives involving regional IOs. On the issue of migration, the EU cooperates with African and southern Mediterranean countries through the Barcelona process.[49]

However, the modalities of tackling the issue are no more important than the infrastructure and resources. In fact, recent experiences show that regional responses have a mixed record. While Africa continues to benefit from the good offices of the OAS, the situation in Latin America is not very encouraging. In a nutshell, there is a complete mismatch between the magnitude of the problem and the efforts summoned by the states and civil society through their various organisations. B. S. Chimni wrote some years ago that the 1951 approach is flawed and the national level remains the most effective to craft responses befitting the needs of the hapless millions in search of safe havens.[50] While this may be truer in the peculiar historical context of South Asia, which was created through partition and witnessed massive population movements across colonial borders, there is a manifest need to beef up regional mechanisms in the light of our collective experiences of humanitarian crises throughout the world. It is a fact that existing political divisions tend to resurface in regional bodies. However, states alone cannot fashion solutions, no matter how well-intentioned they may be.

Africa has continued to witness a significant rise in refugees and internally displaced individuals. Sudan, Somalia, and Niger remain embroiled in domestic conflicts and have in the process generated both IDPs and refugees in huge numbers. According to a report from the Pew Research Center, the information states that the number of forcibly displaced people in Sub-Saharan Africa reached 18.4 million in 2017, up sharply from 14.1 million in 2016. This was the largest regional increase in forcibly displaced people worldwide during that time.[51] However, contrary to popular perception, the sub-Saharan African states—Ethiopia and Uganda, among others—have an exemplary record in hosting refugees. It is a fact that political conflict, resource loot, and natural calamities continue to generate massive population flows throughout much of Africa even today. Yet, any impartial account shows that African states, their poverty notwithstanding, have not shied away from their responsibilities and have hosted refugees created by neighbouring states for years. Sadly, the African record of mitigating the sources of this crisis remains unsatisfactory. The legacies of colonialism and the complications created by artificial borders and resource paucity have conspired to consistently displace people both within and across states, and have also compromised the capacity of states to find a lasting solution to the problem.

Latin America faced its worst displacement crisis in the new millennium from 2017 onwards as domestic conflict ravaged Colombia and political instability and economic crisis pulverised Venezuela. The harsh American policy of closing borders for political asylum seekers under the boorish Trump regime magnified the crisis manifold as resources available for humanitarian action dwindled sharply. Most of the Latin American refugees remain holed up in neighbouring states like Ecuador, Panama, and Costa Rica, and interestingly Venezuela, where many Colombian refugees live pitiable lives. In the words of Robert Muggah, et al.:

> The Northern Triangle countries of El Salvador, Guatemala and Honduras are experiencing the most severe displacement crises since their civil wars of the late 20th century. Roughly 130,000 people applied for asylum from these three countries in 2017—a 1,500 percent increase since 2011. Most of them are seeking protection in Mexico and the U.S., but the majority are being denied.[52]

According to the official statement by Eduardo Stein, Joint UNHCR-IOM Special Representative for Venezuelan refugees and migrants:

> The number of refugees and migrants from Venezuela has now reached 4.3 million and is growing by the day. As of today, there is no end in sight to this massive population movement, which includes an increasing number of people with vulnerabilities, many of them in need of international protection, as well as a large group seeking access to basic services and employment opportunities.[53]

The real problem, however, lies elsewhere. The very category of the refugee is a dehumanisation that will weigh upon our conscience intermittently. Unless we find a way to transcend our differences over selective admission and border closure, international efforts to restore to refugees a life of dignity, capacity, and rights befitting a genuine human existence will remain unsuccessful.

Conclusion

This study is an effort to advance three interrelated arguments. First, global refugee flows have manifestly worsened in the past few years and the crisis appears deeper and more expansive than ever. All the continents are infested with massive displacement and international efforts at all levels remain paltry and inconsistent. I have argued that the modality is not more critical than summoning global actors to prioritise their duty towards humanitarian assistance. For most major powers, humanitarian assistance remains a sad footnote to their international efforts. Realist geopolitics and neoliberal policies combine to make great powers increasingly hostile towards shouldering refugee costs. Global civil society initiatives cannot compensate for the colossal neglect of responsibility by the developed and the developing world.

Second, this chapter has brought together the many theoretical ways of locating the refugee. I have reflected selectively on the liberal, communitarian, post-colonial, and radical tracts to make sense of why the refugee remains a marginal category despite years of efforts to reverse this marginalisation. I largely agree with scholars who emphasise the implicit/undefined labelling of this category as perennial becoming, which oddly absolves those in power of their responsibility to explicitly define and transform it. For what cannot be named cannot be changed.

Third, and as a matter of continuity, this is also a study of the concept of the R2P from its spectacular arrival to an equally striking but inglorious unravelling. Liberal peace projects have met with similar fates before. In a world premised on the arrogance of sovereignty, responsibility is also a function of power. Bereft of any account of which political economy can sustain humanitarian operations across the world, the liberal imagination fails to authorise humanitarian missions to conflict-ridden societies and cannot make states recognise their commitment to uphold the rights of its people in all dimensions of life. Until the refugee, as a category, is humanised and we are able to find a process of normalising the displaced, experiments like the R2P will fall short of their original promise.

ACKNOWLEDGEMENT

The author expresses thanks to Ms Mayuri Banerjee, Research Scholar at the Department of International Relations, Jadavpur University, for research support.

NOTES

1. Michael Walzer, *Spheres of Justice: A Defense of Pluralism and Equality*. New York: Basic Books, 1983, p. 62.

2. Walzer, *Spheres of Justice*, pp. 33, 42–44, 45–48, 55–61.

3. Joseph H. Carens, 'Aliens and Citizens: The Case for Open Borders'. *The Review of Politics* 49(2), Spring 1987, pp. 267–268.

4. David Miller, 'Immigration: The Case for Limits', in Andrew I. Cohen and Christopher H. Wellman (eds), *Contemporary Debates in Applied Ethics*. Malden, MA and Carlton: Wiley-Blackwell, 2005, p. 200.

5. Jeremy Waldron, 'What Is Cosmopolitan?' *Journal of Political Philosophy* 8(2), 2002; Martha C. Nussbaum and Joshua Cohen (eds), *For Love of Country: Debating the Limits of Patriotism*. Boston: Beacon Press, 1996; Martha C. Nussbaum, *Frontiers of Justice: Disability, Nationality, Species Membership*. Cambridge, Massachusetts and London: Belknap Press of Harvard University Press, 2006; Onora O'Neill, *Bounds of Justice*. Cambridge: Cambridge University Press, 2000; Thomas W. Pogge, 'Cosmopolitanism and Sovereignty'. *Ethics* 103(1), 1992, and *Global Justice*. Oxford: Blackwell, 2001.

6. Stephen D. Krasner, *Sovereignty: Organized Hypocrisy*. Princeton, N.J.: Princeton University Press, 1999, p. 9.

7. Edward C. Luck, 'Sovereignty, Choice, and the Responsibility to Protect'. *Global Responsibility to Protect* 1(1), 2009, p. 12.

8. For interesting analyses, see the various essays in Davide Orsi, Janja Rebic Avgustin, and Max Nurnus (eds), *Realism in Practice: An Appraisal*. Bristol: E-International Relations Publishing, 2017.

9. Will Kymlicka, *Liberalism, Community, and Culture*. Oxford: Oxford University Press, 1989, and *Contemporary Political Philosophy: An Introduction*. Oxford: Oxford University Press, 2001.

10. On the varieties of the liberal argument, see Brian Barry, *Culture and Equality: An Egalitarian Critique of Multiculturalism*. Cambridge, MA: Polity Press, 2001; Chandran Kukathas, 'Are There Any Cultural Rights?' *Political Theory* 20(1), 1992, and *The Liberal Archipelago: A Theory of Diversity and Freedom*. Oxford: Oxford University Press, 2003.

11. On this, see the divergent readings of Isaiah Berlin and Bernard Williams, 'Pluralism and Liberalism: A Reply'. *Political Studies* 42(2), 1994; Isaiah Berlin, *Four Essays on Liberty*. Oxford: Oxford University Press, 1969; William A. Galstone, 'Liberalism and Value Pluralism'. *American Political Science Review* 93(4), 1999; John Rawls, *A Theory of Justice*. Cambridge, Massachusetts: Belknap Press of Harvard University Press, 1971, and *Political Liberalism*. New York: Columbia University Press, 1993.

12. As Charles Beitz, commenting on Rawls's *The Law of Peoples* (1993), writes, 'The question is which orientation to the fundamental aims of political life one should embrace—that which regards the flourishing

of domestic society as the ultimate political value or that which judges the importance of any such accomplishment by its consequences for individuals.' Making a claim on global justice and pitching for an ethic of cosmopolitanism, he writes, 'Cosmopolitan theories are committed to justifying and assessing social arrangements by their consequences for individuals. They are also presumably committed to some conception of toleration among individuals in society, a conception which, given the structure of cosmopolitanism, must somehow extend to the international realm.' See Charles R. Beitz, 'Rawls's Law of Peoples'. *Ethics* 110(4), 2000, p. 695.

13. John Rawls, *The Law of Peoples*. Cambridge, Massachusetts: Harvard University Press, 1999.

14. Joseph H. Carens, 'Aliens and Citizens: The Case for Open Borders'. *The Review of Politics* 49(2), 1987, pp. 252–262.

15. On a critique of sovereignty from a post-colonial perspective, see Navid Pourmokhtari, 'A Postcolonial Critique of State Sovereignty in IR: The Contradictory Legacy of a "West-centric" Discipline'. *Third World Quarterly* 34(10), 2013.

16. George Sørensen, 'War and State-Making: Why Doesn't It Work in the Third World?' *Security Dialogue* 32(3), 2001; Mohammed Ayoob, *The Third World Security Predicament: State Making, Regional Conflict, and the International System*. Boulder, CO: Lynne Rienner, 1995.

17. For an excellent post-colonial perspective, see the essays in Sanjay Seth (ed.), *Postcolonial Theory and International Relations*. London and New York: Routledge, 2013.

18. Gurminder Bhambra, 'The Refugee Crisis and Our Connected Histories of Colonialism and Empire'. Available at https://www.sicherheitspolitik-blog.de/2015/10/01/the-refugee-crisis-and-our-connected-histories-of-colonialism-and-empire/ (accessed November 2024).

19. Ranabir Samaddar, 'Power and Responsibility at the Margins: The Case of India in the Global Refugee Regime'. *Refuge* 33(1), 2017, p. 42.

20. Hannah Arendt, *The Origins of Totalitarianism*. New York: Harcourt, Brace, Jovanovich, 1951.

21. Giorgio Agamben, 'We Refugees'. *Symposium* 49(2), 1995, p. 117.

22. Ibid.

23. Ibid.

24. Asher Hirsch and Nathan Bell, 'What Can Hannah Arendt Teach Us About Today's Refugee Crisis?' *Border Criminologies* (blog), 10 October 2017. Available at https://www.law.ox.ac.uk/research-subject-groups/

centre-criminology/centreborder-criminologies/blog/2017/10/what-can-hannah (accessed June 2024).

25. Merkel said, 'An important point yesterday was to make it clear once again: Those in need of protection should get protection. Those who have no prospect of staying will have to leave our country again. Press statements by Chancellor Merkel and Federal Minister of Economics Gabriel on September 7, 2015'. Available at https://www.bundesregierung.de/breg-de/aktuelles/pressekonferenzen/pressestatements-von-bundeskanzlerin-merkel-und-bundeswirtschaftsminister-gabriel-am-7-september-2015-845460 (accessed June 2024). For an excellent historical take on German policies on migration and asylum, which contextualises the policies espoused by Chancellor Merkel, see Joyce Marie Mushaben, 'Wir schaffen das! Angela Merkel and the European refugee crisis'. *German Politics* 26(4), 2017, pp. 516–533.

26. Omri Boehm, 'Can Refugees Have Human Rights?' *Opinionator* (blog), *The New York Times*, 19 October 2015. Available at https://opinionator.blogs.nytimes.com/2015/10/19/could-refugees-have-human-rights/ (accessed June 2024).

27. The UN Charter in Article 2 says: '1. The Organization is based on the principle of the sovereign equality of all its Members; 4. All Members shall refrain in their international relations from the threat or use of force against the territorial integrity or political independence of any state, or in any other manner inconsistent with the Purposes of the United Nations.' Available at http://legal.un.org/repertory/art2.shtml (accessed June 2024).

28. UN Documents, 'Gathering a body of global agreements', United Nations, A/RES/25/2625, Twenty-fifth session, Agenda item 85, 24 October 1970. Available at http://www.un-documents.net/a25r2625.htm (accessed June 2024).

> Convinced that the strict observance by States of the obligation not to intervene in the affairs of any other State is an essential condition to ensure that nations live together in peace with one another, since the practice of any form of intervention not only violates the spirit and letter of the Charter, but also leads to the creation of situations which threaten international peace and security,
>
> Recalling the duty of States to refrain in their international relations from military, political, economic or any other form of coercion aimed against the political independence or territorial integrity of any State,
>
> Considering it essential that all States shall refrain in their international relations from the threat or use of force against the territorial integrity or

political independence of any State, or in any other manner inconsistent with the purposes of the United Nations,

Considering it equally essential that all States shall settle their international disputes by peaceful means in accordance with the Charter,

Reaffirming, in accordance with the Charter, the basic importance of sovereign equality and stressing that the purposes of the United Nations can be implemented only if States enjoy sovereign equality and comply fully with the requirements of this principle in their international relations,

Convinced that the subjection of peoples to alien subjugation, domination and exploitation constitutes a major obstacle to the promotion of international peace and security,

Convinced that the principle of equal rights and self-determination of peoples constitutes a significant contribution to contemporary international law, and that its effective application is of paramount importance for the promotion of friendly relations among States, based on respect for the principle of sovereign equality,

Convinced in consequence that any attempt aimed at the partial or total disruption of the national unity and territorial integrity of a State or country or at its political independence is incompatible with the purposes and principles of the Charter,

Considering the provisions of the Charter as a whole and taking into account the role of relevant resolutions adopted by the competent organs of the United Nations relating to the content of the principles,

Considering that the progressive development and codification of the following principles:

a. The principle that States shall refrain in their international relations from the threat or use of force against the territorial integrity or political independence of any State, or in any other manner inconsistent with the purposes of the United Nations.

29. States, while committed to their own sovereignty, must balance their domestic responsibilities (such as upholding national laws and protecting citizens) with international obligations, including adherence to global treaties, human rights conventions, and international cooperation.

30. For details, see Ramesh Thakur and Thomas G. Weiss, 'R2P: From Idea to Norm—and Action?' *Global Responsibility to Protect* 1(1), 2009; David Chandler, 'The Responsibility to Protect? Imposing the "Liberal Peace"'. *International Peacekeeping* 11(1), 2004, and 'The R2P Is Dead, Long Live the R2P: The Successful Separation of Military Intervention from the Responsibility to Protect'. *International Peacekeeping* 22(1), 2015; Alex J. Bellamy, 'Supreme Emergencies and the Protection of Non-Combatants in War'. *International Affairs* (Royal Institute of International

Affairs 1944–) 80(5), 2004, and 'The Responsibility to Protect and the Problem of Military Intervention'. *International Affairs* (Royal Institute of International Affairs 1944–) 84(4), 2008.

31. Kofi Annan, 'Two Concepts of Sovereignty'. United Nations Secretary-General, 18 September 1999. Available at https://www.un.org/sg/en/content/sg/articles/1999-09-18/two-concepts-sovereignty (accessed June 2024).

32. International Commission on Intervention and State Sovereignty, *The Responsibility to Protect, Report of the International Commission on Intervention and State Sovereignty*. Ottawa: International Commission on Intervention and State Sovereignty, International Development Research Centre, 2001, p. 33:

> 33. Responsibility to protect populations from genocide, war crimes, ethnic cleansing and crimes against humanity
>
> 138. Each individual State has the responsibility to protect its populations from genocide, war crimes, ethnic cleansing and crimes against humanity. This responsibility entails the prevention of such crimes, including their incitement, through appropriate and necessary means. We accept that responsibility and will act in accordance with it. The international community should, as appropriate, encourage and help States to exercise this responsibility and support the United Nations in establishing an early warning capability.
>
> 139. The international community, through the United Nations, also has the responsibility to use appropriate diplomatic, humanitarian and other peaceful means, in accordance with Chapters VI and VIII of the Charter, to help protect populations from genocide, war crimes, ethnic cleansing and crimes against humanity. In this context, we are prepared to take collective action, in a timely and decisive manner, through the Security Council, in accordance with the Charter, including Chapter VII, on a case-by-case basis and in cooperation with relevant regional organizations as appropriate, should peaceful means be inadequate and national authorities manifestly fail to protect their populations from genocide, war crimes, ethnic cleansing and crimes against humanity. We stress the need for the General Assembly to continue consideration of the responsibility to protect populations from genocide, war crimes, ethnic cleansing and crimes against humanity and its implications, bearing in mind the principles of the Charter and international law. We also intend to commit ourselves, as necessary and appropriate, to helping States build capacity to protect their populations from genocide, war crimes, ethnic cleansing and crimes against humanity and to assisting those which are under stress before crises and conflicts break out.

34. United Nations Office on Genocide Prevention and the Responsibility to Protect, 'Framework of Analysis for Atrocity Crimes: A Tool for Prevention', 30 October 2014. Available at https://www.globalr2p.org/resources/framework-of-analysis-for-atrocity-crimes-a-tool-for-prevention/ (accessed March 2025).

35. Arundhati Ghose, Permanent Representative of India to the United Nations, told the Ex. Com of the UNHCR in its 48th session in 1997 that the refugee convention adopted in the European context of political polarisation of the Cold War was irrelevant in the new context and has failed to address the new refugee challenges and realities. She said:

> International Refugee Law is in a state of flux and it is evident that many of the provisions of this convention, particularly those which provide for individualized status determination and social security have little relevance to the circumstances of developing countries today who are mainly confronted with mass and mixed inflows. Moreover, signing the convention is unlikely to improve in any manner the actual protection which has always been enjoyed and continues to be enjoyed by refugees in India. (quoted in Narayan Sharma, 'Refugee Situation in South Asia: Need of A Regional Mechanism'. *Kathmandu Law Review* 1[1], 2008, p. 111).

36. International Commission on Intervention and State Sovereignty, *The Responsibility to Protect*, p. ix.

37. Thomas G. Weiss, 'R2P After 9/11 and the World Summit'. *Wisconsin International Law Journal* 24, 2006, pp. 743–744.

38. Weiss, 'R2P After 9/11 and the World Summit', p. 743.

39. Thakur and Weiss, 'R2P: From Idea to Norm—and Action?' p. 28. Bellamy also makes the same point. The ICISS succeeded in refraining from the humanitarian intervention debate by stressing the primary responsibility that states had towards their own citizens, situating non-consensual intervention within a wider continuum of measures, including prevention, rebuilding, and non-forcible means of reaction, and identifying a range of practices other than armed intervention that could contribute to the prevention and mitigation of genocide and mass atrocities. Bellamy, 'The Responsibility to Protect and the Problem of Military Intervention', p. 621.

40. Thakur and Weiss, 'R2P: From Idea to Norm—and Action?' pp. 24–25.

41. The Afghan military intervention can be differentiated from the Responsibility to Protect framework by emphasising the distinct circumstances surrounding each. While R2P focuses on preventing

atrocities like genocide, war crimes, and crimes against humanity, the intervention in Afghanistan can be said to be driven by different factors, such as counter-terrorism and political regime change. By highlighting these differences in motivations and goals, it becomes clear that the intervention in Afghanistan does not fit neatly within the scope of R2P.

42. Bellamy, 'The Responsibility to Protect and the Problem of Military Intervention', p. 623.

43. Chandler, 'The R2P Is Dead, Long Live the R2P', p. 1.

44. According to the report of the UNHCR available on its portal,

> The Afghan refugee population constitutes the largest protracted situation in the world. Up to 96 per cent of all Afghan refugees live in the neighbouring Islamic Republics of Iran and Pakistan, which have generously hosted them for over three decades.
>
> The Myanmar situation also remains a key operation. An estimated 500,000 refugees from different ethnic groups have been fleeing for several decades in search of protection from ethnic conflict and violence.

'Asia and the Pacific', UNHCR. Available at http://www.unhcr.org/asia-and-the-pacific.html (accessed June 2024).

45. 'Iraq Emergency', UNHCR. Available at http://www.unhcr.org/iraq-emergency.html (accessed June 2024).

46. 'War in Syria and Iraq worsens global refugee crisis in 2016'. *The Indian Express* [online version], 22 December 2016. Available at https://indianexpress.com/article/world/war-in-syria-and-iraq-worsens-global-refugee-crisis-in-2016/ (accessed June 2024).

Karen McVeigh finds that around three-quarters of Afghan refugees were displaced at least twice and the returnees were denied aid and assistance. Karen McVeigh, '"Now is not the time": Violence forces refugees to flee Afghanistan again'. *The Guardian*, 25 January 2018. Available at https://www.theguardian.com/global-development/2018/jan/25/violence-forces-refugees-to-flee-afghanistan-again (accessed June 2024).

47. 'Rohingya Emergency'. UNHCR, 2017. Available at http://www.unhcr.org/rohingya-emergency.html (accessed June 2024).

48. UNHCR, '2018 Joint Response Plan for Rohingya Humanitarian Crisis'. March–December 2018. Available at https://www.unhcr.org/in/media/2018-joint-response-plan-rohingya-humanitarian-crisis-march-december-2018 (accessed March 2025).

49. Zahid Shahab Ahmed, 'The Role of SAARC and EU in Managing Refugees in South Asia and Beyond: Potential for North-South Cooperation'. *Global Policy* 9(5), 2018, p. 77.

50. Bhupinder S. Chimni, 'The Law and Politics of Regional Solution of the Refugee Problem: The Case of South Asia'. *RCSS Policy Studies* 4, Regional Centre for Strategic Studies, Colombo, 1998.

51. Phillip Connor and Jens Manuel Krogstad, 'Record number of forcibly displaced people lived in sub-Saharan Africa in 2017'. Pew Research Center, 9 August 2018. Available at https://www.pewresearch.org/short-reads/2018/08/09/record-number-of-forcibly-displaced-people-lived-in-sub-saharan-africa-in-2017/ (accessed November 2024).

52. Robert Muggah, Maiara Folly, and Adriana Abdenur, 'The Stunning Scale of Latin America's Migration Crisis'. *Americas Quarterly* 20 June 2018. Available at https://www.americasquarterly.org/content/stunning-scale-latin-americas-migration-crisis (accessed June 2024).

53. 'Situation of Venezuelan refugees and migrants needs greater global attention', 29 August 2019. Available at https://www.unhcr.org/news/press/2019/8/5d67c6e94/situation-venezuelan-refugees-migrants-needs-greater-global-attention.html (accessed June 2024).

4

MIGRANTS AND MOVEMENTS ACROSS ASIA

Mobility, Global Migration Governance, and the European Response

ANITA SENGUPTA

> *In the continuum between mobility that is totally voluntary and where the choice and will of the migrant is the overwhelmingly decisive element and totally forced migration where the migrant faces death in remaining in his place of residence, there remains a number of intermediate situations. In fact most movements occur in between the two situations.*[1]

What is termed as the current 'European' migration crisis is in actuality mostly about 'Asian' migrants as well as refugees. Whether it is the elusive Afghan 'peace', manifold levels of conflictual engagement in the case of Syrian refugees, or the unresolved question of the Rohingya refugees of Myanmar, the world has witnessed numerous instances where state borders do not match ethnic boundaries. The trajectories of migration of both Asian migrants and refugees are also interspersed by the fact that in certain situations, short-term migration is the only way to ensure basic economic survival for Asians who are on the move. This movement does not follow a linear Asia to Europe trajectory. Migrants mostly tread traditional routes that were once accepted as 'normal', but have now become problematic with increasing levels of securitisation and the rhetoric that accompanies it. The debate on these movements, however, is clearly oriented towards the lack of mechanisms to deal with 'ethnic' issues in various Asian states, and the subsequent humanitarian problem it poses, which then becomes 'global' and requires a coordinated response. This basic premise itself requires both elaboration and rectification at various levels. These complex mixed migratory movements are only partly motivated by domestic conflicts, which are more often than not compelled by international pressures, great power politics, and an interwoven geopolitical and geo-economic reality. Some, of course, are survivors of the colonial legacy that most Asian states inherited, while others are magnified by the economic interests of the global economy.

Much of the migrant movement is also either domestic or regional, and many more migrants just cross over the border to merge with co-ethnics, thus remaining un-enumerated, rather than undertake a perilous journey across the high seas. There is, therefore, a need to move beyond the rather simplistic assumption that the main division in global migration governance is between the differing interests of states in the global South and the predominantly migrant-receiving states in the global North. In reality, the rhetoric of the 'European' migration crisis can only be understood in terms of the fact that migration holds geopolitical significance, not only in how it is constructed and by whom but also in how it is challenged and subverted. How the concept of the 'migrant' and the 'refugee' is used in different contexts and for a variety of purposes therefore opens up multiple questions about mobility, citizenship, and the nation-state.

Asia extends geographically from the east of the Ural mountain and river across to the offshore islands of Japan and the Asia Pacific (where the ethics of offshore detention centres has resulted in critical debates). While taking note of the fluidity of Asia as a geographical region and its implications for researching forced migration, this chapter restricts itself to the regions traditionally defined as South, Southeast, Central, and West Asia as regions of emigration and transit, but also as the destination for those fleeing conflicts and persecution.[2] It is here that 'durable solutions', resettlement, repatriation and local integration, and the 'right to return' have been tested, with mixed results and responses. Further, it is the supposed paucity of regional, legal, and institutional structures in these regions that have led to debates on the need for creating frameworks to address the consequences of human movements.[3] Yet, more significantly, it is in these regions of Asia that the framing of population movements as a 'crisis' can be best questioned through narratives where mobility is seen as a way of life.

While internal migration in Asia has been significant, this chapter focuses on transnational movements of (forced and illegal) migrants and refugees since it is these processes of relocation that the Global Compact seeks to address. By definition, these transnational movements involve at least two states, and in many cases three or more, as migrants transit through third countries to reach their destination. Further, in each state either travelled through or arrived at, the concern for maintaining particular national identities, widely shared values, and control over political institutions preclude a policy of open entry. As such there is a need to look at the impact of migration beyond the narrowly economic or strategic to include issues of identity and national sovereignty. Migration not only feeds into the nationalist discourses of the sender and receiver states, but it also becomes a lens through which the relationship between the birthplace and the adoptive home is negotiated by the migrants themselves.

There is an ongoing debate within the EU about how to deal with this crisis, with states divided between those who would seek a solution to the conflicts to end migrant movements, and others who are looking for a more equitable way to distribute them across Europe. The EU today is deeply divided over how to cope with the influx of people from West Asia, which is testing the principle of solidarity and making the Union look heartless and ineffective, pitting member states against each other, and fuelling populism and anti-Islamic sentiments. As large parts of what is defined as the greater Middle East gets embroiled in conflicts (resulting in human tragedies and movements across borders), and European states like Hungary respond with measures to confront what they term as threats to European 'security, prosperity and identity',[4] and refuse the right to both resettlement and movement, there is a need to re-engage both with the issue of forced migration in Asia and the reaction of the receiver states in Europe.

'MIXED, MASSIVE AND PROTRACTED': THE FRAMING OF THE ASIAN MIGRATION DEBATE

The framing of the Asian forced migration debate is informed by repeated references to the lack of a formal structure for protection—including developed asylum policies, procedures, and process systems—and the fact that there seems to be little interest in developing them. A 'mixed record of protection of human rights', isolated borders, and irregular movements are said to have brought into sharp focus the interconnections between statelessness, an absence of protection, and irregular migration in the region.[5] Much of the discourse is about people who have been marginalised, and the muted regional response where the right of the migrant is concerned. A principal reason for this is identified in the fact that Asian states in general and South Asian states in particular are non-signatories to the 1951 Refugee Convention and its 1967 Protocol, thus allowing the denial of legal status, access to courts, welfare system, religious freedom, freedom of movement, and identity cards to migrants.[6] Since it is 'Foreigners' Acts' that determine the status of the 'refugee', the term itself carries with it the connotation of the 'outsider', which is problematic in cases like the Pakistanis in Bangladesh, for instance, who were stranded in the post-Partition era.

It is also argued that the definition of a 'refugee' in Article 1 of the 1951 Refugee Convention (someone who is 'outside his/her country of nationality' or 'habitual residence', has a 'well-founded fear of being persecuted for reasons of race, religion, nationality, membership of a particular social group or political opinion', and is 'unable or unwilling to avail of the protection of the country or owing to such fear is unable to return to it') does not apply in the South Asian context. In many instances, there is no 'country of nationality' or 'habitual residence' to which they can return, thereby generating the category of stateless people, who are identified as creating another level of complexity. However, as Paula Banerjee argues in her article on 'Forced Migration in South Asia', all South Asian states are signatories to a number of human rights instruments, and states like India have offered refugee status to specific groups of non-citizens—including Partition refugees, Tibetans, people from Bangladesh, Sri Lanka, and Bhutan.[7] Banerjee also argues that refugees are neither the only nor the largest group of forced migrants in South Asia. Internally displaced people (IDPs) are equally important in understanding the 'construction, determination and delineation of the region'.[8] In South Asia, the causes of displacement include conflict, controversial developmental projects, ecological hazards, and changes in laws, such as forest laws.[9]

In South Asia, both the size and the diversity of the region, as well as the multiplicity of local forms that mobility assumes make its study a formidable task. The literature available is large and a significant portion of it is concerned with small areas or individual communities. There are no significant physical boundaries within South Asia and the ebb and flow of peoples and ideas through trade and conquest was the norm. Colonial British rule, common to the region, facilitated movements of labourers, soldiers, and traders, both within the region and to British colonies in other parts of the world. It was the aftermath of Partition that saw the first large irregular migrations, and later, the creation of Bangladesh led to a fresh wave of movements. While significant numbers of the displaced have now been absorbed within host societies or have returned, migration continues to be a political flashpoint with large numbers of displaced populations left outside their 'national' territories—like the Afghans in Iran and Pakistan or the Rohingya in Bangladesh.

Similarly, migration has its own dynamics in Southeast Asia. While sharing a common colonial history and experiences of migration, each of the states also has individual experiences of forced migration that have regional implications. Alistair Cook and Christopher W. Freize argue that in mainland Southeast Asia, forced migration has mostly been the result of the control of the state by elites belonging to particular communities, who have forced minority communities to relocate. In maritime Southeast Asia, it was a consequence of communal violence and resettlement strategies.[10] Cold War power rivalries also resulted in mass movements like the Indo-Chinese exodus. The continuing tensions are reflected in the inherent strains between intervention and sovereignty, and the continuing lack of regard for basic human rights in some states. However, both the South and Southeast Asian regions are also replete with instances of migratory movements like seasonal labour migration, which are accepted as 'normal' and question the logic of Asian human movements being identified primarily as a by-product of civil wars. This ignores the fact that population 'flows' traditionally defined movement in the region now identified as stretching from Afghanistan to Central and West Asia. Movements of nomadic pastoralist societies, along with movements resulting from trade, pilgrimage, and conquest, have marked the landscape of the region since times immemorial. With the colonial redrawing of the political map, these everyday movements were sought to be restricted in a variety of ways.

In the region stretching from the borders of South to Central Asia, sedentarisation, the Soviet collectivisation campaign, forced deportation of minorities during and after the World Wars, and the buffer status that Afghanistan had in the 'great game' has traditionally been identified as the causes of forced migration and displacement. With the disintegration of the Soviet Union and the emergence of new states, a number of issues assumed importance in the interpretation of forced migration and the resultant non-citizen status conferred upon many. State-building processes across the region left people stateless as they fell outside the definition of citizens (for example, the Uzbek brides in Kyrgyzstan),[11] ethnic conflicts encouraged movements across borders that met with resistance from the host state as they upset the demographic balance (Uzbeks who crossed the border into Kyrgyzstan after 2005),[12] and economic imperatives often led to labour migration.

Furthermore, in certain cases, resentment among displaced peoples encouraged them to join resistance movements in other parts of the globe (for instance, the Islamic Movement of Uzbekistan joining the Islamic State). Most of these movements evade comprehension through a statistical approach, since these flows escape official censuses. There also exists the trend of the return of the refugee with all its associated institutional issues (the return of Afghan refugees, for example). In certain cases, states have actively encouraged return for a variety of political reasons (the Uzbek government has asked for the return of migrants from Russia), while migrants have expressed a reluctance to return. In other situations, refugees have become politically significant for states who wish to replace regimes in neighbouring states or even transform border demarcations.[13] All of these cases invite new interpretations in the study of forced migration as well as refugee crises globally, but more particularly in various regions of Asia.

Similarly, the crisis of statelessness is also a significant issue across Asia.[14] While the Rohingya today are identified as a classic example, the Soviet disintegration in 1991 also resulted in large numbers of people, with different ethnic backgrounds and holding Soviet documents, discovering that the new nationality laws of emerging sovereign states have left them out of the definition of a citizen, although in most cases constitutions recognised all people living within its territorial boundaries as citizens. In regions like Central Asia, the rhetoric of citizenship was complicated by the fact that the history of borders in the region is problematic, and the territories of the five states are closely interwoven with the existence of a number of enclaves. Post delimitation (1924–1936), the borders were left flexible within a broader system where people shared a common Soviet passport, and movement and employment were unrestricted. This, of course, changed in the post-1991 period. In most cases, as in the Ferghana Valley where populations were mixed, movements for trade and/or marriages continued unhindered. Since movement across the borders in the valley did not require documentation, old Soviet passports were often not changed to new national ones. From 1999—and particularly since 2005, when borders (like the Uzbek-Kyrgyz or Uzbek-Tajik) were fenced and visa regimes were introduced—large numbers of people found themselves stateless. Statelessness is not only a result of circumstances (like the border brides of Central Asia), but is also the result of events like the Osh riots that left people without documentation. In recent times, citizenship rules have been used in Uzbekistan as a political instrument to punish non-compliance with the establishment, and passports have been cancelled, leaving nationals stranded in third countries.

Statelessness therefore involves legal issues as well as a narrative, and both are equally important.

There is a similar history of movement between, to, and from the region identified as West Asia today. This history, however, is very different from the complicated humanitarian crises that have been unfolding in recent years, leading to growing numbers of refugees, asylum seekers, and IDPs. This jagged trajectory of migration in West Asia has affected the social fabric, security, administrative structures, and economies of a number of states in the region, and has resulted in a tragic loss of life. A significant number of cases of migration delineate those who are displaced due to civil wars and insurgency in Syria, Libya, Yemen, South Sudan, Iraq, and Somalia, as well as the continuing Israel-Palestine conflict. Here, unprecedented violence, identity-based persecution, and repression have resulted in growing numbers of refugees, who are caught in the crossfire between the Islamic State, the Syrian Kurdish army, and states that are reluctant to host them, adding to a conundrum of political, social, and economic issues. Refugee protection systems in the neighbouring states have also differed significantly. Since it is these multiple framings of the refugee protection systems that the Global Compact seeks to institutionalise, it would be useful to examine the case of Syrian refugees in neighbouring Turkey as an example of a particular mode of protection that epitomises not only state policy towards 'guests', but also multiple geopolitical implications both within the region and in terms of Turkey's relations with the EU, in the context of a surging European unease with population movements across its borders. The following segment will therefore argue that the 'whole of society approach' of the Global Compact not only ignores the various protection modes offered in Asian states, but also neglects the multiple ways in which receiving societies deal with the influx and the resultant manifold refugee experiences. Interwoven through this nexus between the state apparatuses and the refugees is a tacit understanding that the responsibility for 'protection' lies within the 'region', and certainly should not extend to Europe or the US.

Societal Approach vs. Protection Modes in Turkey's Migration Debate

Turkey is a classic example of a state bordering a conflict zone, which attempts to deal with repeated waves of refugees, partly on humanitarian grounds as 'guests', but also increasingly as a useful political object vis-à-vis its relations with the EU.[15] Turkey today is host to more than three-and-a-half million Syrian refugees. Furthermore, the country has shifted its policies of identifying migration categories—from being a country of emigration and transit, it has become a destination for migrants and refugees fleeing conflict—thereby requiring an entirely new regime of legislation to deal with people who are identified as 'guests'.[16] Refugees, however, are increasingly being seen as a political liability—especially near border towns, where Syrians can outnumber locals.[17] A bomb blast in the frontier town of Suruc in July 2015, followed by an attack on a peace rally in Ankara's central train station in October 2015, both of which resulted in significant casualties and for which the Islamic State was charged as being accountable, heightened concerns that Turkey's open-door policy for Syrian refugees has made it easier for militants to enter Turkey.

However, more than security concerns, there remains the problem of integrating a significantly large population with concerns like work permits, for the issue of the influx of migrants remains largely unresolved despite recent regulations.[18] Thus, the 'Syrian' refugee was already identified as problematic and largely tolerated as a political leverage vis-à-vis the EU. In any case, the 'refugee question' is not one that is simply ruled by the logistics of a state unable to deal with the large numbers of 'guests'. The country's policies for regulating the flow of migrants and refugees are today intimately connected with the national plan to project the nation in the 'image' of a migrant—as well as a refugee-friendly state. This plan was born out of Turkey's ambitions to join the EU, of the EU's own concerns about the refugee influx, and the discomfort of international human rights organisations with identifying Turkey as a 'safe' country for refugees. It also involves the issue of the development of a parallel economy in Turkey, supported on the one hand by a surfeit of available migrant labour, and on the other hand, by apprehensions about the impact that migrant labour would have on the country's economy.[19]

Turkish ambitions in neighbouring states complicate the issue further, starting with aspirations in Syria, hopes for the swift fall of the Assad regime, and subsequent support for the Syrian opposition. There is also the unexpressed but underlying Turkey-Greece rivalry that is centred on Cyprus, but involves a number of other aspects, such as the Aegean issue as well as those of other minority communities. Through all of this, and until quite recently in 2020, when there were reports of refugees being fired upon and pushed back by border guards, Turkey kept its borders open for refugees. Camps were constructed along border towns, even though large numbers of refugees who did not enter the legal asylum system moved on to larger urban areas. However, as the Syrian civil war continued and hopes of a quick return to civil normalcy vanished, Europe witnessed a surging movement of refugees—one that subsequently took the form of a deluge—towards its own borders. The EU's unease with this movement of refugees brought to the fore the fact that Turkey was identified as the key controller of refugee flows into Europe.

Seeking asylum in Turkey involves a unique arrangement between the UNHCR, Turkey, and the country of resettlement. Turkey does not grant non-European asylum seekers 'refugee status' due to a geographical limitation reservation. As a result, non-European asylum seekers are prohibited from staying in Turkey permanently. Instead, they enter a three-step process of temporary stay in Turkey, followed by further relocation. As they first enter the country, they are allowed to register as 'temporary asylum seekers'. If their application seeking asylum in the country is accepted, they are allowed to stay temporarily in Turkey as they wait for a third country to offer them permanent resettlement. During this process, the refugees are placed in a small city or town in Turkey, or even in a camp, from which they are not allowed to leave. UNHCR pamphlets state that there is usually a three-year waiting period for the entire resettlement process to come to completion. However, in actuality the process takes much longer. What makes the situation of the refugees precarious during this interim period of temporary settlement is that aid from NGOs and the UN is generally insufficient for their families to subsist on. The need to acquire basic forms of sustenance compels them to look for work. But until quite recently, Syrian refugees as 'guests' were not allowed to work legally as they were not granted working permits. In 2016, the Turkish government published new regulations allowing Syrian refugees who have been in the country for more than six months to apply for work permits in the province where they are registered. Further, these work permits came with the provision of at least minimum wages.[20]

However, despite the legislation allowing Syrian refugees work permits, the degree of employer involvement necessary to obtain the permits, and the lack of incentive on the part of the employers to do so, particularly for unskilled or semi-skilled workers, has meant that less than 0.1 per cent of Syrian refugees in Turkey stand to gain from this new legislation. Many employers are unaware of or unwilling to give work permits, as this will necessitate giving the refugee workers minimum wages.[21] More problematically, Turkish law requires an employer to furnish his employees with a contract before they can apply for a permit, an unattractive proposition in the case of Syrian refugees since they are often employed precisely because they can be easily exploited.[22] Further, as Kamyar Jarahzadeh argues in the course of his study of Afghan refugees in Turkey, increasing 'formal citizenship' through registration as a refugee often does not automatically entail the subsequent acquisition of 'substantive citizenship' in Turkey. In fact, in most cases it entails the refugees' sacrifice of the freedom that comes with remaining undocumented, since as a temporary asylum seeker in Turkey, refugees agree to stay in the city to which they are assigned. As such, they consider it a more attractive option to apply for asylum status once they reach Europe. [23]

Most refugees make the precarious decision of initially crossing the Aegean Sea to Greece, and then waiting for entry into other European states. The assumption underlying this decision is that entry into a Schengen state will automatically facilitate movement to their desired destination in Europe. Unfortunately, this has not happened in practice. Hungary's reaction is a classic example of this undesired actuality. Hungary, situated in Central Europe and a Schengen passport–free zone, has in recent times been seen by refugees as a gateway bound for other parts of Europe. However, unfortunately for the migrants, Hungary's negative reception of them is matched by the comments made by the country's Conservative Prime Minister, Victor Orban. Orban clearly indicated in 2015 that Hungary views Muslim migrants as a threat to Europe's Christian heritage.[24] He accused Germany of encouraging the influx of refugees and has rejected the European Commission's proposal for mandatory quotas to distribute refugees throughout the EU. This is probably reflective of the fact that there has always been a 'civilisational' image attached to the EU that requires the recognition of a system of values shared by all members. It was this mandate, for instance, that, more than any other administrative requirement, prevented Turkey's entry into the EU, given the widespread opinion that Turkey, as a 'Muslim' country, has a different set of traditions and values and a different mentality. This lack of 'civilisational' commonality has made the largely Muslim migrants unwelcome, not just by the Hungarian state but also by substantial numbers of its citizens. There has also been opposition to the concept of the 'country of first asylum principle'. This means that if refugees do not get protection in the first country of asylum and continue to proceed to other neighbouring countries, they could be sent back to that first country of asylum. UNHCR officials argue that this only leads to 'asylum shopping', that is, refugees going from one country to another in search of protection.

There is an ongoing debate within the EU about how to deal with the states divided between, on the one hand, those who would seek a solution to the conflicts and end migrant and refugee movements, and on the other hand, those who are seeking a more equitable way to distribute them across Europe.[25] There are a number of reasons why the processes of migration into Europe remain a problem with few solutions. Foremost is the fact that the political chaos in the Middle East shows little signs of abating, while there remains a significant gap between the income levels in Europe and those in parts of Asia, sub-Saharan Africa, and the Middle East. Labour migration will, therefore, continue to persist in the near future. Second, Europe's history has been one of immigration. In any case, sluggish growth in parts of Southern Europe lowers the possibility of jobs for the migrants. Finally, the migrant situation also creates xenophobic conditions and right-wing reactions that encourage a spectrum of anti-immigration policies.[26]

In fact, when EU leaders met in 2003 to draft a European Union Constitution, the weak cooperation among European countries on issues of immigration was brought into focus. The Convention on the Future of Europe considered extending Brussels' control over immigration. However, the harmonisation of the new EU policy was opposed not only by Euro sceptics but also by Germany, who insisted on a 'national veto' on the numbers of immigrants admitted.[27] This has prompted analysts to argue that EU and member states' migration policies converge in one direction: towards effective restrictions and the exclusion of further non-European migrants. Adrian Favell and Randall Hansen further argue that beyond hostility to the sudden arrival of visible minorities, this repulsion of migrants is also conditioned by the fact that asylum channels distort the ability of the market to select the most appropriate workers for the low-level economic opportunities that exist.[28] It is this control of migration processes by the market, rather than European attitudes and policies on migration, that is determining migration policies.

A central issue facing the EU therefore remains the fact that there is no cohesive policy on how to deal with asylum seekers. The lack of a common system has also been compounded by the principle that refugees may apply for asylum only in the country where they land. This assumption places the burden of refugees on Greece, Italy, and Spain, to an extent. However, many refugees wish to travel further north to Germany or Scandinavian countries where they have better prospects. This trajectory of refugee movements has compelled the Italian Prime Minister to issue Schengen visas to them so that they can go wherever they want in

Europe. Josef Janning, senior policy fellow at the European Council on Foreign Relations, argues that EU states will first have to agree on a standard definition of who is eligible for political asylum and then streamline the process for all member-states.[29] Janning argues that in the absence of a common definition of persons eligible for asylum, too many individuals are being allowed entry into the asylum process, which means that many who actually require it are getting stuck in the pipeline. He further states that a single market and a common space also imply a common understanding of how to deal with individuals entering the country. The solution is seen in terms of, on the one hand, a common continent-wide asylum policy, and on the other, a migration policy that acknowledges these flows of refugees rather than resisting them.

Respect for human rights and freedom of expression lie at the heart of what the EU projects as its humanitarian and liberal 'image'. Political analysts are speculating that a deal with Turkey would affect the image of Europe as a normative power. Moreover, the deal also violates EU's own legislation. Under the Asylum Procedures Directive, Turkey has to be recognised either as a safe third country where Syrians could have applied for protection, or as a first country of asylum where they have protection. In either case, the bare minimum requirement for entry is that the applicant be recognised as a refugee who benefits from the principle of non-refoulement (non-return to a safe country). Since Turkey maintains a geographical limitation for non-European asylum seekers, and Syrians can only be recognised as temporary asylum seekers with no access to refugee protection, this basic requirement is not fulfilled in the case of Syrian refugees. In a striking reversal of concern about refugees altering the 'idea of Europe', it now appears that the very person tasked with keeping them out has brought this idea into question. Europe seems to have arrived at the post Schengen era in more ways than one.[30]

The continuing migrant issue, which has gripped the public imagination, has significantly impacted political landscapes, not only in the region but also across Europe and Canada. While it has played a role in reviving Turkish President Recep Tayyip Erdogan's popularity, in many European countries it remains a polarising issue, often used by right-wing parties to boost their support and shape the political narrative. The image of a woman in a red dress being liberally sprayed with gas as she attempted to cross the Gezi Park went viral during the days of the Gezi Park protests. This was identified as the turning point in the support for the AKP (Justice and Development Party) and the beginning of the end for the popularity it had enjoyed for over a decade. The subsequent loss of majority in Parliament, which brought into question President Erdogan's dreams of a Presidential system, could well have been reversed by the other tragic image of a toddler in a red shirt. (Alan Kurdi, a 3-year-old Syrian refugee whose body washed ashore in Turkey in 2015, became a symbol of the Syrian refugee crisis after a photograph of him went viral, influencing public and political discourse on the migrant crisis.) Erdogan's support for the migrants and criticism of the EU policy, along with demands that EU states now take responsibility for the migrants, seems to have struck a chord not only internationally but also within his own country where, after a significant length of time, his actions appear to have met with approval. In any case, the fact that President Erdogan has demanded EU membership and visa-free travel for Turks in Europe in return for stopping the influx of refugees from his country to Europe and readmitting those who have entered Europe from Turkey, is a significant pointer to the fact that the refugee issue will lead to critical changes in more ways than one.

'We Want to go to a Peaceful Place': Migration Governance in the Era of Global Compact

'We want to go to a peaceful place....'
Sahira, a Yazidi in a camp in southeast Turkey[31]

The assumption that the 'cost' associated with migration is that of the state alone is a misnomer, and it is this misnomenclature that then leads to a search for global migration governance, which operates under the assumption that it is the states which, through international cooperation, can maximise the benefits and minimise the costs associated with migration. In response to this assertion, a manifesto on human mobility underlines that a 'reimagining of migration' is required to take note of the fact that it is the people on the move who need to be at the centre of the migration debate and the decision-making process, as opposed to the states with their exclusionary sovereign rights. The need of the hour is to develop more inclusive and creative ways of dealing with human mobility, which take note of individuals, communities, and organisations that live and work in the 'spaces of displacement'. The manifesto further underlines that here, individual narratives assume relevance as reductionist categories limit the understanding of complex migration journeys.[32] The concluding segment of this chapter therefore begins by looking at two studies based on Southeast Asia that focus not just on 'refugees', but on the 'at-risk' populations that are likely to undertake risky journeys as well. In doing so, the coda of this chapter points to the complex ground realities and precarious existence of migrants as well as refugees that global governance would need to take note of.

Meghna Guhathakurta, in her analysis of the discussions that surround protection strategies for the Rohingya in refugee camps in Bangladesh, argues that there is a continuing debate, on the one hand, between international requirements and national interest, and on the other hand, between ideas of 'charity' and 'service'. Based on this observation, Guhathakurta constructs a sense of the extent to which the Rohingya consider themselves protected against the structural violence embedded in the national and local narratives, given the protracted nature of their stay. She focuses on a number of initiatives, including *Kajoli*, which led to empowerment among the most underprivileged of the Rohingya refugees. However, despite this analysis, exit strategies are being sought by large numbers of the Rohingya, who do not benefit from the aforementioned efforts as they reside outside officially recognised camps. As a result, most of the Rohingya refugees avail of trafficking agents who offer jobs in Malaysia/Indonesia, but most such attempts end in disaster as they encounter insecure and violent borderland spaces, where 'institutions, policies and practices are inimical to their existence'.[33] Guhathakurta further argues that these instances prove that prevention of risky behaviour will only be partially successful without a more significant initiative incorporating the development of skills, which would empower the refugees to take control of their own destinies. This, in the long run, will allow them to 'transform themselves from non-citizens to proactive citizens who can demand the protection of the state they inhabit'.[34] While this strategy would work for documented immigrants, who have the protection of international humanitarian regimes and national governments, it still leaves the cases of undocumented refugees (who live a more precarious existence) unresolved. In such situations, Guhathakurta argues that the democratic structures reflecting peoples' voices must reach out to non-citizens, and employ international standards of humanitarianism within a national context.[35]

Developing a better understanding of the demographic composition of people on the move, including age, sex, and nationality, would better facilitate the country's capacity to meet their needs. Marie McAuliff, in her study of Southeast Asian migrants, therefore advocates for the need for demographic analysis and the modelling of populations who have undertaken migration, as well as of people who are likely to undertake high-risk migration journeys. These include populations that McAuliff identifies as straddling the forced-irregular migration nexus.[36] Greater quantitative data would offer perspectives on factors and processes that underline the complex transnational settings in which these movements occur. McAuliff argues that the identification of communities and groups at risk in countries of origin, based on smuggling networks and on how potential migrants assess and re-assess their chances of movement, would allow the development of enhanced policy responses.

Both studies also underline that irregular migration involves facilitators at various levels. Migrant smuggling networks, for instance, involve a complex arrangement of facilitators who move people across borders. Data on migrant smuggling mostly remains underreported, based either on the few interceptions that take place at borders, or in narratives about migrant lives collected through ethnographic studies. Further, when irregular migrants are intercepted at the borders, there is little information about whether their movements were supported by facilitators. In most situations, the facilitators form a network of people, which may include officials who support the entire process, from illegal entry to extended stays, and furnish illegal migrants with accommodation and employment. In any case, the focus of both state and non-state actors remains primarily on human trafficking, with little urgency to identify the linkages that facilitate the process of migrant smuggling. The collection of reliable data on migrant smuggling is also challenged by the fact that the migrant her/himself is an accomplice, and neither the migrant nor the smuggler wishes to be detected. The multiple networks and complicated routes along which this movement happens also prove to be a hindrance. John Salt and Jeremy Stein argue that while migrant smuggling, like trafficking, is a profit-driven business, it carries with itself the assumption of a commercial relationship between the smuggler and the victim, and the fact that the crime is against the state. This is what distinguishes migrant smuggling from trafficking.[37]

However, the differences that apply between trafficking and migrant smuggling may not become evident in all cases. The migrant's initial consent may shift, as what often starts as migrant smuggling can later lead to forced labour, frequently involving little or no pay. All of these instances require multiple responses that take note of the realities of migrant movement on the ground.[38] Most commentaries on global migration governance, however, continue to argue that:

> Fragmentation has characterized the evolution of global migration governance over the past decades. This fragmentation has had both positive and negative implications for cooperation. Sometimes it has allowed 'coalitions of the willing' to build consensus to engage in agenda setting before bringing work into the UN system. At other times it has offered opportunities for states to bypass pre-existing multilateral mechanisms. The Global Compact process presents an opportunity to reconcile these disjointed developments.[39]

The positive arguments supporting the fragmented nature of global migration governance, as highlighted by many commentaries, complicate the understanding of forced migration and the state policies and structures that govern it. An implicit idea in these positive arguments, as seen in the aforementioned quote, is that migration is a 'crisis' that requires 'coalitions of the willing'. In doing so, these arguments fail to recognise processes of migration for the age-old phenomena that they actually are. Such perspectives then lead to the argument that once a global governance system is in place, the 'crisis' will be resolved. These assumptions therefore ignore the fact that within the EU, even with a common refugee and asylum law, questions of interpretation remain with states. Further, despite legal instruments, protection levels vary, even though most states are signatories to common refugee and human rights instruments. Roland Blank argues that UNHCR studies have revealed important discrepancies in the transposition, but more relevantly in the application of secondary EU legislation. This is partly due to piecemeal approaches to EU law, and partly because some of them give member states significant discretion through optional clauses. As a result, chances of protection are determined largely by which country is processing the claim. Frequently, responsibility is determined by the point of first illegal entry into the EU, turning what Blank calls the 'travel route of asylum seekers into a lottery for their chances of positive decision'.[40]

While most European states are members of the Council of Europe and its human rights instruments, Europe's record regarding forced migration has been mixed. Therefore, Blank argues that the process of harmonisation is yet to be complete, and that there is also an urgency to underline that refugee rights need to be seen as inalienable human rights, and not 'humanitarian aid' to be humbly received.[41] Reintegration and resettlement after situations of mass displacement are generally long-term, multi-faceted, and complex processes. Whether it is acceptance in a new society as refugees, migrants, and guest workers, or returning home to post-conflict situations, each scenario involves specific physical challenges and difficult encounters with broader political communities. The systemic denial of access to rights or their selective attribution calls for a reevaluation that links forced migration, labour studies, and debates of citizenship rights, rather than isolating the refugee experience.

The inconsistencies in the protection systems in place and the ones that are now being envisaged are evident in the lines quoted below, which on the one hand recognise the unwillingness of the West to accept refugees and on the other, laud the emerging Global Compact for reiterating that the protection of refugees is a global responsibility.

> Protecting civilians fleeing persecution and generalized violence is a well-established responsibility under international refugee law. At a time when the West is taking in relatively fewer asylum-seekers, it is important that Turkey maintain its open-door policy towards Syrians refugees. Turkey's generosity is widely recognized, and it should be possible to leverage that goodwill to advance burden-sharing with other countries. The nearly finalized Global Compact on Refugees reiterates that the protection of refugees is a globally-shared responsibility.[42]

At one level, these lines specifically refer to the question of Syrian refugees and underline that, as the neighbouring state of Syria, Turkey should maintain an open-door policy. At another level, however, there is a general agreement underlying global migration governance today that the responsibility for refugees is that of the 'region' alone, and the ideal solution should be to restrict them within that particular region. The Global Compact argues for the sharing of 'assistance' but not 'protection', which should be central to any humanitarian response. Speaking in the context of the Rohingya in Bangladesh, Shamsul Bari points to this fact when he states:

> Real capacity for humanitarian response would entail looking at both protection and assistance. In the current discourse one is looking only at assistance. Protection is a political concept that steers one towards a durable solution whereas assistance is merely functional and hence temporary. 'Fortress Europe' meant that no refugees or asylum seekers would enter Europe. Rather regional solutions to refugee problems were sought where people fleeing persecution would

> take shelter in neighboring states and the whole world would act as saviours by helping them. In that way Europe would be saved from refugees without worrying about durable solutions.[43]

It is the resolution of such contradictions and a clear understanding that asylum should be a universal principle and not a xenophobic reaction that will define how successful 'protection' systems will work at the local, national, and international levels, and will thereby inform and shape the success of any attempt at creating a global system of protection.

Acknowledgements

The author wishes to thank Professor Ranabir Samaddar and Professor Meghna Guhathakurta for their comments and suggestions on earlier versions of the chapter and for sharing material relevant to the study.

Notes

1. Graeme Hugo, Mohammad Jalal Abbasi-Shavazi, and Ellen Percy Kraly, 'Introduction: Advancing the Demography of Forced Migration and Refugees', in Graeme Hugo, Mohammad Jalal Abbasi-Shavazi, and Ellen Percy Kraly (eds), *Demography of Refugee and Forced Migration: International Studies in Population*. Cham, Switzerland: Springer, 2018, p. 4.

2. According to UNHCR figures for 2013, there are 2,589,230 refugees in West Asia, 4,810 in Central Asia, 255,570 refugees in South Asia, 206,860 in Southeast Asia, and 344,410 in East Asia and the Pacific. Among the 10 major source countries for refugees globally, five are in Asia: Afghanistan, Syria, Iraq, Myanmar, and Vietnam. And the 10 top refugee-hosting countries include six Asian states—Pakistan, Iran, Jordan, Turkey, China, and Lebanon. This region also has the world's most protracted refugee situation, that of the Afghans in Iran and Pakistan. See Elaine Lynn-Eo Ho, Laura Madokoro, and Glen Peterson,

'Refugees, Displacement and Forced Migration in Asia: Charting An Inclusive Research Agenda'. Asia Research Institute National University of Singapore Working Paper Series, 236, 2015, p. 3.

3. This, of course, ignores non-institutionalised 'regional' initiatives like the fact that founding ASEAN states like Indonesia, Malaysia, Philippines, Singapore, and Thailand served as asylum countries for more than half-a-million Indo-Chinese refugees since the late 1970s, and that Iran and Pakistan have hosted six million Afghan refugees since the beginning of the conflict in Afghanistan. It also overlooks the presence of multiple regimes and modes of protection in Asia and how these have interacted with the international refugee regime. For details of the debate, see Lynn-Eo Ho, et al., 'Refugees, Displacement and Forced Migration in Asia'.

4. P. Krekó and Z. Enyedi, 'Orbán's political legacy: Security, sovereignty, and the crisis of liberal democracy'. *Journal of Democracy* 29(3), 2018, pp. 66–75.

5. See, for instance, Marie McAuliffe, who underlines this in the Southeast Asian scenario in 'Protection Elsewhere, Resilience Here: Introduction to the Special Issue on Statelessness, Irregularity, and Protection in Southeast Asia'. *Journal of Immigrant and Refugee Studies* 15(3), 2017, p. 277.

6. A representative example is a recent book by Navine Murshid, *The Politics of Refugees in South Asia: Identity, Resistance, Manipulation*. Oxfordshire: Routledge, 2014, pp. 4–8.

7. Paula Banerjee, 'Forced Migration in South Asia', in Elena Fiddian Qasmiyeh, Gil Loescher, Katy Long, and Nando Sigona (eds), *The Oxford Handbook of Refugee and Forced Migration Studies*. Oxford: Oxford University Press, 2014, p. 2.]

8. Banerjee, 'Forced Migration in South Asia'.

9. For details, see ibid.

10. For a detailed study of the experiences of forced migration in each Southeast Asian state, see Alistair D. B. Cook and Christopher W. Freize, 'Forced Migration and Terrorism: Southeast Asian Human Security Challenges', in Alistair D. B. Cook (ed.), *Culture, Religion and Identity in Southeast Asia*. Newcastle: Cambridge Scholars Publishing, 2007, pp. 27–47.

11. It was common practice for Uzbek women to be married to Uzbek men who lived across the border in Kyrgyzstan, particularly in the Ferghana Valley. During the Soviet period, most did not register with the Uzbek embassy in Bishkek. As a result, in the post-disintegration period, they were left without valid documentation from either state, making

them stateless. See 'Kyrgyzstan and Uzbekistan: Stateless "Border Brides" Caught in Between'. *Eurasianet.org*, 17 February 2012. Available at https://eurasianet.org/kyrgyzstan-and-uzbekistan-stateless-border-brides-caught-in-between (accessed November 2024).

12. As an aftermath of the Andijan events in 2005, many Uzbeks fled across the border to Kyrgyzstan. However, they were encouraged to move back to Uzbekistan as the Uzbek/Kyrgyz border already has a significant Uzbek population and there was apprehension that further additions would change the demography in favour of Uzbeks.

13. The Turkish government is asking for a buffer zone between Turkey and Syria to restrict the movement of Syrian refugees into Turkey.

14. Globally, there are between 12–15 million people who are stateless. This gap in estimation is not only because of a lack of systematic attention to collecting reliable statistics, but also due to a lack of consensus on whom to include when counting stateless people. The UN in 1948 recognised the right to nationality as well as the right to change nationality, but it does not define how this responsibility for granting citizenship should fall on a particular state. In 1954, the UN adopted the Convention relating to the Status of Stateless Persons, which provides a framework for the protection of stateless persons. Seven years later, the 1961 Convention on the Reduction of Statelessness was adopted, which contains provisions to prevent and reduce statelessness. In contrast to the 1961 Convention, which focuses on reducing statelessness, the 1954 Convention was devoted to protecting stateless people. In addition, there are other provisions like the International Covenant on Civil and Political Rights, the Convention on the Rights of the Child, the Convention on the Elimination of All Forms of Discrimination Against Women, and the Convention on the Nationality of Married Women, which seek to protect against statelessness.

The right not to be stateless or the right to a nationality is recognised as a Fundamental Human Right. This right is important because many states only allow their own nationals to exercise civil, political, economic, and social rights within their territories. Statelessness means that individuals lack state protection and face numerous difficulties in everyday life, such as restricted movement, limited access to employment, healthcare, and education, and are vulnerable to arbitrary treatment, exploitation, and criminal activity. A stateless person also has no access to protection in the international system because only states are subjects of international law. Without identity papers, a stateless person finds it difficult to obtain political asylum. Stateless persons are also denied the right to leave and enter their own country. It is not relevant how the stateless person came to be without a nationality or whether there is a possibility for the person to acquire nationality. It is also not relevant where they are located—it can occur in both migration and non-migration contexts. A stateless person may never have crossed an international border, having lived in the same country their entire life. A stateless person can also be a refugee if, in addition to not being considered a national of any state, they also meet the definition of Article 1 of the 1951 Refugee Convention (having fled their country due to fear of persecution). Generally, stateless refugees are classified and treated as refugees, meaning that in the UNHCR's definition, only stateless individuals who are not refugees are counted as part of the stateless population.

The first step towards addressing statelessness is to identify stateless populations, determine how they became stateless and understand how the legal, institutional, and policy frameworks relate to those causes and offer possible solutions. The best means of addressing statelessness is to prevent it from occurring. States are the principal actors responsible for the prevention of statelessness because they determine how nationality can be acquired, changed, and lost. Human rights treaties contain a number of safeguards, but the most comprehensive set of standards in this domain is contained in the 1961 Convention on the Reduction of Statelessness. The Convention establishes, for example, that children should acquire the nationality of the state in which they are born if they would otherwise be stateless, that individuals cannot renounce their nationality without having acquired another, and that they cannot be deprived of nationality on discriminatory grounds. The Convention on Stateless Persons asks for the right of free movement and residence for stateless people and asks contracting states to provide identity papers and travel documents. Contracting states are also not allowed to expel stateless persons, except on grounds of national security. Contracting states are, however, allowed to make reservations to specific provisions.

15. For a detailed discussion, see Anita Sengupta, 'The Migrant as a Political Object: "Guests" in Turkey, EU Debates and the Middle Eastern Conundrum'. *Refugee Watch, Issue on Migration and Borders of Citizenship* 49, 2017.

16. Rebecca Kilberg, 'Turkey's Evolving Migration Identity'. Migration Policy Institute, 24 July 2015. Available at www.migrationpolicy.org/article/turkeys-evolving-migration-identity (accessed June 2024).

17. For a detailed study, see Sonar Cagaptay, 'The Impact of Syria's Refugees on Southern Turkey'. *The Washington Institute for Near East*

Policy, Policy Focus 130, 2014. She argues that refugees now represent a significant percentage of the population in provinces like Hatay, Kilis, Gaziantep, Sanliurfa, and Mardin, where they are altering the ethnic and sectarian balance. In provinces like Hatay, where the population is mostly Alevi, the situation is further complicated by their traditional dislike of the AKP and its policies in Syria and their support for the Syrian regime.

18. For details, see Ahmet Icduygu, 'Syrian Refugees in Turkey: The Long Road Ahead'. *Migration Policy Institute*, April 2015. Available at www.Migrationpolicy.org/research/Syrian-refugees-turkey-long-road-ahead (accessed June 2024).

19. See, for instance, Oytun Orhan, *Effects of the Syrian Refugees on Turkey*, Report No. 195, Ankara: ORSAM, 2015. Available at chrome-extension://efaidnbmnnnibpcajpcglclefindmkaj/https://www.tesev.org.tr/wp-content/uploads/report_Effects_Of_The_Syrian_Refugees_On_Turkey.pdf (accessed March 2025). Orhan argues:

- If the effect of the Syrian refugees on the Turkish economy is examined in detail, it is apparent that risks and opportunities are closely intertwined.
- There has been an increase in rental prices and, as a result, it is often difficult to find affordable rentals.
- There has been an increase in inflation in border cities.
- Hiring illegal workers is spreading, especially among small businesses.
- There is unfair competition between businesses that hire illegal workers and companies that do not employ illegal workers.
- Locals believe that job opportunities have been taken away from them. However, when investigated, the effect is not existent. People who might lose their jobs under normal circumstances believe that they have lost their jobs because of Syrian refugee workers. In reality, Syrians are generally employed in areas that locals are not willing to work in. Thus, Syrians meet the demand in unskilled labour.
- Syrians filling a demand for labour creates a suitable environment for investment.
- There has been an important decrease in wages in areas with Syrian refugees.
- The fact that humanitarian aid material distributed to the Syrians in Turkey and Syria are supplied from local Turkish firms creates an opportunity for many of them, especially those involved in the food and textile industries.
- Investors and merchants have moved operations from Syria, especially from Aleppo, to Turkey. Mersin's harbour and sea access make it a top

choice for Syrians. Another city attractive to the Syrian investors is Gaziantep.
- The number of Syrian companies registered with the Gaziantep Chamber of Commerce was 60 before the Syrian crisis. By the end of October 2014, the number rose to 209.
- It has been suggested that a large business opportunity has been lost in channelling Syrian investments to Turkey.
- Syrian investors and merchant who have good relations with the Middle East contribute to the commerce and investments in the region.
- Syrians contribute to production related to the smaller businesses (bakery, shoemaking etc.). However, since most of these small shops are unregistered and they also escape legal responsibilities, they result in losses in tax revenues. Both situations cause unfair competition.

20. 'High Commissioner welcomes Turkish work permits for Syrian refugees'. *UNHCR News Stories*, 18 January 2016.

21. See, for instance, this recent report in *The New York Times*: Carlotta Gall, 'Turkey's Radical Plan: Send a Million Refugees Back to Syria', 10 September 2019. Available at https://www.nytimes.com/2019/09/10/world/middleeast/turkey-syria-refugees-erdogan.html?te=1&nl=morning-briefing&emc=edit_MBAE_p_20190910&section=whatElse?campaign_id=7&instance_id=12280&segment_id=16910&user_id=c40f8243ad85dd7f5c3378996f41db70&regi_id=85799083ion=whatElse (accessed June 2024).

22. Patrick Kingsley, 'Fewer than 0.1% of Syrians in Turkey in line for work permits'. *The Guardian*, 11 April 2016.

23. Kamyar Jarahzadeh, 'Identity at the Fringes of Citizenship: Experiences of Afghan Refugees in Turkey'. *Berkeley Undergraduate Journal* 26(3), 2013.

24. P. Kingsley, 'Hungary PM: Muslim migrants threaten Europe's Christian identity'. *The Guardian*, 2015.

25. Christian Joppke, 'Why Liberal States Accept Unwanted Immigration'. *World Politics* 50(2), 1998.

26. Branko Milanovic, 'Five Reasons Why Migration Into Europe Is a Problem With No Solution'. *Social Europe*, 24 June 2015.

27. Adam Luedtke, 'European Integration, Public Opinion and the Immigration Policy: Testing the Impact of National Identity'. *European Union Politics* 6(1), 2005.

28. Adrian Favell and Randall Hansen, 'Markets against Politics: Migration, EU enlargement and the Idea of Europe'. *Journal of Ethnic and Migration Studies* 28(4), 2002, pp. 581–601.

29. Reem Nasr, 'Migrant Crisis Creates Test for the Idea of a Borderless Europe'. *CNBC*, 3 September 2015.

30. For a detailed discussion, see Ranabir Samaddar, 'Human Migration as Crisis of Europe'. *Economic and Political Weekly* L(51), 2015.

31. From Ayla Jean Yackley, 'Four Years After Genocide thousands of Yazidis languish in Turkey'. *Al-Monitor, The Pulse of the Middle East*, 17 August 2018. Available at https://www.al-monitor.com/pulse/originals/2018/08/turkey-iraq-sinjar-thousands-of-yazidis-languish-in-camps.html?utm_campaign=20180817&utm_source=sailthru&utm_medium=email&utm_term=Daily%20Newsletter (accessed June 2024). Sahira is a survivor of the Islamic State's attack on the Iraqi Yazidi community, who had taken shelter in southeast Turkey in 2014. They continue to live there eight months after the Iraqi government's declaration of victory over the Islamic State as they are too terrified to go home. Remaining in Turkey is not an option, neither is returning home, so their lives remain in limbo as they wait for asylum in Europe, where, according to Sahira, their religion is not a problem. One of her brothers moved to Germany crossing the Agean Sea to Greece, a route that Turkey has now sealed. For the UNHCR, the Yazidis are not a problem since it is assumed that the Islamic State has been defeated. Worldwide, the Yazidis number less than a million and are now scattered far from their traditional homelands in the Middle East. With this severance, Sahira knows that her ancient faith is doomed.

32. See 'Human Mobility: A Manifesto for Change'. Available at https://humanemobility.wordpress.com/manifesto/ (accessed June 2024).

33. Meghna Guhathakurta, 'Understanding Violence, Strategizing Protection: Perspectives from Rohingya Refugees in Bangladesh'. *Asian Journal of Social Science* 45(6), 2017, p. 660.

34. Ibid.

35. See the discussion on SVZV Women Without Residence Permit Support Group of Netherlands in Guhathakurta, 'Understanding Violence, Strategizing Protection', pp. 660–661.

36. Marie McAuliffe, 'The Nexus Between Forced and Irregular Migration: Insights from Demography', in Graeme Hugo, Mohammad Jalal Abbasi-Shavazi, and Ellen Percy Kraly (eds), *Demography of Refugee and Forced Migration: International Studies in Population*. Cham, Switzerland: Springer, 2018, pp. 217–234.

37. John Salt and Jeremy Stein, 'Migration as Business: The Case of Trafficking'. *International Migration Review* 35(4), 1997, pp. 467–494.

38. For a detailed study of migrant networks, see Anita Sengupta's segment on 'Central Asia', in A. Triandafyllidou and M. L. McAuliffe

(eds). *Migrant Smuggling Data and Research: A Global Review of the Emerging Evidence Base*, Vol. 2. Geneva: IMO, 2018, pp. 45–63.

39. Alexander Betts and Lena Keinz, 'The History of Global Migration Governance'. *Refugee Studies Centre* Working Paper, 122, 2017, p. 12.

40. Roland Blank, 'Forced Migration in Europe', in Elena Fiddian Qasmiyeh, Gil Loescher, Katy Long, and Nando Sigona (eds), *The Oxford Handbook of Refugee and Forced Migration Studies*. Oxford: Oxford University Press, 2014, pp. 690–702.

41. Paula Banerjee, 'Forced Migration in South Asia'.

42. Kemal Kirisci, 'The Idlib Offensive Could Create A Major Refugee Outflow—What Should Turkey Do?' *Brookings*, 6 September 2018. Available at https://www.brookings.edu/blog/order-from-chaos/2018/09/06/the-idlib-offensive-could-create-a-major-refugee-outflow-what-should-turkey-do/?utm_campaign=Brookings%20Brief&utm_source=hs_email&utm_medium=email&utm_content=65742727 (accessed June 2024).

43. Unpublished interview in Dhaka, 2 April 2018.

5

REFRAMING THE REFUGEE CRISIS

Resistances and Solidarities

PRIYA SINGH

A EUROPEAN REFUGEE CRISIS?

The 'event'—which the refugee crisis is—seems to occupy the 'structure'—which the village community was.[1]

In the summer of 2015, commonly referred to as the 'summer of migration', a supposed 'European refugee crisis' was said to have unfurled both within and outside Europe. It brought to the table a humanitarian and political dilemma, which necessitated comprehension in the context of the policies and practices of European governments in general, and the EU in particular. People were hosted in 'informal camps' or in 'institutionalised spaces' (also known as 'hotspots') in large numbers. In this case, hotspots refer to the EU-run reception centres in frontier member states like Italy and Greece, set up to identify and fingerprint migrants and refugees. Rejection of asylum and the confinement of irregular arrivals in hotspots, the dearth of legal routes to Europe encouraging enterprises of smuggling, the annihilation of living spaces, and the expulsion of people to nations where their rights were not protected are some of the offshoots of the policy pursued by the European governments and the EU. Another aspect which came to the forefront was the politics of 'exhaustion', referring to the sheer fatigue experienced by continually displaced people, living in the shadows of uncertainty and the constant fear of threat to their lives.[2]

According to the UN Refugee Agency, UNHCR, 'persecution, conflict, and poverty' compelled more than a million people to take off to Europe—this was an unprecedented figure as the number of persons displaced by war and confrontation was the highest witnessed in Western and Central Europe since the 1990s, when a number of conflicts erupted in the erstwhile Yugoslavia. By late December 2015, around 972,500 people had crossed the Mediterranean Sea, according to UNHCR estimates.[3] Moreover, the International Organisation for Migration (IOM) estimated that more than 34,000 people had crossed from Turkey into Bulgaria and Greece by land during the same period.[4] The IOM also estimated that around 1,011,700 migrants arrived by sea in 2015, and nearly 34,900 by land.[5] One out of two of those taking the trip to the Mediterranean, that is, half-a-million people, were Syrians attempting to break away from the conflict in their country. Afghans comprised 20 per cent and Iraqis 7 per cent. Thus, the conflict in Syria was the biggest cause for migration to Europe, although continuing hostility in Afghanistan and Iraq also prompted people to look for safer lives in other places. In addition, there were economic migrants from Balkan countries such as Kosovo and Albania.[6]

The IOM further predicted that the incoming refugee rate could be around 17 per cent higher in 2016. Roughly 258,186 migrants arrived in Europe by the end of July 2016, in comparison with the 219,854 refugees that arrived in 2015 during the same time period.[7] According to the 2018 IOM figures, around 3,785 migrants and refugees were estimated to have died in the Mediterranean in 2015 compared to the 3,283 in 2014. Deaths continue to be a reality even after 2015 as IOM estimates that 5,143 people died at sea in 2016, 3,119 in 2017, and in the first two weeks of 2018, 194 people were recorded to have died at sea.[8] The IOM estimated that around 29,844 migrants and refugees arrived in Europe by sea during July 2019, connoting a 36 per cent decline from the 46,441 arrivals in July 2018. Demises documented on the three chief Mediterranean Sea routes during the first six months of 2019 were of 681 individuals, that is, nearly half the 1,414 proven deaths in the equivalent period in 2018.[9]

In summary, since the civil war erupted in March 2011, around 11 million Syrians were forced to flee their homes. In 2016, approximately 13.5 million Syrians required humanitarian support within the country. The majority of those who sought to escape the violence within Syria took refuge either inside the country or in neighbouring states. According to UNHCR estimates, 4.8 million escaped to Turkey, Lebanon, Jordan, Egypt, and Iraq, while 6.6 million were internally displaced inside Syria. Turkey alone played host to more than 2.7 million Syrian refugees. One million people requested Europe for asylum, with Germany being the most sought-after country, followed by Sweden. Around 150,000 Syrians took asylum in the EU region and member states committed to resettle another 33,000 Syrians.[10] In response, the EU provided humanitarian assistance, and also played the role of host. The contribution of individual nations varied, and according to the UNHCR, 70 per cent of the promised funding was pending. All in all, despite the supposed 'European Refugee Crisis' in the aftermath of the exodus of 2015, the number of Syrian refugees in Europe comprised less than 10 per cent of the overall figure of displaced Syrians.[11] For instance, Javier Alcalde observes that the apparent crisis cannot be attributed to the mere number of refugees, and that the phrase 'crisis' has since time immemorial been employed to define migration waves. The truth lay in the unpreparedness and inability of the European governments to provide humanitarian intermediation. In reality, the year 2016 witnessed a humanitarian crisis, prompted by the view 'that the institutional structures and policies in place, at all territorial levels, were unfit to address what was presented as an emergency'.[12]

While the EU only managed to secure a peripheral position in the political sense of the term as far as the Syrian civil war is concerned, the burden of the repercussions of the war in terms of its humanitarian, economic, and security aspects had to be shouldered by the EU, at least in part. As Russia and the US occupied centre-stage in the military aspects of the Syrian crisis, the EU, conspicuous by its 'diplomatic absence', entered into a pact with Turkey with regard to refugees in March 2016. The immediate impact of this pact was a sharp decline in the number of uncontrolled migrants arriving in Greece. However, the pact became mired in litigation over the 'concessions offered by EU and the conditions to be met by Turkey'.[13] This can be partly attributed to the fact that a divided EU entered into negotiations with Turkey in order to secure the retention of refugees in Turkey. Turkey, in return for keeping the Syrian refugees, was assured of financial support and other concessions, such as visa-free travel for its citizens in EU countries, as well as the resumption of the negotiation process related to Turkey's accession into the EU. In addition, the deal was struck amidst a severe political turmoil in the country. The issues in contention were Turkey's non-implementation of certain clauses of the UN Refugee Convention, the revived armed confrontation in southeastern Turkey with its Kurdish minorities, and the increased disrespect for human rights and establishment of the rule of law within the country itself. [14]

This chapter strives to understand the waves of forced migration to Europe since 2015 in terms of the politics, practices, and policies of the EU, particularly with reference to Syrian refugees, who migrated in large numbers as a consequence of the persistent civil war within their country. It is a more elaborate and revised version of an essay written in the aftermath of the 'summer of migration' in 2015.[15] Since then, there have been several attempts to reframe the crisis in terms of multiple constructs, as well as to throw light on the stories of movements of solidarity and resistance, which in turn are intertwined with the policies of the relevant governments as well as regional and global organisations.

Europe Responds: The EU–Turkey Refugee Pact

Europe's refugee crisis initially drove EU member states apart. Confronted in mid-2015 with a mass inflow of asylum seekers who threatened internal political stability, member states returned to the logic of narrow national self-interest. However, as attitudes towards refugees became non-compromising in even the most benevolent nations since late 2015, a new consensus seemed to have emerged.

The policy of shutting out migrants by reinforcing the EU's external borders and persuading third countries[16] to prevent people from crossing into the EU gained ground. While superficially attractive in terms of reuniting the EU, such a Fortress Europe project would shatter the geographic, political, and economic complexities of Europe's neighbourhood. Rather than rebuilding the EU's legitimacy, it would end up stoking more tensions and greater nationalist anger.[17] An insular, restrictive, gated Europe would be detrimental to the flows of people and commodities that are economically crucial for both European nations and the neighbouring nation-states. The latter provide manpower at lower rates and markets for commodities, while conversely, the former benefit in terms of employment and the availability of products. In other words, such a policy works against the principles of both globalisation and glocalisation. The construction of Fortress Europe via both fences and legal restrictions is not in sync with global markets, global communication, or global capital flows. It ignores the fact that migration is profoundly entangled with globalisation and the easing of restrictions in international trade and investment. Keeping in mind the conflicts, civil war, and non-functioning states in Europe's neighbourhood, emphasising legal and material restrictions to immigration in a fortressed Europe would adversely affect the neighbouring spaces in a political sense. Migration has been an intrinsic part of mankind, it involves deep-seated sociological, social, economic, and ideational issues, and these issues almost always transgress national borders. Curbs to such migration will consequently have ramifications for both spaces in myriad ways, as fluid borders ensure a much-needed informal space for engagement.

On the surface,[18] Europe appeared to be grappling with what was perceived as its worst refugee crisis since World War II. By the end of 2015, more than 500,000 people had crossed to Europe by sea and land from surrounding regions. The majority of the forced migrants undertook the arduous journey in order to get away from the civil war in Syria. On 23 September 2015, the EU member states arrived at a consensus to relocate 120,000 of the refugees across the Union.[19] It was decided that 66,000 of them, who had arrived in Greece and Italy after undertaking hazardous voyages across the Mediterranean, would be relocated in the coming months. Fifty-four thousand were to be shifted to other EU states from Hungary, where they had arrived after trekking across the Balkans. The question that instinctively arose was: Even though the Syrian war had been raging for more than four years, why was there a sudden spurt in the flow of refugees to Europe in 2015? A number of factors could be held responsible for this development, the primary reason being that the civil war in Syria showed no signs of abating, thereby prompting Syrians within Syria to leave and those in exile in Turkey to abandon any hope of returning to their land of origin. Turkey, which was home to more than two million refugees at the time, was yet to grant Syrians the legal right to work. The ruling party, AKP (Adalet ve Kalkinma Partisi, or Justice and Development Party [in English]), perceived as friendly towards refugees, had suffered some setbacks at that juncture, leading to unease among the Syrian refugees. Second, the UN refugee agencies in Jordan, Turkey, Lebanon, and Eastern Europe were dealing with financial constraints, and as such, the condition of the refugee camps was deteriorating. The refugees had saved money to pay smugglers—it was estimated that an individual was paying at least $3,000 to reach Germany from the Middle East.[20] Most significantly, the Syrians who were previously unaware of the Balkan land route discovered it during the summer of 2015, and undertook the rather perilous journey to reach Europe. All this happened while the EU was preoccupied, deliberating over the most appropriate course of action.[21]

In 2016, however, the situation began to change. The refugees began searching for alternative routes to reach Europe as a result of a series of developments, such as 'changing visa regulations for Syrians, intensified border controls, the Balkan route closure, the EU-Turkey agreement, and the development of hotspots on Greek islands'.[22] Those stranded in Turkey no longer had the option of using the Turkey–Greece crossing.

In November 2015, an EU–Turkey summit was held in Brussels to discuss the issue of Syrian refugees and the resultant 'crisis in Europe'. [23] This took place almost four years after the first group of

Syrians fled to Turkey. The two sides arrived at an agreement that provided concessions to both. Turkey accepted the task of patrolling the EU's southern border of Greece, containing Syrian refugees within its borders and accepting the return of Syrians who did not qualify for international protection. The EU, on its part, would provide €3 billion as financial assistance to Turkey for addressing the requirements of the Syrian refugees housed in the country. The EU would also be willing to negotiate on the possibility of visa-free travel for Turkish citizens in the EU–Schengen area and begin negotiations on a renewed accession process for Turkey. The dialogue around visa-free travel was initiated in December 2015 as part of the EU–Turkey readmission agreement. October 2016 was set as the likely date for the abolition of visas for Turkish citizens, albeit with the clause that Turkey fulfils the criteria put forth by the EU. Turkey has been negotiating for accession since 2005 and has been a candidate country since 1999. The agreement opened a new chapter in the negotiation process. The protection of basic liberties and human rights were the core issues that were expected to be discussed according to the European Commission's (EC) progress report of 2015.[24]

In the aftermath of the summit, Turkey took some measures to meet its commitments towards assisting Syrian refugees in the country. The Turkish police raided workshops manufacturing faulty life jackets that failed to meet international safety standards and would be unable to keep migrants afloat, especially those taking the perilous but most popular sea route: crossing the Aegean Sea from Turkey to Greece. As many as 300 people had died on that particular route as of January 2016, according to the numbers released by the IOM.[25] On January 2016, the Turkish government took another step: the country introduced a regulation that would relax the process of acquiring work permits for Syrian refugees in Turkey. This was initiated despite the fact that Turkey exercises what is known as the 'temporary protection regime' as far as Syrians are concerned. According to the new procedure, within six months of receiving their temporary identity cards, Syrian refugees would be eligible to apply for work permits. The legislation would benefit the self-employed as well. The caveat was that the refugees would only be allowed to work within their provinces of residence, and the number of Syrian refugees would be limited to 10 per cent of the total workforce.

Although the initiatives taken by Turkey to limit the number of refugees entering Europe were welcomed, certain questions remained unanswered. Human smuggling continued to be rampant in the coastal towns of Turkey bordering Greece. In addition, Turkish authorities took action against the human trafficking of Syrian refugees rather belatedly. Moreover, as Numan Ozcan, the Director of the International Labour Organisation's (ILO) Turkey chapter, pointed out, 'It would be unrealistic to think of work permits for Syrian refugees as a magical wand that will solve all problems', highlighting the limitations of the arrangement.[26] According to the Organisation of Economic Co-operation and Development (OECD), around 10 per cent of the population in Turkey was already unemployed, which was higher than the OECD average of 7 per cent.[27] This implied that the arrangement would benefit those Syrians who possessed resources to start their own business, while the others would continue to struggle for jobs along with the local unemployed.

Significantly, it was also felt that the turn of events in Turkey towards a more authoritarian system of governance could threaten the fundamental rights of the refugees, as cries of human rights abuses reverberated in Turkey.[28] Since July 2016, the country had entered an extended state of emergency, affecting the rights of all of its citizens. While the emergency was lifted on 19 July 2018, nothing much has changed as 'Erdogan remains in charge and is more powerful than ever, after narrowly winning a constitutional referendum in April 2017 that granted him an "executive presidency", abolishing the role of prime minister and parliamentary system of government.'[29] The financial crisis in early 2019, as well as the loss of local elections by his handpicked candidates, has not undermined his grip over the nation, as he continues to reconstruct Turkey's external policy and suppress dissent within,[30] the most recent manifestation being his threat to 'send a million refugees back to Syria'.[31]

Prior to the internal developments in Turkey, however, on 18 March 2016, representatives of EU member states and Turkey entered into a historical pact, committing to 'end the irregular migration from Turkey to the EU', and to substitute it with 'legal channels of resettlement of refugees to the European Union'. The primary objective of the pact was to substitute 'disorganised, chaotic, irregular and dangerous migratory flows by organised, safe and legal pathways to Europe'.[32] The fourth of April 2016 was fixed as the starting date for the return of the Syrian and other migrants to Turkey, who had used it as their first country of arrival. The Commissioner for Migration, Home Affairs and Citizenship, Dmitris Avramopoulos of Greece and the EU, stated that 'we now need to honour our commitments and ensure an orderly, well managed and safe arrival and admission to Europe.'[33] The agreement specifies that all asylum seekers or 'irregular' migrants were to be returned to Turkey, which was termed as a 'third-safe country of residence', supposedly in keeping with EU and international law. Furthermore, according to the draft statement for the agreement on 18 March 2016, 'this will be a temporary and extraordinary measure which is necessary to end the human suffering and restore public order'.[34]

Turkey as a 'third-safe country of residence' denoted a space that was beyond EU jurisdiction, but which operated to control the flows of migration within the EU, restoring the Schengen Area's 'normative order'. As Donald Tusk (president of the European Council) put it, the aim of the agreement was 'strengthening the EU's external borders, keeping the western Balkan's route closed and getting back to Schengen'.[35] Likewise, Turkey, by being categorised as a 'third-safe country of residence', moved away from being a 'neighbour' of the Union to a sphere of active and autonomous administration, wherein she assumed a role for herself in the EU's border agency FRONTEX, subletting border control. This basically created a focal point for the displaced, and also enabled the confinement and scrutiny of those on the lookout for access to Europe. Moreover, the agreement suggested that for every Syrian sent to Turkey, one would be rehabilitated and given asylum in the EU. Any Syrian not granted asylum would be kept in a 'detention camp', partly funded by €6 billion from the EU to assist the estimated 2.7 million Syrians who were stuck in Turkey. The detention camps were termed 'safe zones', but have come under severe criticism for being geopolitical constructs established for security concerns rather than with a humanitarian basis. Bill Frelick, the Refugee Rights Director at Human Rights Watch, said of the process: 'this means using vulnerable civilians like pawns on a chess board.'[36]

It is true that the EU's actions, on the one hand, could perhaps be analysed from a humanitarian perspective, wherein the situation could be considered exceptional, and where the EU felt a sense of responsibility towards the devastating poverty, overwhelming impenetrability of borders, and the overall suffering of the affected migrants stranded along the boundaries of Europe. On the other hand, the migrants gathered on its borders were quickly portrayed as a risk to the security of the EU, and in this sense, the task of the EU shifted from being humanitarian to performing a dual role where internal security became as important as saving human lives. This has been termed as the collapsing of 'security into justice', wherein preserving territorial integrity is pitted against the safety of migrants. This process often plays into 'anti-immigration' rhetoric, where the 'migrant' becomes coterminous with the 'terrorist'.

Against this backdrop, the agreement with Turkey has been interpreted as the EU's quest to strike an equilibrium between maintaining a tight grip over its territory and displaying the bare minimum responsibility towards the new migrants. Nevertheless, the utilisation of Turkey as a 'safe space' was an awkward continuation and aggravation of the exteriorisation of accountability, wherein the EU used it as an enclave of camps and structures in which migrants would remain immobile, while Turkey occupied the role of an independent migration processing entity. In this sense, the instant objective of this pact was to safeguard the unfurling humanitarian calamity that the migration crisis had engendered by employing subtle methods of mass evacuation within the parameters of permissibility through the international treaty law and refugee law.[37]

Reading the Accord

In an interesting piece for *OpenDemocracy*, entitled 'Zones of turbulence in the wake of EU-Turkey's migration agreement', Evan Stanley Jones compares the EU-Turkey deal of March 2016 with the 1838 Treaty of Balta Limani, or the Anglo-Ottoman Treaty.[38] The trade treaty was signed by the British with a view to abolishing all Ottoman monopolies, thereby facilitating equal levels of taxation and full access to Ottoman markets for British traders. The purpose of this analogy is to state that liberalisation is a method used to capitalise on turmoil. The uncertainty of that period, when the Ottomans felt threatened by Egypt and by the prospect of a Russian involvement, led to the signing of this treaty, which enabled the British merchants to benefit from trade with the Ottomans, culminating in a boost for the British economy. The political turbulence of the time was exploited by the British in an economic sense, and led to a widening disparity between the British and the Ottoman Empires. Jones contends that in the contemporary context, the 'restoration of order' as a consequence of the EU-Turkey pact in practice facilitates a 'return of order for liberal markets and political economy' in a similar fashion. While the Ottomans lost out as a consequence of the Balta Limani treaty back in 1838, the real losers of the EU-Turkey pact would be the migrants. Particularly after the failed coup attempt in Turkey, President Recep Tayyip Erdogan consolidated his authority and became even more of a central player in EU-Turkey dealings. Despite the authoritarian measures that he adopted, he faced limited criticism by the EU. Thus, Jones concludes,

> The comparison I want to make between the EU and the British in 1838 lies in how the economisation of regional instability makes acceptable the braiding of human rights-violating exceptional measures with liberal humanitarianism, a mechanism which is playing itself out with massive consequence, not only on the borders of the Mediterranean, but on the streets and in the schools of Turkey.[39]

Needless to say, the EU-Turkey deal on refugees has come under close scrutiny. It has been extensively analysed and written about. Thus far, the agreement has been widely labelled as an attempt by EU members to regulate the influx of refugees and asylum seekers to their advantage. According to Jeff Crisp, for instance, the three main features of the deal between the EU and Turkey clearly reveal the intent of the industrialised world in the Global North to look for other options and methods to restrict the entry of asylum seekers:[40]

> The first is the establishment of 'safe zones' in countries of origin limiting the need and ability of people to seek asylum in other states. The second is that of 'migration management' and 'offshore processing' agreements, usually involving cooperation between the industrialised states and less prosperous countries in the same region. The third is that of legitimising state strategies by securing the involvement of the United Nations High Commission for Refugees (UNHCR), the International Organisation for Migration (IOM) and other international organisations.[41]

Crisp also refers to the ambiguity of some of the other clauses, such as the EU's commitment 'to work with Turkey in any joint endeavour to improve humanitarian conditions inside Syria which would allow for the local population and refugees to live in areas which will be more safe.'[42] It is difficult to conceive in a concrete sense how conditions within Syria can be improved by outside involvement. Moreover, the EU-Turkey deal envisions the automatic and immediate return of refugees from Greece to Turkey, which is difficult to comprehend, considering the exorbitant costs and perilous nature of the journey that the refugees have to undertake to reach Greece, if the boats are flagged while at sea. While the UNHCR and the IOM have been eagerly courted by the EU to accord legitimacy and competency to the pact, the cumbersome question that arose was how these organisations would then deal with the resettlement clause. The UNHCR stated that 'resettlement should not be conditional on external factors, and the protection needs of the individual remain the priority', a statement itself rooted in ambiguity.[43]

As Defne Gonenc points out, Syrian refugees were acutely aware of the deteriorating condition inside Syria and, as such, were on the lookout for a new life in a new homeland. The risks involved in the arduous journey were no secret to them. Under these circumstances, would they want to leave Europe after having undertaken a death-defying trek? Moreover, the legality of this deal continues to be questionable. Although Turkey has ratified the 1951 Refugee Convention and its 1967 Protocol, there is a major constraint: Turkey only grants refugee status to people of European nationality and/or origin and as a consequence of an alteration in domestic law, it only offers temporary protection to Syrians. As such, it need not treat Syrians in conformity with the Geneva Convention or the Refugee Convention. This is apparent in the way Turkey has been handling at least some of the Syrian refugees, through the use of coercive measures and arbitrary detentions.[44] Some of the migrants have been sent back to their country of origin due to security reasons. Protests within Turkey against the refugees and the general discontent about the admissions *en masse* is at least partly because the EU-Turkey pact is perceived as discriminatory, with Turkey having to bear the responsibility for the bulk of Syrian refugees. However, critics contend that the agreement is in reality more unfair to the migrants than to Turkey or the Turkish people *per se*. Turkey is not a preferred destination for migrants due to its heavy-handed government exercising autocratic measures, its rather inefficient education system which might be unable to accommodate millions of Syrian children, and the rampant inequality and unsafe conditions for the refugees. Turkey, on its part, could make amends by not being involved in the civil war in Syria or elsewhere, and most importantly by addressing the vital question of inequality in living standards in the country.[45]

The EU, in its bid to control the massive influx of refugees, concluded that cooperation with Turkey should be a priority as it would facilitate the fulfilment of its immediate objective of reduced or even zero refugee entries, as well as an increase in the rate of evictions. However, Sergio Carrera and Aikaterini Drakopolou opine that the transfer of responsibility in providing protection, and the decline in the numbers of those who require such protection as they move from Turkey to Greece, were achieved at the expense of deep political, legal, and ethical costs. These costs include grave 'political instability and insecurity in Turkey', which did not constitute a safe haven for refugees; an incapacitated Greece, which was not in a position to receive and provide international protection to the refugees and asylum seekers; and the emergence of a new politics and policies of crisis management in the EU and EC, which perceived the rights of the refugees and the rule of law as negotiable.[46]

The Aftermath

The image of 3-year-old Alan Kurdi, who drowned while trying to escape to Greece and ended up washed back to the shore of a fancy Turkish beach resort, brought the world's focus back on Europe's Middle Eastern refugee crisis. This was despite the fact that the crisis was not 'Europe's own' but of Europe's making. Issues of compassion and humanitarian assistance are no doubt very important, but equally significant is the fact that the Global North is all too keen to abandon their role in the amelioration of lives affected by the Syrian crisis. It would be foolish to think that what happens in the Middle East will remain confined to the region, be it terror groups or refugees.[47]

As the supposed European 'migration crisis' escalated, some of the refugees embarked on a quest for new/alternative routes, others were trapped in transit, while still others tried to run away from Europe to North America. In this context, Vicki Squire and Vasiliki Touhouliotis raise the following questions that remain germane to the subject:

> How far is Europe willing to go to fulfil its deterrent migration agenda? If the aim is to create such dire conditions that people are forced to take flight in the opposite direction, Europe may finally be succeeding with its otherwise failing approach. Yet success and failure are hard to disentangle in this context. Where

> deterrence fails it can still have productive effects for architecture of coercion that thrives on precariousness. And where it succeeds, deterrence fails so many people in so many ways. Driving people away or leaving them in a social and legal limbo is not an answer to Europe's so-called 'migration crisis.' A new agenda on migration is long overdue, and needs to be grounded in an appreciation of each person's inherent potential rather than in a drive to deter 'unwanted' people.[48]

As the much-hyped EU-Turkey deal started to falter, a number of Syrian as well as other refugees began fleeing from Turkey to Greece yet again. In its initial period, the deal seemed to be working well, with the number of migrants fleeing to Europe dipping. In September 2016, only 1,000 or so Syrians, Afghans, Pakistanis, and Iraqis arrived in Greece. It became evident that the animosity between Turkey and Europe was on the rise, since the Turkish state under Erdogan's presidency reacted to a failed coup attempt with extensive purges. As a consequence, the EU-Turkey migrant deal appeared progressively more dubious, and Europe faced the prospect of rekindling a disaster. In an effort to thwart this, European officials were quick to begin negotiations with Turkish leaders yet again. The foreign policy head, Federica Mogherini, and its enlargement commissioner, Johannes Hahn, paid a visit to Turkey, becoming the highest-level European leaders to visit Turkey since the unsuccessful coup attempt.[49] Analysing the series of political manoeuvres in the aftermath of the 'summer of migration' leading to the refugee agreement, Lucy Williams observes that by using Turkey merely as an expedient safeguard against surplus refugees, the EU is playing into the Turkish government's domestic politics, which will keep migrants disenfranchised and under state control, likely to be used for additional votes for the upcoming referendum seeking a regime change. As in other places, migrants in Turkey are valuable as scapegoats, who render cheap labour to the market but who have no say as far as the use of state resources are concerned. EU's policy in the context of Turkey is, therefore, perceived as temporary and cynical in nature, stimulated by the aspiration to find a collaborator to repress the 'human product of global security', rather than seeking a compassionate solution to the actual needs of Syrians on the move.[50]

****

In Syria, we may die one day. Here we die every day.[51]

Between 1–3 September 2016, there were widespread protests and demonstrations by Syrian refugees in the different cities of Greece they were residing in. The demanded that the Greek borders be opened to arriving Syrians and those wishing to leave Greece, and for better care to be taken of refugees in the camps. They also urged the authorities to treat the refugees with dignity. The underlying message to the EU was to open the Greek border so that they could access the rest of Europe; they also urgently requested the EU to improve conditions in the camps, some of which were devoid of even basic facilities. Above all, they pointed to the critical need for monetary assistance, so they could make use of their skills and support themselves in the long run.[52]

Nine years have passed since the world was flooded with distressing images of frantic men, women, and children pouring into Europe. Today, interest in their plight has waned considerably. Borders have been shut and Syrian arrivals to Europe are mostly restricted to camps. Moreover, anti-immigrant sentiments have escalated in many European countries, particularly after people who came to Europe with the Syrian exodus were accused of alleged criminal links and, in some instances, of terrorist attacks planned by groups such as the Islamic State. Neither the affluent countries of Western and Northern Europe, which refugees want to inhabit, nor Turkey, their point of exit for the continent, appears to be in the mood to keep their promises of aid and assistance in full.[53] In the words of a Syrian refugee:

> We fled a war, and now the European Union is making war against us, a psychological war. When we hear rumours that we'll be let into Europe, we celebrate. These leaders give us new hope, then they

> extinguish it. Why did you open the door to refugees? Why did you welcome people? If they had stopped it before, we would not have come. We would not have risked death, me and my children, and thousands of others, to make the crossing.[54]

It has been over eight years since the EU-Turkey refugee agreement was signed and yet disagreements between the two parties persist. On the one hand, figures released by the UN state that Turkey has been hosting 2,900,000 refugees.[55] Turkey, on the other hand, contends that their number of late has risen to around 3,500,000, and has occasionally threatened to call off the agreement as the EU has not paid the specified amount due to her, nor has the removal of visa restrictions for Turkish citizens stipulated in the agreement been executed.[56] For the EU, the problem centres on how to obtain the money, whereas for Turkey, the more significant question has been when the money would come. As part of the settlement, Turkey was assured of €6 billion in financial assistance, to be used by the Turkish government to fund schemes for Syrian refugees. The EC states that €3 billion have been given to Turkey to bear the expenses of educating half-a-million Syrian children.[57] The Turkish government, in contrast, protest that it has so far obtained €1.85 billion from the EU. Turkey receives monetary aid from the EU by way of projects, and the aid is not supplied to the government's reserves.

Since 2016, in the aftermath of the agreement, the number of refugees arriving in Europe illicitly through the Aegean Sea declined. Despite the figures being far below those of 2015 when the crisis arose, Gerald Knaus, the architect of the refugee deal and chairman of the European Stability Initiative (ESI), considers the agreement to be in jeopardy. In his opinion, during the first six months of 2017, nearly 9,000 people arrived in Europe through the Aegean Sea, while in the next six months the number rose to 20,000.[58] However, the EC contends that the number of refugees who reached Greece declined by 97 per cent, in contrast to the period prior to the agreement. Meanwhile, Syrians in Turkey continue to be deprived of official refugee status and, consequently, do not meet the international criteria for protection. It is estimated that almost 1,000 Syrians are placed under temporary protection per day, with merely 20,000 of them possessing work permits and no less than 800,000 working illegitimately, a sizeable number of whom are children.[59] While the impasse between the signatories to the agreement continues, the plight of the refugee persists.

James Hathaway observes that the model approach to implementing the Refugee Convention should take cognisance of a few core principles. Any reform programme should take into account the situation of all states and not merely the few powerful nations. The international refugee system should plan for, rather than merely respond to, refugee movements. Any international protection programme for refugees should include a 'common but differentiated responsibility', that is, not all states involved in the movement of the refugees should have to play the same protection roles. There should be a move away from a national towards an international system of administration of refugee protection, preferably in the form of a rejuvenated UNHCR. Finally, according to Hathaway, migration is to be seen as a 'means to protection and not as an end in itself'. In other words, 'protection is for the duration of risk, not necessarily permanent immigration'.[60] In the same spirit, the following words of the *Open Society Initiative* underline the necessity to look for an alternative migration and asylum policy:

> The EU should commit to building a single asylum and migration system that establishes safe, legal means of migration. This requires the political will to recognise that existing approaches to migration have created the appearance of failure and crisis. Europe needs sustainable, affordable migration systems and popular understanding and support for these.[61]

Marc Pierini aptly sums up the imbroglio:

> The most tragic consequence of the war in Syria is the unspeakable suffering of Syrians of all creeds and ages, a trauma bound to generate frustration and resentment for generations to come. And inevitably, the EU's foreign policy ambitions will be judged at least in part on its contribution to the alleviation of Syrians' suffering, while at

home, EU leaders seem set to pay a heavy political price for not finding a course of action that European citizens deem appropriate.[62]

Why is the Summer of Migration Exceptional?

This certainly is not the first time, nor will it be the last, that migrants in sizeable numbers have entered Europe or elsewhere as a result of multiple factors. However, as Manuela Bojadžijev and Sandro Mezzadra assert, the 'geography of the current crisis is significantly different'.[63] Three crucial events initiated what could be termed as the European 'migration crisis' in 2015. The first took place on 19 April 2015, when a ship carrying around 800 migrants and refugees sank on the way from Tripoli to Italy. There were only 27 survivors.[64] It is supposed to have been the worst incident on the Mediterranean and prompted considerable debate regarding the condition of the vessels transporting migrants across the sea in inclement weather conditions, devoid of technical equipment, safety amenities, and so on. The second occurrence, which took place on 3 September, was the image of the drowned Syrian child, Alan Kurdi, whose body was swept back to the shore near Bodrum in Turkey after his family's unsuccessful attempt to reach the Greek island of Kos.[65] The poignant and disturbing image transformed how these events were viewed, and as Bojadžijev and Mezzadra observe, 'it is impossible to underestimate the effect of the circulation of that photo'.[66] Even though anti-immigrant sceptics blame the father and the family, questioning 'what kind of father would make such a hazardous journey with a small child',[67] the prevailing reaction was a request for empathy, and for unity with the predicament and cause of asylum seekers crossing the waters.

The third event that reinforced the narrative of the refugee crisis occurred on 5 September. Countless migrants and refugees had been encamped at the Budapest Keleti railway station, and the Hungarian police began refusing them entry into the trains, redirecting them to detention camps beyond the city.[68] This spontaneously instigated a large number of refugees to mobilise—

they began chanting 'freedom!' and quickly marched on to the road that led toward Vienna in what came to be referred to as 'the March of Hope'. The Hungarian authorities yielded and turned the marchers toward Austria and Germany, who then called for their borders to be opened. The event indicated two simultaneous corollaries. Due to the failure of the Dublin process, the EU structure was incapable of contending with the circumstances. The 'long summer of migration' of 2015 signified a conflict between the principles of Schengen, suggesting that asylum seekers could move to their chosen places after arriving in the EU, and those of the Dublin II processes. In one go, the marchers pressed for European solidarity, embodied by a man holding the flag of the EU at the head of the march, prompting the creation of a throng of solidarity systems; alternatively, it reinforced the existence of the prevailing ones, making them discernible throughout Europe.[69]

Reframing the 'European Migration Crisis': Emerging Tropes

As the debate on the nature of the European 'migration crisis' in the aftermath of the influx of refugees in 2015 continues, one is reminded of the words of Giorgio Agamben on the 'state of exception' and the consequent control regime that it establishes:

> The concept 'crisis' has indeed become a motto of modern politics, and for a long time it has been part of normality in any segment of social life. [...] 'Crisis' in ancient medicine meant a judgement, when the doctor noted at the decisive moment whether the sick person would survive or die. The present understanding of crisis, on the other hand, refers to an enduring state. So this uncertainty is extended into the future, indefinitely. It is exactly the same with the theological sense; the Last Judgement was inseparable from the end of time. Today, however, judgement is divorced from the idea of resolution and repeatedly postponed. So the prospect of a decision is ever less, and an endless process of decision never concludes. Today crisis has become an instrument of rule. It serves to legitimise

> political and economic decisions that in fact dispossess citizens and deprive them of any possibility of decision.[70]

A short piece by Prem Kumar Rajaram, written in the wake of the 'summer of migration', follows the same trajectory as Agamben, as Rajaram too dismisses the crisis theory completely:

> The refugee crisis in Europe is fabricated. Like most 'crises,' the recent onset of people from Syria, Iraq, Afghanistan, Bangladesh, and Pakistan trying to cross into the European Union is a representation. Anxiety and specific readings of law and humanitarianism frame this issue. This framing works inward as well as outward. Inward, it establishes a dominant regulating norm—an idea of 'the refugee'—that allows for internal comparison and inequalities (people are said to have varying rights to protection). Outward, the framing helps create an understanding of a complex situation—an *abstracted* understanding—and allows for policy makers and commentators to treat 'the refugee crisis' as an exceptional condition.[71]

On the one hand, most academics accept that Europe has been experiencing what has been termed as a crisis. On the other hand, there is not much unanimity on the kind of crisis Europe is undergoing, and the way it should be construed and constructed.[72] There appears to be a plethora of transposable dialogues, constructs, and accounts, all of which imply precise interpretations as well as extrapolative and analytical constructs. Though the concept of 'refugee crisis' has possibly been the overriding construct, other terms have also been in vogue, such as 'migrant crisis', which in fact appropriately includes both the refugee issue and migration to Europe in a wider sense. At times, the concept of a 'humanitarian crisis' has been espoused which also underlines discrimination and creates divisions among 'wanted and unwanted migrants', and eventually is connected to a 'crisis of the asylum system' and/or a 'crisis of the European border' and 'border control'.[73] An indication of a breakdown in the 'border regime' converts the crisis into a 'crisis of the EU', of 'the Schengen zone', and in the final analysis, a 'crisis of the political idea of Europe'.

These interchanging constructions of the crisis are also connected to other interpretations. Therefore, the refugee crisis is linked to concepts such as 'the economic crisis', 'the financial crisis', 'the debt crisis', the 'banking crisis', 'the housing crisis', and so on. In this sense, the refugee crisis is connected to the neoliberal expressions of essential austerity measures. Greece, for example, is cited as the case study of a nation incapable of dealing with the influx of refugees, owing to a historic lack of economic accountability, and is in danger of additional economic sanctions if it fails to contend with the refugee issue.[74] The fusion of austerity measures along with refugee safeguards reinforces divisions between 'genuine' refugees and 'economic migrants', who have migrated solely for money; desirable and undesirable migrants; and essentially those who are justified as migrants and those who are not.

The most recent development is possibly around the construct of 'security crises' in the aftermath of the unfortunate events in Paris and Brussels, where refugees by and large were instantly viewed as prospective extremists, notwithstanding the fact that the culprits and planners of these attacks had been European residents for a considerable period of time. The cultural undertone with respect to the crisis has led to various kinds of stereotyping, of 'Muslim extremism', and the notion of fanatics 'hiding' amongst the refugees in search of safety in Europe. The descriptions and categories of 'strangeness', 'ontological difference', and 'un-Europeanness' of the refugees were reinforced after the episode in Cologne during the public celebrations of New Year's Eve of 2015/2016, when a few predominantly North African (Moroccan and Tunisian) migrants were blamed for sexually abusing revellers. This in turn conjured the idea of a 'moral crisis'. Then again, the failures of the EU and European nations to regulate the crisis in terms of offering feasible answers/alternatives have created another category—'the crisis of legitimacy'. The crisis continues to be constructed and reconstructed in myriad new ways.[75]

Ranabir Samaddar, terming 'Europe as the last liberal empire' and migration 'as the unconscious tool of history to end the last liberal empire in the modern age', [76]explicates the contradictory tendencies and practices that are inherent in and have been adopted by the EU with respect to immigration and refugees, and which have in turn contributed to the so-called European 'migration crisis'. Samaddar therefore believes that the supposed European migration crisis is intertwined with the currency crisis:

> Europe achieved continental unification through economic means, liberal constitutionalism, and currency union. It sets goals of peace and security that encourage everyone to be a liberal with unfettered freedom to access the market and, on the other hand, allow the European Union to follow interventionist policies near abroad. The consequences of the union are to be found in Europe's restrictive and contradictory policies and programmes relating to immigration and refugee protection. European migration crisis originates from this.[77]

Samaddar elaborates upon the reason behind the categorisation of the migration that took place from 2015 onwards as a crisis, as it was superimposed on multiple inherent fault-lines within the European space.

> Europe was the last liberal empire in history. It had achieved unification after the Second World War through dialogues on coal and steel, peace, and economic means, it established a charter of rights, it founded a European Court of human rights, it curbed nationalism, it broadly attained currency union and held peace and security as the goal of the union, and finally as Lord Dahrendorf remarked after the annus mirabilis of 1989, it encouraged everyone to be a liberal with unfettered freedom to access the market so much so that countries in the east of Europe joined one after another the union to make it a true empire two centuries after Napoleon Bonaparte had failed to create one and had provoked unwittingly the first concert of the continent in 1815. Yet crucial fault lines remained. The peaceful empire was built in the last fifty years on whiteness of skin, a particular faith called Christianity, anti-communism, stringent anti-immigration laws and practices, neoliberal tools of economic coordination, massive banks, and geopolitically what turned out to be most uncertain for the fate of the continent, that is doing away with the old fuzzy division of the continent into west, middle, and the east. The present crisis of Europe in the wake of the entry of massive numbers of migrants from the Middle East and North Africa is perched on all these fault

lines. The immigrants are non-Europeans, they are predominantly Muslims, quite a lot of them are not white, and they have disturbed the seamless nature of the united space called Europe, because the old divisions into west, middle, and the east have now resurfaced in the wake of the migrant rush.[78]

SOLIDARITIES AND RESISTANCES

'We are facing the biggest refugee and displacement crisis of our time. Above all, this is not just a crisis of numbers; it is also a crisis of solidarity. [...] We must respond to a monumental crisis with monumental solidarity.'[79]

Even as refugees continue to occupy the lowest rungs of the social and economic fabric in the host states, the plethora of activities and initiatives being undertaken to support the refugees who have completed the perilous journey to Europe in search of asylum, travelling through the Mediterranean Sea or South-Eastern Europe, necessitates a second look at the so-called European 'migration crisis'.[80] There have been sustained efforts to include migrants in the realm of citizenship rights, as Engin Isin and Bryan Turner point out:

> From aboriginal rights, women's rights, civil rights and sexual rights for gays and lesbians to animal rights, language rights and disability rights, we have experienced in the past few decades a major trend in Western nation-states toward the formation of new claims for inclusion and belonging.[81]

At the same time, Jef Huysmans and Xavier Guillaume point to the sustained attempts at retaining the exclusive nature of citizenship vis-à-vis the migrants:

> While citizenship has been an instrument of crafting a people of equals, in which rights are universal and not a privilege, historically it has also been a vehicle for working differentiations within this

> universal people. On the one hand, citizens comprise a people united around a body of law and rights and/or a set of narratives about its origins. Both allow the people to recognise themselves as a collective unity with political status. On the other hand, citizenship is constituted in relation to those without rights or limited rights, those who remain outside of the narratives of the people's community of origin. In this continuum between inclusion and exclusion citizens are actually stratified, rather than dichotomised. Rights are often assigned differentially and citizens do have different capacities to claim rights within the citizenry body.[82]

In addition to citizenship discourses, studies on migrant movements have also emphasised the equation between 'states and markets', defining critical moments globally. In other words, research on migration has explored the consequences of capitalism on the movements for citizenship. In the context of the large-scale migration into Europe in the summer of 2015, the demonstrations or solidarity movements have also been examined in terms of a crisis of neoliberalism, as changes in the capitalist methods of utilisation began to have a profound impact on the mobilisation of migrants. Early attempts at mobilisation have articulated the need to absorb migrants into the economy. In the aftermath of the 'global crisis of 1970', a restrictive policy towards migrants was adopted, which triggered a spate of demonstrations demanding a more inclusive approach. It was neoliberalism that changed the scenario of migration. On the one hand, there were clamours against the discriminatory approach towards migrants, who were vilified and looked upon as intruders and criminals, detrimental to global security and stability. On the other hand, states began to adopt increasingly restrictive border policies, even as the neoliberal economy continued to augment the demand for inexpensive, malleable, and acquiescent labour.[83] Migration policies within the neoliberal paradigm recognise a degree of fluctuation in migration, but at the same time are founded on suppression, in the process denying migrant rights—for instance, as personified by EU's restrictive border policies and surveillance of the Mediterranean Sea. Parallely, a limited movement is also acceptable, as echoed by Sandro Mezzadra,

> European policies on migration, despite their rhetoric, do not aim to hermetically seal European borders. Their objective and their effect is the establishment of a system of dams and eventually the production of an active process of inclusion of migrant labour by means of its criminalisation.[84]

Didier Fassin contends that migrants who do not have documents at their disposal are denied basic rights and their movements are controlled.[85] Davide Pero and John Solomos opine that demonstrations have demanded basic human rights and have opposed the abuse of such rights in makeshift detention centres, occasionally assuming a global character.[86] Simultaneously, as Anne McNevin sums it, 'the militarisation of state and regional borders represents performances of political closure designed to assuage those made vulnerable by neoliberal economic trajectory.'[87]

Certain decisive moments can be identified as far as the migration of 2015 is concerned, which indicate a more inclusive political participation. For instance, 12 September 2015 was an important date in the context of solidarity movements. In more than 85 cities in 30 countries across Europe, a massive number of protesters demonstrated with placards stating 'Refugees Welcome' and 'Europe Says Welcome'. In numerous European nations, enterprises have been initiated that involve the innovative practices of daily politics that symbolise solidarity. There are countless instances of such acts, for instance, the 'Austrian lorry drivers who joined a campaign to pick up refugees stranded in Budapest to locally organised mobilisations which provided support for arriving refugees, donating food, water, clothes, and other supplies to those in need.'[88] There is a growing perception that across Europe and beyond, the 'refugee crisis' is in fact encountering a 'welcoming culture'.[89] The phrase 'welcome culture' (*Willkommenskultur*) refers to Germany's initial public discourse and official response to the refugees who arrived in the country in 2015, as a consequence of the Syrian civil war. The term has been used to indicate that it was increasingly being replicated in Europe and beyond. Donatella Della Porta observes that the humanitarian crisis in 2016 strengthened the opinion that formal structures, at all levels, were inept at dealing with this predicament. Furthermore, according to Porta, 'political opportunities are, therefore, to be located within a critical juncture that challenged existing institutions'.[90]

The evolution of a 'welcoming culture' can be traced to the political spaces provided by both the crisis and the inability of member states as well as the EU to provide a logical and reasonable resolution. For Stuart Hall, crises are instants of impending transformation, minus a specified purpose. A confluence indicates shifts amid political instants and can be explained as 'a period during which the different social, political, economic and ideological contradictions that are at work in society come together to give it a specific and distinctive shape'.[91] Solidarity in the intersection of the economic crisis and the 'refugee crisis' can lead to the creation and conversion of political spaces that can now be accessed as 'opportunity spaces'. Founded on Massey's notion of enunciating convergences in distinct and fruitful ways, David Featherstone and I. Karaliotas underline the significance of accepting the reasoning of the crisis, and its ramifications on divergent sections to 'envision articulations of solidarities/alternatives across differences in the context of the European crisis'.[92]

Even as the state and individuals continue to restrict and resist the inflow of migrants, the network of solidarities appears to gain momentum.

> [There are] no Border activists, activists of self-organised migrant groups, feminists and others who identify as part of the undogmatic or party-political left and who increasingly campaign for refugee rights. Moreover, supporters include also many NGOs, church-based charities, established migrant organisations, left-wing academics and artists, as well as some groups within trade unions and political parties. In 2015, the long summer of migration has demonstrated that many of those who are not explicitly organised in political parties, religious organisations or civil society seek to help refugees based on humanitarian or other concerns. And, not least, many refugees or those who once personally experienced flight in their past have become supporters of today's refugee and with them transversal forms of politics that do not essentialise differences

but acknowledge the different experiences and realities of those encountering one another. [93]

NOTES

1. Efthimios Papataxiarchis, 'Being "There": At the Front Line of the "European Refugee Crisis"'. *Anthropology Today* 32(2), 2016, p. 7; Donatella della Porta, 'Contentious Moves: Mobilising for Refugees' Rights', in Donatella della Porta (ed.), *Solidarity Mobilisations in the 'Refugee Crisis': Contentious Moves*. Cham, Switzerland: Palgrave Macmillan, 2018, p. 5. This explains the fundamental change that took place in the island of Lesbos, where millions of refugees entered Europe in 2015.

2. Leonie Ansems De Vries and Marta Welander, 'Refugees, displacement, and the European "politics of exhaustion"'. *Open Democracy*, 30 September 2016. Available at https://www.opendemocracy.net/mediterranean-journeys-in-hope/leonie-ansems-de-vries-marta-welander/refugees-displacement-and-europ (accessed July 2024).

3. 'A million refugees and migrants flee to Europe in 2015'. *UNHCR/IOM*, 22 December 2015. Available at http://www.unhcr.org/news/press/2015/12/567918556/million-refugees-migrants-flee-europe-2015.html (accessed July 2024).

4. Ibid.

5. 'Migrant Crisis: Migration to Europe explained in seven charts'. *BBC News*, 4 March 2016. Available at http://www.bbc.com/news/world-europe-34131911 (accessed July 2024).

6. 'A million refugees and migrants flee to Europe in 2015'.

7. Susmita Baral, 'Refugee Crisis 2016 in Europe: Death Toll and Migrant Arrival Increases, Statistics Show'. *International Business Time*, 10 August 2016. Available at http://www.ibtimes.com/refugee-crisis-2016-europe-death-toll-migrant-arrival-increases-statistics-show-2399933 (accessed July 2024).

8. 'Missing Migrants—Tracking Deaths Along Migratory Routes'. IOM, 2018. Available at https://missingmigrants.iom.int/ (accessed July 2024). The latest figures from the International Organization for Migration indicate that the Mediterranean Sea remains one of the deadliest migration routes in the world. In 2023, at least 3,129 migrants and refugees were reported dead or missing while attempting to cross the Mediterranean. This marks the highest toll since 2017. Tragically,

this death toll is part of a broader global trend, with over 8,500 migrant deaths recorded worldwide in 2023 alone, a 20 per cent increase from the previous year. See https://www.iom.int/news/deadliest-year-record-migrants-nearly-8600-deaths-2023; https://missingmigrants.iom.int/region/mediterranean (accessed November 2024).

9. 'Mediterranean Migrant Arrivals Reach 29,844 in 2019; Deaths Reach 681'. IOM, 7 May 2019. Available at https://www.iom.int/news/mediterranean-migrant-arrivals-reach-29844-2019-deaths-reach-681 (accessed July 2024).

10. 'Syrian Refugees: A Snapshot of the Crisis—in the Middle East and Europe'. *Syrian Refugees*, September 2016. Available at http://syrianrefugees.eu (accessed July 2024).

11. Ibid.

12. Javier Alcalde, 'Why the Refugee Crisis Is Not a Refugee Crisis'. *Peace in Progress* 29, 2016. Available at http://www.icip-perlapau.cat/numero29/articles_centrals/article_central_2/ (accessed July 2024); della Porta, 'Contentious Moves: Mobilising for Refugees' Rights', p. 6.

13. See The Parliamentary Assembly of the Council of Europe (PACE) report. See https://assembly.coe.int/nw/xml/XRef/Xref-XML2HTML-EN.asp?fileid=22738 (accessed November 2024). This has been referred to in multiple recent articles, including S. Gürkan and R. Coman, 'The EU–Turkey deal in the 2015 "refugee crisis": When intergovernmentalism cast a shadow on the EU's normative power'. *Acta Polit* 56, 2021, pp. 276–305.

14. Marc Pierini, 'In Search of an EU Role in the Syrian War'. *Carnegie Europe*, August 2016. Available at https://www.jstor.org/stable/resrep12824 (accessed October 2024).

15. Priya Singh, 'Politics and Policy: Syrian Refugees and the European Union'. Mahanirban Calcutta Research Group, *Refugee Watch Catalogue* 48, 2016, pp. 7–19. The article has been published as a working paper: 'Reflections on the Mediterranean Refugee Crisis', *Policies and Practices* 105, December 2018.

16. In the context of the EU-Turkey deal, 'third countries' refers to countries outside the European Union where migrants or asylum seekers can be sent after arriving in the EU. Specifically, it involves the designation of certain countries as 'safe third countries', meaning these countries are deemed capable of offering adequate protection and rights to refugees, similar to what they would receive in EU member states. In the case of the EU-Turkey agreement, Turkey was classified as a 'safe third country', whereby irregular migrants and asylum seekers arriving in Greece could be returned to Turkey on the assumption that Turkey would provide

them with adequate asylum procedures and protection. However, this designation was controversial, with critics arguing that Turkey did not fully comply with international standards of refugee protection, raising concerns about potential violations of non-refoulement (the principle that refugees should not be sent back to a country where they face serious threats to their life or freedom). See the PACE report, available at https://assembly.coe.int/nw/xml/XRef/Xref-XML2HTML-EN.asp?fileid=22738 (accessed March 2025), and Gürkan and Coman, 'The EU–Turkey deal in the 2015 "refugee crisis"'.

17. Stefan Lehne, 'The Tempting Trap of Fortress Europe'. *Carnegie Europe*, 21 April 2016. Available at https://carnegieendowment.org/research/2016/04/the-tempting-trap-of-fortress-europe?lang=en&center=europe (accessed November 2024).

18. The extent and impact of the refugee crisis have been debated extensively, which has included the contention that while the magnitude of the crisis cannot be denied, the coverage by the media has been both extensive and dramatic (images in particular), as we are living in a digitalised era, while the continuous trickling or even spurts of similar migrations from multiple spaces across the Global South have not been given as much weightage.

19. 'Sharing the burden: EU finalises refugee redistribution plan'. *The Hindu*, 26 September 2015. Available at http://www.thehindu.com/news/international/syrian-refugee-crisis-explained/article7621867.ece (accessed July 2024).

20. Ibid.

21. Ibid.

22. Vicki Squire and Vasiliki Touhouliotis, 'Fleeing Europe'. *openDemocracy*, 3 August 2016. Available at https://www.opendemocracy.net/5050/jane-freedman-vasiliki-touhouliotis/fleeing-europe (accessed July 2024).

23. Elif Mendos Kuskonmaz, 'What can we expect from the EU-Turkey deal over the lives of Syrian refugees?' *openDemocracy*, 15 February 2016. Available at https://www.opendemocracy.net/can-europe-make-it/elif-mendos-ku-konmaz/what-can-we-expect-from-eu-turkey-deal-over-lives-of-syrian (accessed July 2024).

24. Ibid.

25. Ibid.

26. Ibid.

27. Ibid.

28. Ibid.

29. Holly Ellyatt, 'Turkey lifts state of emergency but nothing much has changed, analysts warn'. *CNBC*, 19 July 2018. Available at https://www.cnbc.com/2018/07/19/turkey-lifts-state-of-emergency-but-nothing-much-has-changed-analysts.html (accessed July 2024).

30. Kaya Genc, 'Erdogan's Way: The Rise and Rule of Turkey's Islamist Shapeshifter'. *Foreign Affairs*, September/October 2019. Available at https://www.foreignaffairs.com/articles/turkey/2019-08-12/erdogans-way (accessed July 2024).

31. Erdogan, in fact, is promoting a 'radical' resolution of refugee resettlement in a strip of Syrian space occupied by the United States and its Kurdish associates. If refused, he is threatening to redirect a million Syrian refugees to Europe. Erdogan has been pressing for a 'buffer zone' between Turkey's borders with Syria to stop the Kurdish militia from entering its territory. The concept of a zone has been reconstructed as a 'refuge' for Syrians escaping the war, as supposedly, antipathy towards Syrians in Turkey has amplified, and a Syrian and Russian attack in Syria has compelled hundreds of thousands of refugees to take off towards the Turkish border. See Carlotta Gall, 'Turkey's Radical Plan: Send a Million Refugees Back to Syria'. *The New York Times*, 10 September 2019. Available at https://www.nytimes.com/2019/09/10/world/middleeast/turkey-syria-refugees-erdogan.html (accessed October 2024).

32. Evan Stanley Jones, 'The EU-Turkey migration agreement and its humanitarian masquerade'. *openDemocracy*, 15 June 2016. Available at https://www.opendemocracy.net/arab-awakening/evan-stanley-jones/eu-turkey-migration-agreement-and-its-humanitarian-masquerade (accessed July 2024).

33. Ibid.

34. Ibid.

35. Ibid.

36. Ibid.

37. Ibid.

38. Evan Stanley Jones, 'Zones of turbulence in the wake of EU-Turkey's migration agreement'. *openDemocracy*, 26 July 2016. Available at https://www.opendemocracy.net/arab-awakening/evan-stanley-jones/zones-of-turbulence-in-wake-of-eu-turkey-s-migration-agreement (accessed July 2024).

39. Ibid.

40. Jeff Crisp, 'Protection and pragmatism: The EU-Turkey refugee deal in historical perspective'. *openDemocracy*, 21 March 2016. Available at https://www.opendemocracy.net/en/openglobalrights-openpage/

protection-and-pragmatism-eu-turkey-refugee-deal-in-historical-perspecti/ (accessed November 2024).

41. Ibid.

42. Ibid.

43. Ibid.

44. The phrase 'the use of coercive measures and arbitrary detentions' refers to actions taken by Turkish authorities that have reportedly involved forcibly controlling or restricting the movement of Syrian refugees. This included forcing refugees to return to unsafe areas, restricting their freedom of movement, or pressuring them into accepting unfavourable conditions and holding refugees without clear legal reasons or due process, often in detention centres or camps, sometimes for extended periods without justification.

45. Defne Gonenc, 'The Turkey-EU refugee deal and how to really solve the problem'. *openDemocracy*, 26 April 2016, Available at https://www.opendemocracy.net/en/north-africa-west-asia/turkey-eu-deal-for-refugee-crisis-and-how-to-really-solve-problem/ (accessed July 2024).

46. Sergio Carrera and Aikaterini Drakopolou, 'Unsafe Turkey, unsafe Europe'. *openDemocracy*, 29 September 2016. Available at https://www.opendemocracy.net/en/unsafe-turkey-unsafe-europe/ (accessed November 2024).

47. 'The West's Refugee Crisis: What Happens in the Middle East Doesn't Stay in the Middle East'. *The Wall Street Journal*, 6 September 2016.

48. Squire and Touhouliotis, 'Fleeing Europe'.

49. Ceylan Yeginsu, 'Refugees Pour Out of Turkey Once More as Deal With Europe Falters'. *Jadaliyya*, 14 September 2016.

50. Lucy Williams, 'Turkey is doing the dirty work of Europe's immigration control'. *openDemocracy*, 22 January 2016. Available at https://www.opendemocracy.net/en/can-europe-make-it/turkey-is-doing-dirty-work-of-europe-s-immigration-control/ (accessed November 2024).

51. A young Kurdish woman quoted in Ludek Stavinoha, 'Europe's Greek tragedy deepens out of sight'. *openDemocracy*, 15 September 2016. Available at https://www.opendemocracy.net/can-europe-make-it/ludek-stavinoha/europe-s-greek-tragedy-deepens-out-of-sight (accessed July 2024).

52. Yazan Al-Shrif, 'I am a human, speaking to you'. *openDemocracy*, 9 September 2016. Available at https://www.opendemocracy.net/en/can-europe-make-it/i-am-human-speaking-to-you/ (accessed November 2024).

53. Liz Alderman, 'Aid and Attention Dwindling, Migrant Crisis Intensifies in Greece'. *The New York Times*, 13 August 2016. Available at http://www.nytimes.com/2016/08/14/world/europe/migrant-crisis-greece.html (accessed July 2024).

54. 'A Syrian Refugee's Message to the European Union'. *New York Times*, 31 March 2016. Available at http://www.nytimes.com/2016/04/01/opinion/a-syrian-refugees-message-to-the-european-union.html (accessed July 2024).

55. 'The EU-Turkey refugee agreement: A review'. *DW*, 18 March 2018. Available at https://www.dw.com/en/the-eu-turkey-refugee-agreement-a-review/a-43028295. (accessed July 2024).

56. Ibid.

57. Ibid.

58. Ibid.

59. Ibid.

60. James C. Hathaway, 'A global solution to a global crisis'. *openDemocracy*, 29 February 2016. Available at https://www.opendemocracy.net/openglobalrights/james-c-hathaway/global-solution-to-global-refugee-crisis. (accessed July 2024).

61. 'Understanding Migration and Asylum in the European Union'. Open Society Initiative for Europe, Magyar, October 2015.

62. Pierini, 'In Search of an EU Role in the Syrian War'.

63. Manuela Bojadžijev and Sandro Mezzadra, '"Refugee Crisis" or Crisis of European Migration Policies?' *Focaalblog*, 12 November 2015. Available at http://www.focaalblog.com/2015/11/12/; (accessed July 2024).

64. Ibid.

65. Ibid.

66. Ibid.

67. Ibid.

68. Ibid.

69. Rainer Bauböck, 'Europe's Commitments and Failures in the Refugee Crisis'. *European Political Science* 17(1), 2017, pp. 1–11; Bojadžijev and Mezzadra, '"Refugee Crisis" or Crisis of European Migration Policies?'; Allesandra Bonomolo, 'UN Says 800 Migrants Dead in Boat Disaster as Italy Launches Rescue of Two More Vessels'. *The Guardian*, 20 April 2015. Available at https://www.theguardian.com/world/2015/apr/20/italy-pm-matteo-renzi-migrant-shipwreck-crisis-srebrenica-massacre (accessed July 2024); Óscar García Agustín and Martin Bak Jørgensen,

Solidarity and the 'Refugee Crisis' in Europe. Cham, Switzerland: Palgrave Macmillan, 2019, pp. 8–9.

70. Giorgio Agamben, 'The Endless Crisis as an Instrument of Power: In Conversation with Giorgio Agamben'. *Verso* (blog), 4 June 2013. Available at https://www.versobooks.com/blogs/1318-the-endless-crisis-as-an-instrument-of-power-in-conversation-with-giorgio-agamben. Accessed July 2024; Agustín and Jørgensen, *Solidarity*, p. 5.

71. Prem Kumar Rajaram, 'Beyond Crisis: Rethinking the Population Movements at Europe's Border', 19 October 2015. Available at https://www.focaalblog.com/2015/10/19/prem-kumar-rajaram-beyond-crisis/ (Accessed July 2024). The post is part of a series on migration and the refugee crisis, moderated and edited by Prem Kumar Rajaram (Central European University); Agustín and Jørgensen, *Solidarity*, p. 4.

72. Magnus Dahlstedt and Anders Neergaard, 'Crisis of Solidarity? Changing Welfare and Migration Regimes in Sweden'. *Critical Sociology* 2016, pp. 1–15; Agustín and Jørgensen, *Solidarity*, p. 3.

73. Maribel Casas-Cortes, et al., 'New Keywords: Migration and Borders'. *Cultural Studies* 29(1), 2015, pp. 7–14; Agustín and Jørgensen, *Solidarity*, p. 3.

74. Pietro Castelli Gattinara, 'The "Refugee Crisis" in Italy as a Crisis of Legitimacy'. *Contemporary Italian Politics* 9(3), 2017, pp. 318–331; Agustín and Jørgensen, *Solidarity*, p. 4.

75. Agustín and Jørgensen, *Solidarity*, pp. 3–4.

76. Ranabir Samaddar, *A Post-Colonial Enquiry into Europe's Debt and Migration Crisis*. Singapore: Springer, 2016. pp. 87–88.

77. Ibid.

78. Ibid., p. 89.

79. UN Secretary-General Ban Ki-moon, 'Refugee Crisis about Solidarity, Not Just Numbers, Secretary-General Says at Event on Global Displacement Challenge'. *United Nations*, 15 April 2016. Available at https://www.un.org/press/en/2016/sgsm17670.doc.htm (accessed July 2024).

80. Porta, *Solidarity Mobilisations*, p. 1.

81. Engin S. Isin and Bryan S. Turner, 'Citizenship Studies: An Introduction', in Engin S. Isin and Bryan S. Turner (eds), *Handbook of Citizenship Studies*. London: Sage, 2003, p. 1; Porta, *Solidarity Mobilisations*, p. 2.

82. Jef Huysmans and Xavier Guillaume, 'Citizenship and Securitising: Interstitial Politics', in Xavier Guillaume and Jef Huysmans (eds),

Citizenship and Security. London: Routledge, 2014, p. 24; Porta, *Solidarity Mobilisations*, pp. 2–3.

83. Porta, *Solidarity Mobilisations*, pp. 3–24.

84. Sandro Mezzadra, 'Citizenship in Motion', *Make World* 4, 2004, Arianna Bove (trans.). Available at http://www.makeworlds.org/node/83 (accessed July 2024); Porta, *Solidarity Mobilisations*, pp. 3–24.

85. Didier Fassin, 'Compassion and Repression: The Moral Economy of Immigration Policies in France'. *Cultural Anthropology* 20(3), 2005, pp. 362–387; Porta, *Solidarity Mobilisations*, pp. 3–24.

86. Davide Però and John Solomos, 'Introduction: Migrant Politics and Mobilisation: Exclusion, Engagement and Incorporation'. *Ethnic and Racial Studies* 33(1), 2010, pp. 1–18; Porta, *Solidarity Mobilisations*, pp. 3–24.

87. Anne McNevin, 'The Liberal Paradox and the Politics of Asylum in Australia'. *Australian Journal of Political Science* 42(4), 2007, p. 611; Porta, *Solidarity Mobilisations*, pp. 3–24.

88. Agustín and Jørgensen, *Solidarity*, p. 29.

89. Ilker Ataç, '"Refugee Protest Camp Vienna": Making Citizens through Locations of the Protest Movement'. *Citizenship Studies* 20(5), 2016, pp. 629–646; U. Hamann and S. Karakayali, 'Practicing Willkommenskultur: Migration and Solidarity in Germany'. *Intersections: East European Journal of Society and Politics* [S.l.] 2(4), 2016, pp. 69–86; C. Hann, 'The Fragility of Europe's Willkommenskultur'. *Anthropology Today* 31(6), 2015, pp. 1–2; L. Zamponi, 'From Border to Border: Refugee Solidarity Activism in Italy across Space, Time and Practices'. in Donatella della Porta (ed.), *Solidarity Mobilisations in the Refugee Crisis: Contentious Moves*. London: Palgrave Macmillan, 2018, pp. 99–123; Agustín and Jørgensen, *Solidarity*, p. 29.

90. Porta, *Solidarity Mobilisations*, p. 18.

91. S. Hall and D. Massey, 'Interpreting the Crisis'. *Soundings* 44, 2010, p. 57; Agustín and Jørgensen, *Solidarity*, p. 29.

92. D. Featherstone and L. Karaliotas, 'Challenging the Spatial Politics of the European Crisis: Nationed Narratives and Trans-Local Solidarities in the Post-Crisis Conjuncture'. *Cultural Studies* 32(2), 2018, p. 294; Agustín and Jørgensen, *Solidarity*, p. 29.

93. Ilker Ataç, Stefanie Kron, Sarah Schilliger, Helge Schwiertz, and Maurice Stierl, 'Kämpfe der Migration als Un-/Sichtbare Politiken'. *movements. Journal für kritische Migrations-und Grenzregimeforschung* 1(2), 2015. Cited in Della Porta, *Solidarity Mobilisations*, p. 21.

6

On the Edge of Law and Society

Stateless People in a Westphalian Order

Sabyasachi Basu Ray Chaudhury

In contemporary times of mixed and massive flows of people across the globe, hundreds and thousands of people are trying to move from one country or one part of the world to another even without documents, and refugees, stateless persons, asylum seekers, and economic migrants are looking forward to 'greener pastures' elsewhere—either seeking a safe haven from the atrocities back home, or in search of livelihood. In the evolving phase of capitalist globalisation, where the traditional Westphalian systems of state and sovereignty are being challenged, the existing international and regional legal mechanisms that ensure rights and security for these different categories of people often prove insufficient, ineffective, and in some cases, outdated or unable to fully address the current complexities. In these changing times, therefore, we need to search for fresh alternatives to guarantee the basic rights to stateless persons, who in most cases are either at the margins of municipal laws or simply beyond them. In such a scenario, the definitions of statelessness, as well as their legal implications, need to be thoroughly revisited.

The Westphalian order came into being with the signing of the treaties of Munster and Osnabruck in 1648. This new order facilitated the system of sovereigns signing treaties with other sovereigns and devising policies to rule inside a territory. This also managed to exclude other authorities from interfering in 'domestic politics'. Accordingly, even today, Article 2 (7) of the Charter of the United Nations (UN) states that the UN has no authority to intervene in matters which are within the domestic jurisdiction of any state, although this principle shall not prejudice the application of enforcement measures under Chapter VII of the Charter. In other words, the Westphalian order has practically turned into a point of departure for a system of territorially organised states that still largely prevails in this latest phase of globalisation. This has, in turn, generated an utterly paradoxical situation, given that capital and technology have become mobile, while labour, the third dimension of production, is still not allowed to cross international borders in the face of the 're-territorialisation' of states.

The year 2018 was the 370th anniversary of the Treaty of Westphalia. Interestingly, 2018 was also the 70th anniversary of the Universal Declaration of Human Rights, and the world celebrated this through several programmes. On the contrary, the Treaty of Westphalia was hardly rejoiced in by anyone, although it has been systematising the dominant political ideas for the last four centuries. The Treaty of Westphalia installed a system of sovereign states where a single authority is supreme and sacrosanct within a set of borders. In other words, the Treaty of Westphalia foreclosed the visions of limiting sovereignty for basic human rights.

Since the rise of the nation-state in the eighteenth century, the right to nationality has, in practice, become integral to the enjoyment of almost all other rights. International law has traditionally allowed states the broad discretion to define the contours of and delimit access to nationality. Nonetheless, the recognition of the inherent link between the right to a nationality and the enjoyment of other human rights has confirmed that nationality laws and practices must be consistent with the principles of international law. International law limits state sovereignty to regulate citizenship. This was first made clear in the early 1920s by the Permanent Court of International Justice in its ruling, which said: '[t]he question of whether a certain matter is or is not solely within the domestic jurisdiction of a State is an essentially relevant question; it depends on the development of international relations.'[1] Article 1 of the 1930 Hague Convention on Certain Questions relating to the Conflict of Nationality Laws affirmed this principle:

> It is for each State to determine under its own laws who are its nationals. This law shall be recognized by other States in so far as it is consistent with international conventions, international custom, and the principles of law generally recognized with regard to nationality.[2]

Subsequently, in response to the mass atrocities of World War II and the refugee crisis involving millions of displaced persons throughout Europe, the international community declared its commitment to the protection of human rights, while recognising the critical role that nationality plays in ensuring individual access to the enjoyment of these rights. In this very context, Article 15 of the Universal Declaration of Human Rights (UDHR) guaranteed that '[e]very one has a right to a nationality', and that '[n]o one shall be arbitrarily deprived of his nationality nor denied the right to change his nationality.'[3] The right to nationality gained further recognition through international and regional human rights instruments in the decades after World War II.[4]

The international legal instruments, such as the International Covenant on Civil and Political Rights (ICCPR) and the Convention on the Rights of the Child (CRC), further guarantee the right of every child to acquire a nationality and indicate the duty of states to respect this right as it pertains to children.[5] Moreover, a few international legal restrictions on state sovereignty over the regulation of citizenship have emerged:

(a) prohibition against racial discrimination
(b) prohibition against statelessness
(c) prohibition on arbitrary deprivation of citizenship.

The Inter-American Court of Human Rights has later indicated prohibitions in the realm of nationality law. It says that, although 'the determination of who is a national of a particular state continues to fall within the ambit of state sovereignty, *states' discretion must be limited by international human rights that exist to protect individuals against arbitrary state actions*.' According to this Court, 'states are particularly *limited in their discretion to grant nationality by their obligations to guarantee equal protection before the law and to prevent, avoid, and reduce statelessness.*'[6] State sovereignty over nationality is quite clearly restrained by the prohibition of racial and ethnic discrimination. The principle against racial discrimination is integral to all international and regional human rights instruments, representing a customary rule of international law.[7]

However, in the contemporary world, new forces of globalisation are providing fresh challenges for international and domestic governance. As a consequence, the state has been required to cede sovereignty on certain issues, mainly economic, and relinquish many business decisions to transnational business corporations. This, though, has not led to the free mobility of people, be they economic migrants, refugees, asylum seekers, or stateless populations. The instance of the Rohingyas, labelled 'the most persecuted minority' by the UN, highlights how international legal principles are often inadequate to ensure that stateless populations around the world can exercise 'the right to have rights' in the face of state sovereignty.

Differential Treatment

India, though a member of the Executive Committee of the UNHCR, has ratified neither the 1951 UN Convention on Refugees nor its 1967 Protocol. One of the major recipients of refugees in South Asia, India has been treating refugees in a differential manner. In 1996, the National Human Rights Commission (NHRC) of India filed a Public Interest Litigation (PIL) in the Supreme Court to enforce the basic human rights of the Chakma people, who were displaced during the construction of the Kaptai dam over Karnaphuli river in erstwhile East Pakistan (now Bangladesh) in 1964. Some of them crossed the international border and were resettled by the Government of India in Arunachal Pradesh (then the North East Frontier Agency or NEFA). After three decades of their stay in Arunachal Pradesh, in 1996, the All Arunachal Pradesh Students' Union (AAPSU) asked them to quit the state as they were foreigners. The Government of Arunachal Pradesh also considered them 'foreigners' and, therefore, not entitled to any rights whatsoever.

The Supreme Court observed that the notices to the Chakma to quit the state amounted to a violation of Article 21 of the Indian Constitution, and that no person can be deprived of their right to life and liberty except according to the due process of law. Therefore, it was the duty of the state government to protect the Chakma from such threats to their lives and liberty, as well as bring to book those who had threatened to violate these rights. It was further held that by not forwarding the Chakmas' citizenship applications to the concerned department within the Union government, their constitutional and statutory right to be considered for citizenship was being denied to them. This decision of the Supreme Court was crucial in the consideration of the legal future of the Chakma refugees or stateless persons.

Similarly, a judgment by the Delhi High Court in 2011 in *Namgyal Dolkar v. Government of India* generated new hopes among those facing questions relating to nationality and statelessness in India. Namgyal Dolkar was born in 1986 in Himachal Pradesh, India and her parents were both Tibetan refugees. In 2005, she had obtained an identity certificate under the Passports Act of India after submitting a formal application for the same. Later, while trying to submit an application for an Indian passport, she was refused by the Regional Passport Office, and the reason cited was that her parents were Tibetan. Since Namgyal Dolkar had identified herself as a 'Tibetan national', the passport authorities invoked Section 6(2) of the Passports Act, whereby a passport application can be rejected if the applicant is not a citizen of India. The Delhi High Court observed that the concept of a 'national' is not recognised or defined under the Citizenship Act. Therefore, Namgyal Dolkar's identification of herself as a 'Tibetan national' in her application for an identity certificate is of no legal consequence under the Citizenship Act. The Court further observed that Namgyal was an Indian citizen by birth, under Section 3(1)(a) of the Citizenship Act, and that her statement could not be treated as a renunciation of Indian citizenship. Such a renunciation could only occur as envisaged under Section 8 of the Citizenship Act. Moreover, according to the Delhi High Court, Section 9 of the Citizenship Act made it clear that Namgyal Dolkar's citizenship had not been terminated either. The Court mentioned that there is no need for an Indian citizen, who is a citizen 'by birth' (*jus soli*) under Section 3 of the Citizenship Act, to apply for citizenship of India. Therefore, the passport authorities were citing unfair and erroneous grounds. The Court directed the Regional Passport Office to process Namgyal Dolkar's application for her passport. This judgment of the Delhi High Court was quite significant, in the sense that it highlighted the absence of any legal framework in India to date to deal with refugees or stateless persons.

On 7 October 2018, seven Rohingya men—Mohammad Jalal, Mokbul Khan, Jalaluddin, Mohammad Younus, Sabbir Ahamed, Rahimuddin, and Mohammad Salam—who were arrested in 2012 for entering India without documents, were deported to Myanmar. This deportation took place a few hours after the Supreme Court of India refused to intervene in a plea to allow these Rohingya men to remain in India. These men ultimately were taken to the border town of Moreh in Manipur, where they were handed over to the Border Guard Forces of Myanmar. They had been arrested initially on charges of illegal entry into India in 2012, after they were caught by the police in the Shilchori-Nagatila region of Assam. They were detained under the Foreigners Act and served a sentence of three months for the 'crime' of entering India without valid documents. However, after they completed this sentence, they were incarcerated for a further six years at the detention centre in Silchar Central Jail. This probably marked the beginning of a large-scale deportation process that would target to push back all 40,000 Rohingya refugees living across India.

The Rohingya are people who had fled Myanmar on account of serious violations of human rights and the fear of persecution. Therefore, the rationale behind their deportation when no arrangement had been made between India and Myanmar for the repatriation of the refugees, and with no prior assessment on how far the current political and human rights situation in Myanmar had improved, remains in question. Even the UNHCR had been denied access to assess these men's claim to international refugee protection. The UNHCR's official statement also raised concerns that these men did not have access to lawyers from state legal services, which could have helped to get their asylum claims assessed in India.

Moreover, while hearing a petition filed in 2017 challenging such a deportation plan, a Bench of the Supreme Court of India, headed by former Chief Justice Deepak Mishra, clearly mentioned that although the problem of Rohingya refugees is of 'great magnitude', there is a need to strike a balance between the human rights of refugees and national security concerns. This petition is still pending in the Supreme Court of India. Since 2017, the Government of India has maintained its plan to deport 'all illegal immigrants', including an estimated 40,000 Rohingya refugees living across the country. In an order issued by the Ministry of Home Affairs in August 2017, state governments were instructed to 'identify and deport all illegal immigrants', with specific reference to the Rohingya community. This policy has continued to generate controversy and legal challenges in subsequent years. The Ministry of Home Affairs as well as the leaders of the ruling party in India insisted that illegal migrants posed a threat to national security, as they were understood to be more vulnerable to potential recruitment by terrorist organisations. Even of late, the Government of India has asked states to identify members of the Rohingya refugee community, record their biometric details, and report them to the Union government. To quote Rajnath Singh, Home Minister of India: 'Advisories have been issued to states. They need to identify the Rohingyas, take their biometrics and send us a report.'[8]

Similar attitudes are visible elsewhere in India, even in the non-government circles. Jammu's Chamber of Commerce and Industry threatened to launch an 'identify and kill movement' against the settlers in 2017, which it claimed pushed the government into taking the issue of Rohingya people more seriously. Rakesh Gupta, the President of the Jammu Chamber, said that there was nothing new in taking the law into one's hands if 'someone becomes a threat to our security, to the nation's security, and the security forces don't tackle them.'[9] Incidentally, the unquiet, insurgency-prone Himalayan state of Jammu and Kashmir, which is adjacent to Pakistan, has the biggest population of Rohingya refugees in the country, with around 7,000 people scattered in various makeshift settlements, largely in the Jammu region.

On the other hand, in a section of the Indian media, the Rohingya were accused of trafficking in drugs and humans, apart from being involved in terrorist and anti-national activities. It is therefore not surprising that the Rohingya are considered 'a problem', 'radicalised Islamist extremists' who need to be dealt with ruthlessly, or simply 'economic migrants' that India cannot afford to help. New Delhi also mentioned in 2017 that it shared Myanmar's concern about 'extremist violence' by Rohingya militants. The Ministry of Home Affairs, Government of India, also informed the country's Supreme Court that it had reports from the country's security agencies and 'other authentic sources' indicating linkages between some unauthorised Rohingya immigrants with 'Pakistan-based terror organizations and similar organizations operating in other countries'.[10]

More recently, a confidential letter addressed to the Divisional Security Commissioners of Indian Railways in Madurai, Thiruvananthapuram, and Palakkad alerted them to a mass movement of the Rohingya from India's Northeast to Kerala on several long-distance trains. The letter, signed by P. Sethu Madhavan from the office of the Principal Chief Security Commissioner of the RPF, said:

> All Rohingyas are travelling in groups along with their families. Officers and staff under your control may be sensitized about their movement. If they are found in trains, they may be handed over to the police having jurisdiction for further action. Action taken report may be sent to this office at the earliest for the perusal of ....[11]

The letter also listed 14 trains connecting India's east and/or Northeast with Kerala as potential trains that might carry the suspected Rohingyas. It is interesting to note that many of these trains run along the migrant corridor, which witnesses mass movement of labourers from states like Assam, West Bengal, Odisha, and Bihar to the southern state in search of work.

As it is, the issue of cross-border undocumented migration from Bangladesh to India has been a sensitive one in Indian politics, particularly during the poll seasons. It is not surprising, therefore, that while addressing an election rally in Madhya Pradesh, a senior member of the government stated that all illegal immigrants were 'like termites eating into the nation's security'. Therefore, panic has spread among the Rohingya refugees, who fled to India either directly from Myanmar or through Bangladesh. Moreover, most of the Rohingya refugees who had earlier taken shelter in the Baruipur region of South 24 Parganas district of West Bengal (the state perceived to be 'slightly friendly' to the Rohingyas) have 'disappeared' from the region, probably in view of the growing panic regarding deportation to Myanmar.[12] After all, the present government in India has taken an unsympathetic position on the issue, and made it clear that the Rohingya cannot be given refugee status in the country on account of perceived threats to the country's national security, and should be deported to Myanmar *en masse*.

India's Home Minister Rajnath Singh said, during an event of the NHRC on 12 October 2018, that action against 'illegal immigrants' should not be seen from the prism of human rights. Subsequently, a senior official of the Ministry of Home Affairs said that the principle of *non-refoulement*, which basically relates to human rights, was applicable to those who seek asylum, and one needs to remember that no Rohingya has so far sought it.[13]

In this emerging scenario of the securitisation of Rohingya refugees and other migrants, particularly from Bangladesh, and in view of the growing erasure of concern for human rights, the core issue concerning the Rohingya remains marginalised in the context of the deportation of these seven Rohingyas to Myanmar. These seven men have not been officially termed by either India or Myanmar as 'citizens' of Myanmar, but have been called 'residents' of the latter. After all, the matter of citizenship lies at the core of the entire Rohingya issue. This is clear from the observation of the Supreme Court of India, which quoted the affidavit of the

Ministry of Home Affairs, Government of India, in defending the deportation of the seven Rohingyas, indicating that 'they have been identified as residents of Myanmar'.[14]

Old Questions, New Contexts

The deportation of seven Rohingyas back to Myanmar in October 2018 raised fresh issues on India's stand regarding the refugee/stateless/migrant with its legal, ideological, and diplomatic implications. The deportation clearly amounts to a violation of the principle of *non-refoulement* or the prohibition against forcible return to a state where a person fears persecution, a customary principle of international law that is binding in nature for all countries, irrespective of whether or not the 1951 Refugee Convention or its 1967 protocol had been signed and/or ratified by the country concerned. Moreover, there is hardly any provision in the Indian immigration rules under which a stateless person may apply for leave to enter or remain in the country. We need to recall that the Rohingya are often referred to as the world's most persecuted minority, having settled for generations in Myanmar's restive Rakhine state. Since 25 August 2017, the large-scale migration of this community to Bangladesh and also to India began in the face of a heavy army crackdown in Myanmar on the Rohingya in the name of rooting out terrorist elements. This decision of the Government of India contradicted India's long tradition of providing shelter to those fleeing their own countries after serious human rights violations—be it from Tibet, Bangladesh, or Sri Lanka.

Consequently, Aakar Patel of Amnesty India said that the '... decision by the Supreme Court marks a dark day for human rights in India.' He rightly pointed out that 'This decision negates India's proud tradition of providing refuge to those fleeing serious human rights violations. It endangers the most persecuted population in the world and is bereft of any empathy.'[15] So far as the Rohingya refugees in India are concerned, they were predetermined to be 'illegal immigrants'. Therefore, they were to be deported (including those who are registered with the UNHCR), despite heavy criticism from both within and outside the country for blatantly ignoring the plight of those who had fled from a 'well-founded fear of persecution', and who as such were 'refugees' and not illegal immigrants. Official statements were also made, indicating clearly that the plan to deport Rohingya refugees would be executed, even against those registered with the UNHCR or considered at risk of persecution. India's Home Minister promised that the Union government would initiate action through diplomatic channels with Myanmar and get the issue resolved. It is interesting to note that in the pending case of the *en masse* deportation of Rohingya people before the Supreme Court of India, the Government of India has already identified them as a threat to the country's national security. A senior official of the Ministry of Home Affairs, Government of India, further said that the principle of *non-refoulement* was applicable to only those who seek asylum, and that no Rohingya has so far sought it.

The *de facto* stateless Rohingya refugees have been facing similar situations in almost all the countries they have sought refuge in, after being removed from their traditional homeland. This is only one classic example to indicate the inadequacies of international law. Millions of Rohingya and others elsewhere are living 'outside normal legal protection' and without 'elementary rights'. Non-recognition of the Rohingya in India or in any other country as 'stateless' means deportation, as has already been noticed, to their country of origin (in this case, Myanmar), which refuses to recognise them as citizens, and where they are likely to be persecuted.

International legal principles are quite inadequate in offering a solution to refugees and stateless persons as international law continues to operate in terms of reciprocal agreements and treaties between sovereign states. In reality, the right to have rights can primarily be obtained through citizenship guaranteed by nation-states, and for the time being, there is no sphere above the nations. Therefore, even after 70 years of the UDHR, nationality and citizenship continue to be fundamental elements of human security as they tend to provide people with a sense of belonging and identity. As citizenship provides the legal basis for the exercise of most human rights, persons without a nationality are, in reality, denied the basic human rights which citizens take for granted. These basic rights include, among others, access to schools and medical care, ownership of property, marriage and the foundation of a family, and the enjoyment of legal protection.

Refugees and the Stateless

Historically, refugees and stateless persons are closely interlinked. Both have received protection and assistance from international refugee organisations. Although refugees have existed almost since the advent of the modern nation-state, after World War II, the needs of refugees appeared dominantly in an Euro-centric world. When the 1951 Refugee Convention was drafted, a protocol relating the status of stateless persons, attached to the draft convention, was postponed for consideration at a later date. International Conventions on Statelessness were adopted in 1954 and 1961, but as the international community did not pay much attention to statelessness at the time, few countries became parties to these treaties. The UNHCR was entrusted with certain responsibilities with regard to stateless persons, but for many years the organisation devoted little time, resources, and efforts to address the issue of statelessness.

With increasing numbers of stateless people around the world and the implications this might have for national and regional security, the international community needs to revisit international instruments that deal with issues relating to nationality and citizenship. The end of the Cold War led to a profound change in international relations and forced the issue of statelessness onto the agenda of the international community. These changes included the disintegration of several states, the rise of ethnic consciousness in many parts of the world, and the fear of large-scale population movements involving stateless persons. This prompted the UNHCR and other humanitarian organisations to address the issue of statelessness in a more urgent and systematic manner, by trying to avert situations that can lead to statelessness, protecting stateless persons, and seeking adequate solutions to their problems. Ultimately, however, the problems of statelessness and disputed nationality can only be effectively addressed by states themselves in a Westphalian order. A brief perusal of some of the major international legal instruments indicates that there is no dearth of laws ensuring basic rights. However, these rights still elude the stateless and refugees. Being stateless means having no nationality, and having no nationality means having no documents to prove one's identity.

Two primary universal instruments on statelessness are the 1954 Convention relating to the Status of Stateless Persons and the 1961 Convention on the Reduction of Statelessness. Article 1 of the 1954 Convention defines a stateless person as a person not considered a national (or citizen) under the law of any state. In addition to providing a definition of statelessness, the Convention seeks to improve the status of stateless persons and helps ensure that stateless persons enjoy fundamental rights and freedoms without discrimination. It regulates, *inter alia*, the legal rights of stateless persons and their access to work and welfare, and urges states to facilitate their assimilation and naturalisation.

Despite the absence of a strong non-discrimination clause, the 1954 Convention contains a number of important provisions that require the treatment of stateless persons to be at least as favourable as that accorded to nationals. These provisions apply in respect to the freedom of religion, artistic rights and industrial property, access to courts, rationing, elementary public education, public relief and assistance, labour legislation, and social security (subject to state discretion in the case of non-contribution benefits). However, aside from these enumerated rights, the central point of departure for the 1954 Convention is Article 7(1), which stipulates that except where the Convention contains more favourable provisions, states 'shall accord to stateless persons the same treatment as is accorded to aliens generally'. Moreover, many of the provisions of the 1954 Convention, including those that confer no better treatment than that afforded to aliens generally, explicitly require that the individual is lawfully staying in the territory of the state.[16] This problem is further compounded because states differ in their approach as to what constitutes 'lawful stay' and may, for example, require the individual to be granted a residence permit before they are considered as 'lawfully staying'.[17]

The 1954 Convention defines a stateless person as one 'who is not considered as a national by any state under the operation of its law'. Therefore, the Convention requires states to guarantee its provisions to *de jure* stateless persons, a group defined in a narrow, strictly legal manner, which does not usually accommodate persons who have become *de facto* stateless as a result of not enjoying the core minimum state protection linked with nationality. Indeed, it has been argued that this technical definition ignores the power of states to politically manipulate citizenship in both law and practice. States are encouraged, but not obliged, by virtue of a recommendation of the Final Act of the Convention, to extend the provisions of the Convention to *de facto* stateless persons wherever possible.

In sum, despite containing important provisions to regularise the status of stateless persons and to ensure basic rights, the 1954 Convention has significant weaknesses. Many of the protections apply only to stateless persons who are considered to be staying lawfully in a particular country, many provisions require that no more preferential treatment be extended to stateless persons than to 'aliens' generally, and fundamentally, it does not contain a comprehensive non-discrimination provision. Perhaps most importantly, it categorises the stateless into two groups (*de jure* and *de facto* stateless) and affords protection only to one, thus creating a hierarchy within statelessness, further complicating the (in)equality puzzle.

Regardless of whether a state is party to the 1954 Convention, the right to non-discrimination would require a procedure that enables states to respond to the specific needs of stateless persons in a timely manner. The first step would be a formal recognition procedure for stateless persons. This is based on the fundamental principle of equality and non-discrimination, which asserts that equal treatment does not necessarily mean identical treatment.[18] To realise full and effective equality, it would be necessary to treat people differently according to their different circumstances, to assert their equal worth, and to enhance their capabilities to participate in society as equals.[19] This understanding of equality may be applied by states when responding to statelessness, in order to ensure that their particular vulnerabilities are taken into account when dealing with the stateless and resolving the problems specific to them.

The 1954 Convention requires state parties to extend protection to *de jure* stateless persons, defined as those who are 'not considered as a national by any state under the operation of its law'. Only in the non-binding Final Act does the 1954 Convention encourage states to extend Convention provisions to *de facto* stateless persons. Although the Final Act does not provide a definition of the latter, the UNHCR has defined a *de facto* stateless person as one who is 'unable to demonstrate that he/she is *de jure* stateless, yet he/she has no effective nationality and does not enjoy national protection'.[20] The fact remains that while there are clear cases of *de jure* statelessness, most cases of *de facto* statelessness fall in a grey area. The consequence is that many persons are genuinely in need of protection as they are in effect stateless, but cannot provide legal proof that they have no nationality. Therefore, they are simply excluded from the purview of the 1954 Convention. The provisions of the 1954 Convention seem to be insufficient in responding to questions like: '(1) how to identify its beneficiaries and (2) how to interpret the meaning of "stateless person"'. The definition of statelessness, by its nature, is a negative concept, making it difficult to prove and apply consistently.[21] One of the most contested questions that the drafting process of the 1954 Convention dealt with was whether the *de facto* category should also be included in its provisions.[22] To avoid confusion, the drafters decided against it.[23] The members of the drafting committee were also perhaps apprehensive of a decline in the number of signatories to the Convention, which therefore led to their avoiding the inclusion of *de facto* statelessness in the definition.[24]

Carol A. Batchelor is of the opinion that the lack of an effective nationality causes a particular problem for individuals outside their states of origin, who cannot obtain assistance or documents to return. She argues that a person who is unable to obtain an effective nationality due to administrative obstacles should be fairly considered *de facto* stateless.[25] She also argues that although Article 1(1) of the 1954 Convention refers to *de jure* stateless persons, the resolutions attached to the Final Act of the 1954 Convention and to the 1961 Convention on the Reduction of Statelessness recommend that persons who are *de facto* stateless should be treated as *de jure* stateless as far as possible to enable the acquisition of an effective nationality, and that states ought to implement it.[26] On the other hand, Laura van Waas is apprehensive that cases of ineffective nationality will often be confused with cases of *de facto* statelessness. She points out that the question of whether these individuals are *de jure* or *de facto* stateless is somewhat irrelevant. In the end, the challenge is to identify them as stateless through appropriate procedures and well-defined rules of evidence.[27]

Other international instruments dealing with the right to nationality include, *inter alia*, Article 15 of the UDHR, which stipulates the right to a nationality, and the right not to be arbitrarily deprived of nationality. Further, Article 5 of CERD (International Convention on the Elimination of All Forms of Racial Discrimination), signed in 1965, seeks to 'prohibit and to eliminate racial discrimination in all its forms and to guarantee the right to everyone, without distinction as to race, colour, or nationality or ethnic origin, to equality before the law'. International legal instruments dealing specifically with the right to a nationality with regard to women and children also include the Convention on the Nationality of Married Women (1957), Article 9 of the CEDAW (Convention on the Elimination of all Forms of Discrimination Against Women), and Articles 7 and 8 of the CRC. The instruments concerning women seek to ensure that they enjoy equal rights to acquire, change, or retain nationality, while those covering children deal mainly with the right of children to be registered and to acquire a nationality from birth. At the regional level, the European Convention on Nationality (1997) embodies principles and rules applying to all aspects of nationality. The Convention on the Avoidance of Statelessness in relation to State

Succession (2006) establishes more detailed rules to be applied by states with a view to preventing, or at least reducing to the extent possible, cases of statelessness arising from state succession.

However, like the situation of IDPs (Internally Displaced Persons), to date there is no specific international institution dealing with the problem of statelessness, or supervising the 1954 and 1961 Conventions relating to statelessness. The UNHCR was provisionally assigned to assume the responsibilities referred to in Article 11, indicating 'a body to which a person claiming benefit of this convention may apply for the examination of his claim and for assistance in presenting it to the appropriate authority', in order to fill this gap with the entry into force of the Convention on the Reduction of Statelessness in 1975.[28] However, no mention was made of UNHCR's competence regarding the Convention relating to the Status of Stateless Persons, and it was not given wider responsibilities relating to statelessness.

Meanwhile, recent times have witnessed a steep rise in the number of stateless persons and a growing securitisation of these stateless people. This has probably led the UNHCR's Executive Committee and the UN General Assembly to adopt and endorse the 'Conclusion on the Prevention and Reduction of Statelessness and the Protection of Stateless Persons' (Resolution 50/152). In addition, the UNHCR was requested to 'actively promote accession' to the 1954 and 1961 Conventions on statelessness, 'as well as to provide relevant technical and advisory services pertaining to the preparation and implementation of national legislation'.

To this end, the UNHCR has taken a number of practical steps to strengthen its efforts with regard to stateless persons. It has appointed a legal expert on the problem of statelessness, and has actively assisted governments in the preparation and implementation of nationality legislation while encouraging them to accede to the 1954 and 1961 statelessness Conventions. A key provision of the 1961 Convention categorically asks states not to create statelessness through the deprivation of nationality. Article 8(1) of the Convention mentions that a 'Contracting State *shall not* deprive a person of his nationality if such deprivation would render him stateless'. In addition, the UNHCR has also strengthened its working relationship with a number of organisations involved in this issue, such as the Office of the United Nations High Commissioner for Human Rights (OHCHR), Council of Europe and the Organization for Security and Co-operation in Europe (OSCE).

In 2014, the UN launched a global campaign to end statelessness by 2024. At the same time, the crises of the Rohingya from Myanmar and the displacement of people from Syria started unfolding. Populist responses to globalisation and migration, as well as securitisation and digitisation have probably placed greater pressure on citizenship policies and made the task of promoting fair, inclusive, and non-discriminatory rules and practices ever more difficult. Post-colonial societies have been dealing with the demarcation of new boundaries created at the time of decolonisation, which also ignore natural and historical frontiers. The fresh geopolitical calculations of the post-colonial states have attached less importance to different communities who have been inhabiting a territorial area, often for centuries, and have begun emphasising the importance of the territory itself (which may be stacked with different natural resources), its integrity, and 'national security'. Under these circumstances, Hannah Arendt's observation, in an earlier generation, seems to be quite relevant: '[T]he moment human beings lacked their own government… no authority was left to protect them and no institution was willing to guarantee them… [what was] supposedly inalienable.' After all, modern international law still grants states the right to set citizenship rules, and to revoke citizenship.[29] This power allows states to divest their citizens of citizenship, or 'denationalise' them, despite the work of the international community to eliminate statelessness.

New Horizons

In an emerging anti-immigrant and xenophobic world, the *jus sanguinis* theory of citizenship is becoming more popular, where citizenship is limited to those with an ethnic or racial tie to the country concerned. Such laws usually grant citizenship to the foreign-born children of non-resident nationals, and also create statelessness amongst children born to members of minority groups and refugees. The USA, under President Donald Trump, was contemplating changing the US citizenship from a *jus soli* system to a *jus sanguinis* one. This would have the obvious and intended effect of stripping the 'outsiders', who are not 'real Americans', of their citizenship and its connected rights. The history of the world is witness to the application of the *jus sanguinis* principle of citizenship, and the production of large stateless populations. It would probably not be an exaggeration to say that if states had defined citizenship solely on a *jus soli* principle, statelessness would have been a less serious problem. At least, all the children born to stateless people would have been citizens of the state of their birth.

So far as the Rohingya in India are concerned, the gap in the international protection regime is apparent as India's attitude towards the refugees is ambiguous or entirely hostile. Restrictive trends in refugee determination procedures mean that more and more people (at present the Rohingya) are refused refugee protection, and they cannot return home because they fear persecution and are concerned about their safety. This trend highlights the heightened necessity for a well-built framework of protection for *de facto* stateless persons, who do not strictly fit the refugee criteria and yet cannot return home, and others who, while not at risk if returned, cannot return home for legal reasons.

The world has been witnessing mixed and massive flows of people since the 1990s. Since then, it has become quite difficult to make a clear distinction between refugees and asylum seekers, normally protected by international refugee law, and economic migrants, who usually do not enjoy that level of protection. In other words, the earlier categorisations of people on the move are becoming blurred and sometimes irrelevant in dealing with evolving situations worldwide. Consequently, the interplay between security, and economic, political, and humanitarian concerns is becoming increasingly complex. The states or governments usually focus on frameworks and procedures to 'disaggregate and manage mixed migration',[30] whereas a rights-based approach must address basic human needs beyond such considerations. Therefore, in order to address the basic needs of people on the move, on the one hand we need to look beyond international refugee law *per se*, and must take into consideration international human rights and humanitarian laws and other international and regional legal frameworks. On the other hand, we need to address the Westphalian order and the question of state sovereignty from an absolutely fresh perspective.

Notes

1. 'Nationality Decrees Issued in Tunis and Morocco—Advisory Opinion'. *Permanent Court of International Justice* 3(24), 4 October 1922.

2. League of Nations, *1930 Convention on Certain Questions relating to the Conflict of Nationality Laws*, Treaty Series, Vol. 179. The Hague: League of Nations, 1930. LNTS 80; 1930 Can. T.S. No. 7.

3. Although the Declaration itself is not legally binding, international jurists argue that it has acquired the status of customary international law. See United Nations, *Universal Declaration of Human Rights*. Paris: United Nations, 1948. Available at https://www.ohchr.org/EN/UDHR/Documents/UDHR_Translations/eng.pdf/ (accessed July 2024).

4. For instance, Article 4 of the European Convention on Nationality states: '(a) Everyone has a right to a nationality; (b) statelessness should be avoided; (c) no one shall be arbitrarily deprived of his or her nationality.' See Council of Europe, *European Convention on Nationality*, European Treaty Series, No. 166. Strasbourg: Council of Europe, 1997. Available at https://rm.coe.int/168007f2c8. (accessed July 2024).

Similarly, Article 20 of the American Convention on Human Rights affirms the general right to a nationality and the prohibition against arbitrary deprivation, mentioning that '[e]very person has the right to the nationality of the state in whose territory he was born if he does not have the right to any other nationality'. See Organization of American States, *American Convention On Human Rights 'Pact Of San Jose, Costa Rica'*. San Jose: Organization of American States, 1969. Available at https://treaties.un.org/doc/Publication/UNTS/Volume%201144/volume-1144-I-17955-English.pdf. (accessed July 2024).

5. See Article 23(3) of the International Covenant on Civil and Political Rights (ICCPR), Office of the High Commissioner for Human

Rights (OHCHR), *International Covenant on Civil and Political Rights*, 1966. Available at https://www.ohchr.org/Documents/ProfessionalInterest/ccpr.pdf. (accessed July 2024); Aee also Articles 7(1) and 8(1) of the Convention on the Rights of the Child (CRC), Office of the United Nations High Commissioner for Human Rights (OHCHR), *Convention on the Rights of the Child (CRC)*, 1989. Available at https://www.ohchr.org/Documents/ProfessionalInterest/crc.pdf. (accessed July 2024).

6. *Dilcia Yean and Violeta Bosico v. Dominican Republic*, Int. Am. Ct. H.R. Case No. 12.189, 8 September 2005; emphasis mine.

7. The prohibition on racial and ethnic discrimination is enshrined in the following provisions of international and regional human rights instruments: Article 1(3) of the *United Nations Charter* (the purpose of the Charter is to promote and encourage 'respect for human rights and for fundamental freedoms for all without distinction to race, sex, language or religion'). See United Nations, *United Nations Charter*. San Francisco: United Nations, 1945; Article 55(c) of the *United Nations Charter* (committing the United Nations to promote non-discrimination); Articles 2 and 7 of the Universal Declaration of Human Rights, see United Nations, *Universal Declaration of Human Rights*. Articles 2 and 26 of the *International Covenant on Civil and Political Rights* (ICCPR); Article 2(2) of the International Covenant on Economic, Social and Cultural Rights, United Nations, *International Covenant on Economic, Social and Cultural Rights*, 1966. Available at https://www.ohchr.org/Documents/ProfessionalInterest/cescr.pdf. (accessed July 2024); Article 14 of the European Convention on Human Rights (ECHR), Council of Europe, *European Convention on Human Rights*. Strasbourg: Council of Europe, 1950; Articles 1 and 2 of *Protocol No. 12 to the ECHR*; Article 21 of the *European Charter of Fundamental Freedoms*; Chapter 1, Article 2 of the *African Charter on Human and Peoples' Rights*; see Organisation of African Unity, *African Charter on Human and Peoples' Rights*, 1981. Available at https://au.int/sites/default/files/treaties/36390-treaty-0011_-_african_charter_on_human_and_peoples_rights_e.pdf (accessed November 2024); and Articles 1(1) and 24 of the *American Convention on Human Rights 'Pact Of San Jose, Costa Rica'*. See Organization of American States, *American Convention On Human Rights 'Pact Of San Jose, Costa Rica'*. San Jose: Organization of American States, 1969. Available at https://treaties.un.org/doc/Publication/UNTS/Volume%201144/volume-1144-I-17955-English.pdf. (accessed July 2024).

Also see *Restatement (Third) The Foreign Relations Law of the United States*, 702, 1987 ('Customary International Law of Human Rights: A state violates international law if, as a matter of state policy, it practices, encourages, or condones … systematic racial discrimination'); *R. v. Immigration Officer at Prague Airport*, UKHL 55(46), 2004.

> The great theme which runs through subsequent human rights instruments, national, regional and international, is the legal right of equality with the correlative right of non-discrimination on the grounds of race…. It is true that in the world, as we know it, departures from this norm are only too many. But the international community has signed up to it. The moral norm has ripened into a rule of customary international law. It is binding on all states.

8. *Hindustan Times*, 'Govt tells states to collect biometrics of Rohingyas', 2 October 2018. Available at https://www.hindustantimes.com/india-news/govt-tells-states-to-collect-biometrics-of-rohingyas/story-PyRqA1jw9JbPfQivAMo4rJ.html (accessed November 2024).

9. *Scroll.in*, 'Jammu commerce chamber says it will identify and kill Rohingya Muslims if state does not deport them', 8 April 2017. Available at https://scroll.in/latest/834067/jammu-commerce-chamber-says-it-will-identify-and-kill-rohingya-muslims-if-state-does-not-deport-them (accessed November 2024).

10. *Aljazeera*, 'India: Rohingya have "terror" ties', 18 September 2017. Available at https://www.aljazeera.com/news/2017/9/18/india-rohingya-have-terror-ties (accessed November 2024).

11. *Financial Express*, 'In missive to states, Modi government seeks biometric details of Rohingyas to tackle immigrants issue', 2 October 2018. Available at https://www.financialexpress.com/india-news/in-missive-to-states-modi-government-seeks-biometric-details-of-rohingyas-to-tackle-immigrants-issue/1333871/ (accessed November 2024).

12. Snigdhendu Bhattacharya, 'Rohingya refugees find a safe haven near Kolkata'. *Hindustan Times*, 17 March 2018. Available at https://www.hindustantimes.com/india-news/rohingya-refugees-find-a-safe-haven-near-kolkata/story-Do4kKTU8PkXJV9JORN6LfL.html (accessed November 2024).

13. ICJ, 'India: Immediately halt forced returns of Myanmar refugees in Manipur and respect the non-refoulement principle', 10 May 2024. Available at https://www.icj.org/india-immediately-halt-forced-returns-of-myanmar-refugees-in-manipur-and-respect-the-non-refoulement-principle/ (accessed November 2024).

14. Human Rights Watch, 'India: 7 Rohingya Deported to Myanmar', 4 October 2018. Available at https://www.hrw.org/news/2018/10/05/india-7-rohingya-deported-myanmar (accessed November 2024).

15. Amnesty International, 'India: Protection of the humans rights of the people of Jammu and Kashmir must guide the way forward', 11 December 2023. Available at https://www.amnesty.org/en/latest/news/2023/12/india-protection-of-the-human-rights-of-the-people-of-jammu-and-kashmir-must-guide-the-way-forward/ (accessed November 2024).

16. Several articles of the 1954 Convention, including Article 15 (Right of Association), Article 17 (Employment), Article 21 (Housing), Article 23 (Public Relief), Article 24 (Social Security), Article 26 (Freedom of Movement), Article 28 (Travel Documents), and Article 30(1) (Non-Expulsion), are significant in this context. See UNHCR, *1954 Convention Relating to the Status of Stateless Persons*. Available at https://www.unhcr.org/ibelong/wp-content/uploads/1954-Convention-relating-to-the-Status-of-Stateless-Persons_ENG.pdf (accessed July 2024).

17. See Carol A. Batchelor, 'The 1954 Convention relating to the Status of Stateless Persons: Implementation within the European Union Member States and Recommendations for Harmonisation'. *Refuge* 22(2), 2005. This review of EU state practice indicates that, 'the majority of countries in the EU do not anticipate an automatic right to residence based on recognition as a stateless person'.

18. In *Thlimmenos v. Greece*, application no. 34369/97, judgment of 6 April 2000, where the European Court of Human Rights observed that, '[t]he right not to be discriminated against in the enjoyment of the rights guaranteed under the Convention is also violated when States without an objective and reasonable justification fail to treat differently persons whose situations are significantly different.' Cited in Amal de Chickera and Katherine Perks, 'The Silent Stateless and the Unhearing World: Can Equality Compel Us to Listen?' *The Equal Rights Review* 3, 2009, p. 48.

19. The Equal Rights Trust, *Declaration of Principles on Equality*. London: The Equal Rights Trust, 2008, Principle 2: Equal Treatment, 5.

20. UNHCR, Inter-Parliamentary Union, *Nationality and Statelessness: A Handbook for Parliamentarians*. Geneva: UNHCR, Inter-Parliamentary Union, 2005, p. 11. Available at http://archive.ipu.org/PDF/publications/nationality_en.pdf. (Accessed July 2024).

21. For a detailed and comprehensive discussion on this issue, please see Laura van Waas, 'The UN Statelessness Conventions', in Alice Edwards and Laura van Waas (eds), *Nationality and Statelessness under International Law*. Cambridge: Cambridge University Press, 2014.

22. See UN Doc E/CONF.17/L.6 in UNHCR, *Convention Relating to the Status of Stateless Persons: Its History and Interpretation*, A Commentary

by Nehemiah Robinson, World Jewish Congress 1955, Institute of Jewish Affairs, reprinted by the Division of International Protection of UNHCR, 1997, pp. 3, 7; United Nations General Assembly (UNGA), Conference of Plenipotentiaries on the Status of Stateless Persons, Summary Records (13–23 September 1954), UN Doc E/CONF.17/SR. 1–15, SR. 2; SR.11–15; SR. 11, 5–8; SR.13, 5–16, cited in Katia Bianchini, 'The "Stateless Person": Definition in Selected EU Member States: Variations of Interpretation and Application'. *Refugee Survey Quarterly* 36(3), 2017, p. 87.

23. David Weissbrodt and Clay Collins, 'The Human Rights of Stateless Persons'. *Human Rights Quarterly* 28(1), 2006, pp. 245–243.

24. For details, see Carol A. Batchelor, 'Stateless Persons: Some Gaps in International Protection'. *International Journal of Refugee Law* 7(2), 1995, pp. 232–248.

25. For details, see Carol A. Batchelor, 'Statelessness and the Problem of Resolving Nationality Status'. *International Journal of Refugee Law* 10(1/2), 1998.

26. Paragraph 3 of the 1954 Convention's Final Act recommends that the benefits of the Convention should be extended to individuals whom states consider to have had valid reasons for renouncing the protection of their state of nationality. The Final Act of the 1961 Convention does not mention *de facto* statelessness, but rather recommends that such persons benefit from the provisions in the 1961 Convention so as to obtain an effective nationality. Final Act of the United Nations Conference on the Status of Stateless Persons, 360–9 UNTS 118, 6 June 1960.

27. Cited in Bianchini, 'The "Stateless Person"', p. 88.

28. Article 11 of the 1961 Convention on the Reduction of Statelessness establishes that a mechanism must be created for stateless individuals to present their claims. The UNHCR was provisionally assigned to fulfil this role, allowing individuals who claim the benefits of the Convention to apply to a designated body for examination and assistance. The purpose of this assignment was to ensure that stateless persons could seek remedies and resolution of their status, particularly after the Convention came into force in 1975.

29. UNHCR, Division of International Protection, *UNHCR Action to Address Statelessness: A Strategy Note*, 22 INT'L J. REFUGEE L. 297, 299, 2010 (explaining the international legal framework regarding the loss and acquisition of nationality).

30. Thomas Linde, 'Mixed Migration: A Humanitarian Counterpoint'. *Refugee Survey Quarterly* 30(1), 2011, p. 89.

7

Responsibility to Protect

Questions of Race, Religion, Resource, and the Unspoken Fourth

Paula Banerjee

In April 2010, Jan Brewer, the Governor of Arizona, signed a bill which proposed that for migrants, failure to carry immigration documents is a crime. This bill gave the police broad powers to detain anyone suspected of being in the country illegally, and was clearly aimed at the 'illegal' entry of the growing Hispanic population in the United States of America. It was also alleged that 'proponents and critics alike said that this bill was the broadest and strictest immigration measure in generations'.[1] Importantly, the question that remained was: How were these migrants to be identified? The presumable answer was: but of course, migrants will look different and act differently. Thus, could any non-Caucasian in the wrong place and at the wrong time be branded 'illegal', unless proven otherwise? Micky Hammon, the Alabama House of Representatives' Republican majority leader, allegedly asked his fellow legislators to draft a bill that would so terrify the Hispanic population that they themselves would leave. 'This bill is designed to make it difficult for them to live here so they will deport themselves,' said he.[2] Mary Bauer, a pro-immigrant activist and the legal director of Southern Poverty Law Centre in Montgomery, Alabama, bemoaned:

> Tens of thousands of people have been estimated to leave the state including many U.S. citizens. It has divided the people of Alabama.... This law was about vilifying a vulnerable group of

> people; scapegoating them for the state's economic problems and the acts of really small minded demagogues who want to point the finger at vulnerable people and blame them for the state's problems.[3]

The Hispanic population of the state, it is said, were dreadfully frightened. This bill clearly made a suspect of anyone who seemed alien.

However, this was not the first effort to control immigration on the basis of race, nor will it be the last. In this chapter, I contend that both citizenship and migration rest on a triad of the axes of race, religion, and resources, and gender remains the unspoken fourth axis. So migration and forced migration studies become meaningless if these extremely volatile issues are not considered in their proper perspectives. Race and religion create the alien body that is forced to move and cross borders. Yet, this very act of crossing borders can also create further borders—as SB 1070 of the United States of America proves, particularly in the context of Arizona. Therefore, without understanding the ramifications of race, religion, resource, and gender one cannot understand forced migration, and such an analysis fails to give forced migration studies its proper credence. The present study elaborates on this complex interplay of factorial prefectures through a case study of the performativity undergirding the selection of who belongs in the politico-geographical polarities of the Global North and the Global South, but also how intra-regional conjectures in South Asia are played out.

Race and Belonging: Citizenship in the West

Forced migration is a fairly recent field in pedagogy. It began in the Global North after World War II as 'refugee studies'. It became clear that modern state formation was often accompanied by large-scale population displacement, resulting in large population groups becoming refugees. Suddenly, there was an upsurge in interest in who these people were. When it became evident that these people were different, racially and perhaps even by religion, this population movement came to be recognised as a crisis. What was ignored, however, was the knowledge that population movements have happened in all historical periods, and not especially during and immediately after World War II. Forced migration in the context of the known history of Europe largely comprised of movements of white people. Thus, it was never considered a problem or a crisis. Contrary to this pattern of movement, the end of colonialism witnessed partitions that often went hand-in-hand with hordes of non-white people moving in the Global South. Many of these people aspired to move to the Global North because they correctly associated their marginality with colonial rule, which made race the bedrock for the acquisition of benefits such as citizenship, power sharing, and material wealth and resources. As a result, countries in the Global North marked such movements as a 'crisis' that necessitated policies and laws, which in turn gave the respective states the authority to decide who should be welcomed and who shunned. Because more people were stopped from entering the northern borders, policies and laws were formulated and the hordes that were moving were homogenised as a faceless and nameless mass. In no way were they humanised in the narratives because the moment they appeared as individuals, their claims for rights and resources could not legitimately be ignored. At the centre of resource sharing was the question of citizenship, and who belonged was a conscious decision made by the ruling elite. Those who were considered unworthy of being recognised as citizens were either to be tolerated as a precarious group that might provide cheap labour, or were to be forced out, to join the ranks of the 'nowhere' people.

According to social scientists such as Manuela Boatca and Julia Roth, 'an entire Occidentalist tradition of citizenship theory viewed citizenship as a modern, progressive institution that helped overcome particularities of unequal social origin'. However, contrary to that claim, Western scholarly tradition makes it obvious that 'the institution of citizenship has developed in the West through the legal (and physical) exclusion of non-European, non-White and non-Western populations from civic, political, social and cultural rights'.[4] Citizenship from the time of Max Weber was posited against the institution of slavery, and the institutionalisation of citizenship was portrayed as progress from bondage to freedom. As an institution, citizenship was considered an equaliser and a paradigmatic shift from the spectrum of social hierarchies, at the other end of which was slavery. This was highlighted even more in colonial times, when aliens were denoted first, and then it was indicated who could be a citizen.[5]

Race, religion, and resources were the three pillars on which citizenship was perched. In the case of the colonising countries, where the modern capitalist world order was in the making, resources became a key question for the acquisition of citizenship. Yet, in the colonies it was often race and religion that were privileged, and resource was usually the third signifier of citizenship. For example, in the case of the French colony of Saint Domingue, where a revolt of the enslaved resulted in the liberation of slaves in 1794, the question of citizenship was hotly contested between the white settlers and the native mulattos. Even though the contribution of the former slaves dominated the rhetoric of freedom, notions of colour took precedence over those of property when the question of citizenship was decided. Although many mulattos were property owners, it was the white population that was privileged when citizenship was awarded.[6]

In the USA, too, the question of who should get the material and ideological benefits of citizenship was intensely debated. Questions of citizenship came up at a time when African-American people, recently liberated from slavery, were moving to the northern and western cities of the US from the rural south, and the country was also facing an influx of migrants from Europe, who were not quite in the same category of people who had migrated earlier. According to some social scientists, it was a time when 'the category of "white" was subject to challenges brought about by the influx of diverse groups who were not of the same Anglo-Saxon stock as the founding immigrants'.[7] The African-Americans created a major hurdle in denoting who could be a citizen because in most instances, they were markedly the alien. This provided scholars with a particularly rich topography for an examination of the dynamics of racialisation. However, according to iconic

African-American writer Toni Morrison, 'blackness' was both a hurdle and a harbinger for creative imagination on the question of who belonged:

> Black slavery enriched the country's creative possibilities. For in that construction of blackness and enslavement could be found not only the not-free but also, with the dramatic polarity created by skin colour, the projection of the not-me. The result was a playground for the imagination. What rose up out of the collective needs to allay internal fears and to rationalise external exploitation was an American Africanism—a fabricated brew of darkness, otherness, alarm, and desire that is uniquely American.[8]

The American view of 'otherness', when juxtaposed with a sense of 'alarm', created vulnerabilities that could consciously be exploited for ages. The legitimisation of hierarchies created out of such attitudes ensured that American democracy was premised on the constant creation of minorities who were kept out of equations of power sharing.

While the African-Americans were decidedly vulnerable, they were still accommodated within the American mindset. They entered American homes, albeit as domestic workers, but at least found a space in the American imagination. As early as 1905, single black women in the city of New York were hired as domestic workers. Most of the African-American migrants moved to big cities such as New York, Philadelphia, Boston, etc.[9] Although they were quite low in the power hierarchy, their presence within white American homes saved them from invisibility and complete subjugation. In W. E. B. Du Bois' seminal work, *The Philadelphia Negro* (1899), we learn that these former slaves were not just tolerated but rather, encouraged in the white American homes. An employer commented on one 'coloured' domestic help:

> Our experience of them is that they are infinitely cleaner than the white Irish, both in their work and personally; they are more self-respecting and better mannered—more agreeable in manners; indeed, I have found them capable of the very highest cultivation of manner.[10]

Perhaps even more than 'blackness', as Toni Morrison puts it, the fear of migrant aliens was more palpable. From Du Bois' exposition, one gets some insight into how Irish migrants were viewed, even though they were 'almost white'.

Very little can be learnt about non-white migrant groups in the US in the early nineteenth century, which was a high point in migration to the free world. Around the 1850s, Chinese peasants were arriving in the US in fairly large numbers. They were engaged as miners and railroad workers, and faced tremendous repression. A legal analyst, Mae Ngai, discusses how the 'Asian' migrants led to the concept of 'ineligibility to citizenship'. She says that such a construction was applied 'to all Asians, justifying and perfecting their exclusion from imagination, and that completed the "Asiatic" as a peculiarly American racial category'.[11] About the Chinese migration in particular, a migration that ultimately necessitated the construction of the 'Asiatic', Leland Stanford, the Governor of California, announced in his inaugural address in 1862 that:

> ... the settlement among us of an inferior race is to be discouraged by even legitimate means. Asia with her numberless millions, sends to our shores the dregs of her population. Large numbers of this class are already here; and, unless we do something early to check their immigration, the question, which of the two tides of immigration, meeting upon the shores of the Pacific, shall be turned back, will be forced upon our consideration, when far more difficult than now of disposal. There can be no doubt but the presence of numbers among us of a degraded and distinct people exercise a deleterious influence upon the superior race, and, to a certain extent, repel desirable immigration.[12]

The troubles faced by the Chinese workers were stupendous, and yet, that history is all but obliterated. One way of unearthing knowledge about minority groups, especially those that have been on the move, is by acquiring knowledge regarding their resistance to persecution. Much of this understanding came from the field of gender and labour studies. However, little is known about the resistance, if any, that was surmounted by the Chinese railroad workers. Ranabir Samaddar writes:

> ... very little of the resistance of the Chinese labour except the famous strike in 1876, when on 25 June the Chinese workers left their grading work along a two-mile stretch on the eastern Sierra slope and went back to their camp. They demanded $40 a month instead of $35, and a reduction in hours. A workday on the open Sierra lasted from dawn till dusk; the Chinese labourers wanted to work no more than 10 hours daily. They also asked for shorter shifts in the cramped, dangerous tunnels. The company bosses responded with stopping food supply at the heights and deployed white strongmen.[13]

From these writings, it is clear that race dominated the construction of both the citizen and the migrant in the colonial period.

CITIZENSHIP: A SOUTH ASIAN PROBLEM

If one looks at the question of citizenship from the perspective of South Asia, once again the issue of race rears its head. When one looks at India's Northeast in the colonial period, the issue becomes even clearer. To understand how differences were created, which were ultimately racialised and then nationalised, one needs to study colonial administration and the creation of differences, as was done in the Northeast of India in the eighteenth century. The colonial administration had introduced in that period the notion of 'racial difference' between the plains and the hills. The hill people belonged to the 'Mongolian areas', they belonged 'neither historically nor racially' to 'India proper' or its 'backward area' (that is, plains in the Northeast). Therefore, as one colonial administrator, R. N. Reid, noted, while power would soon be transferred in the country, the people of the 'non-Indian Mongolian areas' should not be made to negotiate with 'alien politicians'. Another administrator, J. P. Mills, noted the 'sharp cultural distinctions ... (which) needed little re-emphasis'. The 'languages of the hills with the exception of the Khasis were all Tibeto-Burman'; the indigenous system of self-government was 'vigorously alive' in the hills while it had 'disappeared from the plains'; the 'hills were clearly different', in that 'self-sufficiency was greater, artistic development was higher, squalor and misery rare, and sense of social responsibility … high'. Just as Hinduism and Islam covered all aspects of life in the plains, 'Christianity or animism' covered the tribal way of life.[14] In the context of what the colonial administration saw as racial, ethnic, and cultural differences, J. H. Hutton, the then Deputy Commissioner of the Naga Hills, recommended that the entire hill area between the two countries of India and Burma be turned into a crown colony (like Singapore and Swaziland) after the transfer of power.

Yet, as we know, the nationalist pressure proved too strong to retain such an indirect and graded system of rule. The Government of India Act, 1935 had, with respect to Assam, designated the Northeast Frontier Tracts, the Naga Hills District, the Lushai Hills District, and the North Cachar Sub-division of the Cachar District as 'excluded areas'. The Garo Hills District, the Mikir Hills in Nowgong and Sibsagar Districts, and the British portion of the Khasi and Jaintia Hills District, besides Shillong Municipality and the Cantonment, became the partially excluded areas. A special cadre for the frontier area was created in Burma, and India followed suit. The only nagging problem remained the issue of slavery. The Government of India adhered to the League of Nations' Slavery Convention (1926). Slavery, practised by many hill communities, could therefore not be allowed to continue indefinitely. However, control over slavery and human sacrifice was only the beginning of the march towards extending full administrative control over and settlement of the area. World War II became the second occasion.

Finally, the third occasion was provided by the argument voiced by Gopinath Bordoloi and the Khasi leader Nichols-Roy, which gained ground after the war ended in that area. They noted that with independence, the fruits of self-rule and democratic institutions could no longer be denied to the hill people of that region. By the time the Indian Constitution came to be framed, the political exclusion of the hill areas (including Manipur and Tripura, which had evolved along different historical lines) was out of the question. The end of political exclusion also meant the end of autonomy. In free India, the race card regarding the Northeast was played to deprive rather than to include.

It was during the debate on the provisions of the Sixth Schedule of the Indian Constitution that this mentality of officials from the plains became apparent, particularly among members of the dominant religious, caste, and ethnic/race groups. When there were discussions about making the Naga Hills an autonomous council, some responses from the members of the Assembly reflected the attitude of the architects of the Constitution towards the Naga people. Kuladhar Chaliha from Assam was particularly vocal. He said:

> The Nagas are a very primitive and simple people and they have not forgotten their old ways of doing summary justice when they have a grievance against anyone. If you allow them to rule us or run the administration it will be a negation of justice or administration and it will be something like anarchy.[15]

Although not as loud as Kuladhar Chaliha, there were many others who made it obvious that the Nagas did not belong among those who could govern. Brajeshwar Prasad from Bihar stated during the same debate:

> responsibilities of parliamentary life can be shouldered by those who are competent, wise, just and literate. To vest wide political powers into the hands of the tribals; is the surest method of inviting chaos, anarchy and disorder throughout the length and breadth of this country.[16]

Even Gopinath Bordoloi, who drafted the Sixth Schedule, commented that at the time, hardly any of the tribes could be called self-governing, but 'the time may come when they may become fit to govern themselves'.[17]

The discussions on the Sixth Schedule were a precursor of things to come. The members of the Constituent Assembly, who were deliberating on the creation of a democratic Constitution for India, were not just obsessed with the idea of maintaining order, as Paul Brass has suggested. That was only one of the things that they concerned themselves with. They were also in the business of constructing a citizenry loyal to the order they were seeking to maintain. On the basis of such criteria, they constructed notions of and discourses around who belonged and who did not. They created a hierarchy of citizenship in which many Northeastern tribal groups found themselves on the bottom rung. Their avowed difference was considered deviant and their physical appearance also marked them as alien. They were at best patronised and at worst, vilified. At the back of everyone's mind was the fact that these people were not *us*, and thus were unworthy of any autonomy or self-rule. Even as early as in the Constituent Assembly, the nation's leaders were using the language of their colonisers to deal with all those whom they considered *other*/deviant. This was decisive in shaping the state attitude towards the region. If one studies the history of the Rohingyas in Myanmar, one begins to understand how race and religion were used to dis-empower groups in colonial and post-colonial periods.

Arguably, the word 'Rohingya' came from the word 'Rohang', which was the historical name given to Arakan. The 1826 Treaty of Yandaboo led to the absorption of the Arakan Hills into the British Empire. The border between Arakan and Bengal was always porous, leading to cross-border exchanges. During the nineteenth century, the Arakan region witnessed the migration of Bengali Muslims hailing from Chittagong into the Arakan Hills. However, there is enough evidence to suggest that there was a Muslim presence in the Arakan Hills even before the arrival of these Bengali Muslims from Chittagong.[18] Today, the Arakan Hills are in the Rakhine state in Myanmar. Most of the people in the Rakhine state are either Buddhist Rakhine or Islamic Rohingya. Other than these communities, also present in this area are the ethnic groups of Chin, Mro, and Khami. The Arakan Hills retained their autonomous administration until 1784, when the Burman King Bodawpaya defeated the Arakan King Thamada. Later, the Arakan King took shelter in Bengal and the British became involved in the conflict. After 1826, the Arakan Hills became part of the British Empire.

After Burma's independence in 1948, the political demands of the Buddhist and the Muslim people from the Arakan Hills were never met. In 1962, when Ne Win seized power, the situation of ethnic and religious minorities became precarious. In 1982, the new Citizenship Act made it impossible for Muslims to become full citizens. At best, they were given the status of associate citizen. As for the Rohingya, they became a stateless community in 1982 when the Myanmar Citizenship Law excluded them from the list of 135 national ethnic groups.[19] The situation of the Rohingya became progressively more precarious. For decades, the Rohingya have been subjected to excessive violence. In 1989, the Myanmar government issued colour-coded scrutiny cards for citizens, but the Rohingya were not issued any card. On 21 February 1992, U Ohn Gyaw, the Foreign Affairs Minister of Myanmar, announced:

> Historically, there has never been a 'Rohingya' race in Myanmar. Since the first Anglo-Myanmar War in 1824, people of Muslim faith from the adjacent country illegally entered Myanmar Naing-Ngan, particularly Rakhine State. Being illegal immigrants they do not hold immigration papers like other nationals of the country.[20]

This has been the official statement since. From 1995, as a result of enormous pressure from the UNHCR, the Rohingya were given a white card (that functioned as temporary registration cards), which nevertheless could not be used to claim citizenship. The situation of the Rohingya failed to improve at all.

The trials and tribulations of the Rohingya became known to the world in 2015, when it was discovered that hundreds of them were perishing in boats as they tried to escape persecution in Myanmar. None of the other countries in the region was willing to take them in. With the Rohingya were many Bangladeshi forced migrants. Not only were they being denied safe haven, but they were also denied resources essential for survival. In these boats were women, children, the maimed, the sick, one and all trying to escape persecution and survive. Their first port of entry was Bangladesh due to its geographical proximity and religious affinity, but in this case, because of ethnic/racial differences, religious affinities were forgotten by 2009, and from that year onwards, even Bangladesh refused to accept Rohingya refugees. The plight of the Rohingyas in high seas led to protest by the international human rights regime when open graves were discovered in Thailand. This, more than any other event, revealed the precarious situation of the Rohingya population. In March 2017, another state-sanctioned crackdown on Rohingya Muslims was defended by the Myanmar government as a counter-insurgency operation. Social scientists call the Rohingya 'the world's most persecuted minority without citizenship'.[21]

As for Rohingya women, their situation is even worse. According to one observer, 'because of the diversity among Burma's 135 officially-recognised ethnic groups generalizing about them is risky. However, there clearly exists a country-wide pattern to the abuses suffered by Karen, Karenni, Mon, Shan, Kachin, Chin, Arakanese, Rohingya, and other ethnic women.'[22] Among the groups mentioned, the Rohingya women are worst-off because they belong to a stateless community. A 440-page report by the UN Human Rights Council (UNHRC), released in August 2018, details the persistence of crime against Rohingya women in Myanmar. The report

> includes accounts of women tied by their hair or hands to trees then raped; young children trying to flee burning houses but forced back inside; widespread use of torture with bamboo sticks, cigarettes and hot wax; and landmines placed at the escape routes from villages, killing people as they fled army crackdowns.[23]

A UNFPA report states that even in camp sites, 'women and girls report being harassed while attempting to access humanitarian services or perform essential tasks, such as collecting water or using the latrine. Many lack adequate clothing and essential hygiene items.'[24] It is obvious that the situation of women, and crimes against them, worsen when their communities are under siege.

The Unspoken Fourth

According to Carolyn Merchant, in discussions on how certain groups were perceived as aliens, there were debates on the nature of women in Europe. In the terms of this debate, women were considered essentially emotional and fragile, needing firm control to guide them. Just as nature's disorder necessitated order, the woman's chaos presaged control, and that which was wild needed to be tamed. Merchant notes that mastery over women coincided with mastery over nature in European society. In this way, Merchant argues, women became an emotional resource for men, but like other resources, this too needed to be harnessed.[25] Women were increasingly restricted, not only in production, but in reproduction as well. Their economic role was made necessary by the poverty in their families. Thus, women remained economic resources, but their control was justified by highlighting their ability to be emotional resources for their husbands. If women were not viewed as emotionally imbalanced, their subjugation to their husbands within the institution of marriage could be questioned, and the entire family structure challenged. Husbands were considered superior beings, ordained to control. Marriage and family were institutions meant to maintain the social order imbued with religious values. In this sort of gendered and orthodox framework, women living alone were also perceived as a social threat. In 1492, an ordinance was passed in Coventry forbidding women under the age of 50 to live alone. Instead, they could go into service until marriage. However, within a century, economic independence for women was becoming increasingly difficult.[26] With the arrival of the modern era, women began to lose out even more. The French Revolution legitimised the de-politicisation of French women by denying them the vote. How could they be a citizen (*citoyenne*) without the vote? Women were also progressively losing out in participation in the workforce and work culture because of middle-class domesticity. The pejorative argument that women lacked professional skills was advanced to deny opportunities to women, who were deemed unfit for prime jobs.

In 1990, Ronnie J. Steinberg uncovered the often arbitrary and subjective basis of skill determination, and its relationship to job awards. She concluded that males exerted considerably more power over the definition of skills, and the maintenance of those definitions.[27] Apart from Steinberg, P. Sawchuk highlighted the fallacy of the skills debate:

> the failure to recognize the socially situated and collaborative nature of all skill performance; the failure to openly address the imbalances of power and thus the tendencies to reproduce inequities; the failure to recognize economic, sectoral, organizational dynamics; and finally the failure to address the conflation of 'actual skill/competency' versus relations of 'power/control'.[28]

By exposing the caveat—that skills are not gender-neutral and are influenced by one's location and situation—in the skills debate, feminist authors were able to argue that skills are defined as a non-racial and un-gendered concept because of the conscious decision of certain groups. Where migration is concerned, the skills debate proved to be particularly problematic for women. It could be used to both displace and deny asylum. Even when the skills of forced migrants are considered real, they can be viewed with suspicion. Skill was used as a construct particularly to deny 'aliens', and among all 'aliens', the skill regime deprived women the most. Most forced-migrant women lost out when skills were considered crucial for asylum. The qualities they did not possess were often defined as skills, whereas racial threat perceptions made the qualities they did possess suspect.

The entire construction of the skills regime played into the fear of migrants. During his first term as President, Donald Trump's response to the caravan people portrayed the racial connotations of forced migration. According to one feminist social scientist:

> ...both sensationalist and more moderate immigration restriction efforts rely upon seemingly identity-neutral narratives of protecting the well-being of a vulnerable national citizenry to justify the illicitly racialized and gendered treatment of undocumented immigrants and their citizen children. Commonsensical notions of biological reproduction are welded to emotional distress over national precariousness, weighing down abstract claims that immigration generates a national state of emergency.[29]

Compounding this is the notion that forced migrants, particularly forced-migrant women, lack the necessary skills.

FORCED MIGRATION AND SOUTH ASIA

In the context of South Asia, forced migration was closely related not only to race and religion, but also to gender. We have already discussed the issue of race. Now let us turn to the issue of gender. Modern states that are built on gender differences develop a precarious relation with its women. Women become both subjects of the state and its other. In pluralistic societies such as those found in South Asia, 'the modern projects of national independence, state building, and economic development have had distinctive gender implications and outcomes'.[30] The nation-building projects in South Asia have led to the creation of a homogenised identity of citizenship. State machineries seek to create a 'unified' and 'national' citizenry that accepts the central role of the existing elite. This is done through the privileging of majoritarian, male, and monolithic cultural values that deny space to differences. Such a denial has often led to further segregation of the marginalised, on the basis of caste, religion, and gender, from the collective 'we'. One way of marginalising women from the body politic is by targeting and displacing them in times of state versus community conflict.[31] As a refugee, a woman loses her individuality, subjectivity, citizenship, and her ability to make political choices. As political non-subjects, refugee women emerge as the symbol of difference between us/citizens and the other/refugees/non-citizens. Refugee women become the material for the symbolic construction of the nation's boundaries.

By studying women's displacement in South Asia, literary writers and social analysts alike have come up with theoretical assumptions about the position of women in discourses on citizenship, state, and statelessness. In discussing women's experiences of displacement, scholars have portrayed how, as dislocated subjects, women negotiate spaces to retrieve agency in the face of institutional apathy. Sri Lankan analysts were the first to privilege women's experiences in refugee discourses in South Asia. Selvy Thiruchandran, Sasanka Perera, and others have claimed the centrality of women as dislocated subjects. Perera, in his study on the districts of Monaragala and Hambantota, worked on households that were formerly headed by male members but are now headed by female members. He foregrounded women's experiences of coping with trauma, and how they still manage to continue with their everyday lives in the face of depression, and the lack of economic opportunities and justice. Perera called for people working with displaced populations to be more sensitive to women, as in most cases it is the women who have taken up the burden of providing stability to their families.[32] Darini Rajasingham Senanayake wrote on how strongly women occupied the front stage during the civil war in Sri Lanka. Women stood out as individuals or as small groups, exposing atrocities and violations of dignity. Senanayake says that women's history does have triumph. There is powerlessness and disappointment, but also dreams and hopes.[33] The aforementioned scholarship thus recognised that even in their marginality, refugee women are never merely victims.

Bolan Gangopadhyay's essay on women refugees from East Pakistan portrays how women exert agency even in situations of marginality.[34] It has been recognised that women refugees from East Pakistan/Bangladesh have altered the work pattern of women in Bengal, and changed the definition of what constitutes a *bhadramahila*.[35] Women have often used their marginality to retrieve agency; Prem Nath Bazaz's *Daughters of the Vitasta: A History of Kashmiri Women from Early Times to the Present Day* (2011) is a case in point with regard to women in Kashmir. Afghan women in Pakistan have for long agitated for their voices to be heard in peace-making. Dislocation is without doubt a debilitating experience, but there are many exceptions where women have transformed it into an empowering one, often assuming new roles as heads of households. Such experiences have increased their confidence, although at times they might even have contributed to their trauma. To reinforce this scholarly narrative with a personal anecdote: I have met a number of women in camps in Sri Lanka who have used dislocation as an empowering incident. They have willingly assumed the role of breadwinners. When these women take refuge in a different country, they assume agency even in the face of opposition from asylum-giving states because in a new location, they are able to transcend patriarchal control. Sometimes repatriation can seem problematic because these women are then forced back within the control of traditional patriarchy.

The aforementioned studies on women's forced displacement work against a state-centric narrative that views refugee women as mere victims. They direct attention towards the argument that state policy often results in the creation of refugees. State policy is not un-gendered. It results from a political effort to homogenise citizenship—the ruling elites decide who belongs and who does not. Rape, sexual assault, and other gendered crimes are perpetrated against women to dislocate civil society. Crimes against women are then trivialised as a natural result of conflict. Therefore, death or serious threat to liberty becomes a reason for asylum, but rape or vulnerability to human trafficking does not. Such a value judgement makes it even more difficult for women to seek asylum. This is a way of reducing the importance of crime against women, and then marginalising women and reducing them to the status of political non-subjects. Narratives based on the responses of South Asian states fail to do so because governmental discourse reduces women to the status of victims, and then justifies their experiences as marginal and hence unimportant. Only by retrieving refugee women's own voices, and not dismissing their individual experiences as anecdotal, can we centre the marginal.

Eileen Pittaway and Linda Bartolomei say that for too long, the prevailing discourse has portrayed refugee women and girls as a vulnerable minority. This has been reinforced by media stories and fundraising advertisements, which depict them as helpless and hopeless. It is true that these women are vulnerable, but so are the men who become victims of forced migration. An often asked question is: Why must women's experiences be privileged? To answer this question, I draw attention to the differences in the needs of men and women. While sharing with men and boys the same basic needs of food, water, shelter, sanitation, and security, women also have additional and significantly different needs. The most important difference is that of endemic and often systemic sexual and gender-based violence against women and girls. Men and boys are also victims of sexual and gender-based violence, which again generates the need for varied and appropriate responses to the different layers and levels of sexual abuse and assault that men and women have to face.[36] If one negates the sexual abuses faced by Rohingya women, both in their state of origin and in their host countries, then one misses the larger picture of why a gendered analysis is important.

To concentrate only on the vulnerability of refugee women through the axis of race, religion, or gender can be a disservice to these women. As many feminist scholars have shown us, the service that these women provide to their host countries as well as to their families is testimony to their strengths. In the post-Partition days, refugee women and girls entered the workforce in large numbers, thereby allowing middle-class women to access other forms of work. Ishita and Deepita Chakravarty write,

> the three decades after independence were crucial in shaping domestic service as a strongly feminized area of work with a large-scale presence of girl children working in the urban areas. The high rate of participation by very young girls in paid work, in a state which historically has a low female work participation rate, has made the case unique.[37]

Other authors also talk about the emancipating experience of the *bhadramahila* joining the workforce in the post-Partition period.[38]

Forced-migrant women perform enormous services for their families. They concentrate 'all their efforts on bringing up their children in a safe and stable environment'.[39] In the case of Sri Lankan refugees, we have seen, more often than not, how many more women sought work than the men in their families. Women take up temporary labour to cope with material difficulties. Even in the camps in Gujarat after the riots in 2002, women were continuously looking for work.[40] It is the women who 'maintain cohesiveness within the family by consciously assessing the situation and deciding that their duty is to provide their dependents with financial and emotional security'.[41] Regarding the situation of women in Sri Lanka, one analyst has commented: 'displacement and camp life had also provided spaces for empowerment for several Tamil women who had taken on the role of head of household for various reasons'.[42] Women have had a great impact both in displacement and in rehabilitation, and the masculinist and mainstream narratives have often forgotten that.[43]

The Intersection of Race and Gender: The Forced Migrant

In this chapter, I have tried to show how race and gender have impacted the citizenship question, thereby impacting questions of forced migration. Race becomes the ground for deciding who belongs and who does not. Forced migrants are created as a result of conscious will, and gender becomes the axis along which groups are made vulnerable. Women's bodies are transformed into borders placed at the centre of the debate on belonging. On the intersection of race and gender in the refugee question, Pittaway and Bartolomei comment:

> During armed conflict, women can become the targets of 'ethically motivated gender-specific' forms of violence. Ideological frameworks developed by extreme forms of nationalism and fundamentalism that reify women's image as 'bearers of the culture and values' have led to widespread sexual assaults against women as political acts of aggression. Such acts of sexual aggression are often fuelled by race and gender based propaganda. An additional intersection of race and gender is the forcible impregnation of females from one ethnic group by males from another group as a form of genocide. Women bear the direct impact of these actions. Racism, racial discrimination, xenophobia, and related intolerance have increasingly been used to incite armed conflicts over resources and rights within and between countries around the world.[44]

In the recent past, Donald Trump's views on South American and Mexican refugees portray how questions of race and migration are intertwined. Our own work on jailed Bangladeshi women and Rohingya women portray how gender and race impact women migrants. In these jails, their children are removed from them, thereby casting suspicion on their capability to be mothers. Therefore, any discussion on forced migration or refugee studies remains incomplete without an analysis of the matrix formed by race and gender, particularly without studying the intersections of race, gender, labour, and migration.

Notes

1. Randal C. Archibold, 'Arizona Enacts Stringent Law on Immigration'. *The New York Times*, 23 April 2010. Available at https://www.nytimes.com/2010/04/24/us/politics/24immig.html (accessed July 2024).

2. Micky Hammon, quoted in Kenneth Jost, 'Should states crack down on unlawful aliens'. *CQ researcher*. Available at https://library.cqpress.com/cqresearcher/document.php?id=cqresrre2012030900 (accessed July 2024).

3. Ryan Vasquez, 'SPLC Legal Director Mary Bauer Talks Civil Rights and Immigration'. Alabama Public Radio, 17 August 2012. Available at https://www.apr.org/politics-government/2012-08-17/splc-legal-director-mary-bauer-talks-civil-rights-and-immigration (accessed March 2025).

4. Manuela Boatca and Julia Roth, 'Unequal and Gendered: Notes on the Coloniality of Citizenship'. *Current Sociology Monograph* 64(2), 2016, pp. 191–212.

5. Paula Banerjee, 'Aliens in the Colonial World', in Paula Banerjee (ed.), *Borders Histories Existences: Gender and Beyond*. New Delhi: Sage, 2010.

6. Robin Blackburn, *The Overthrow of Colonial Slavery*. London: Verso, 1988.

7. Michael Omi and Howard Winant, *The Racial Formations in the United States: From the 1960s to the 1990s*. New York: Routledge, 1994, 2nd edn, pp. 64–65.

8. Toni Morisson, *Playing in the Dark: Whiteness and the Literary Imagination*. New York: Vintage, 1993, p. 38.

9. Kimberly L. Phillips, *Alabama North: African–American Migrants, Community and Working Class Activism in Cleveland, 1915–1945*. Urbana: University of Illinois Press, 1999, p. 40.

10. W. E. B. Dubois, *The Philadelphia Negro: A Social Study*. Philadelphia: University of Pennsylvania, 1899, pp. 487–488.

11. Mae M. Ngai, 'The Architecture of Race in American Immigration Law: A Reexamination of the Immigration Act of 1924', in Ian Haney Lopez (ed.), *Race, Law and Society*, Burlington: Ashgate, 2007, pp. 354–355.

12. Leland Stanford, 8th Governor of the Republican Party, 1862–1863, Inaugural Address, 10 January 1862, California State Library, 2018. Available at http://governors.library.ca.gov/addresses/08-Stanford.html (accessed July 2024).

13. Ranabir Samaddar, 'Histories of the late nineteenth and early twentieth century immigration and our times'. *Current Sociology Monograph* 66(2), 2018, pp. 192–208.

14. J. P. Mills, 'A Note on the Future of the Hill Tribes of Assam and the Adjoining Hills in a Self-Governing India', and R. N. Reid, 'A Note on the Future of the Present Excluded, Partially Excluded and Tribal Areas of Assam', in Fuji Takeshi (ed.), *Mirrors of the Colonial State: The Frontier Areas between North East India and Burma*. New Delhi: Manohar Publishers, 2001, pp. 203–205.

15. Shri Kuladhar Chaliha, in *The Constituent Assembly Debates*, Vol. IX, Tuesday, 6 September 1949, pp. 1–2. Available at http://parliamentofindia.nic.in/debates/vol9p27a.htm (accessed July 2024).

16. Shri Brajeshwar Prasad, in *The Constituent Assembly Debates*, Vol. IX, Tuesday, 6 September 1949, p. 3. Available at http://parliamentofindia.nic.in/debates/vol9p27a.htm (accessed July 2024).

17. Shri Gopinath Bordoloi, in *The Constituent Assembly Debates*, Vol. IX, 8 September 1949, p. 4. Available at http://parliamentofindia.nic.in/debates/vol9p27a.htm (accessed July 2024).

18. See Sabyasachi Basu Ray Chaudhury and Ranabir Samaddar (eds), *The Rohingya State in South Asia: People Without a State*. Oxon and New York: Routledge, 2018, p. 8. Much of what is discussed here is taken from this book.

19. Ibid., p. 12.

20. Md. Razidur Rahaman, 'Rohingya: The Community of No Human Rights'. *The Daily Observer*, 13 April 2017.

21. Ibid., p. 4.

22. Brenda Belak, 'Double Jeopardy: Abuse of Ethnic Women's Human Rights in Burma'. *Cultural Survival Quarterly Magazine* 24(3), 31 October 2000, p. 24.

23. Michael Safi, 'Tied to trees and raped'. *The Guardian*, 18 September 2018. Available at https://www.theguardian.com/world/2018/sep/18/tied-to-trees-and-raped-un-report-details-rohingya-horrors (accessed July 2024).

24. 'One Year on, Rohingya Women and Girls Seek Safety and a Chance to Heal'. *United Nations Population Funds, News Section*, 24 August 2018. Available at https://www.unfpa.org/news/one-year-rohingya-women-and-girls-seek-safety-%E2%80%93-and-chance-heal (accessed July 2024).

25. Carolyn Merchant, *The Death of Nature: Women, Ecology and the Scientific Revolution*. New York: Perennial Library, 1980, p. 155.

26. Boatca and Roth, 'Unequal and Gendered', p. 193.

27. Ronnie J. Steinberg, 'Social Construction of Skill: Gender, Power and Comparable Worth'. *Work and Occupations* 17(4), 1990, pp. 449–482.

28. P. Sawchuk, 'Labour Perspectives on the New Politics of Skill and Competency Formation: International Reflections'. *Asian Pacific Education Review* 9(1), 2008, p. 54.

29. Katie E. Oliviero, 'The Immigration State of Emergency: Racializing and Gendering National Vulnerability in the Twenty-First-Century Citizenship and Deportation Regimes'. *Feminist Formations* 25(2), 2013, p. 3.

30. Valentine M. Moghadam, quoted in Paula Banerjee, 'Women, Trafficking and Statelessness in South Asia', in Ranabir Samaddar and Sanam Roohi (eds), *State of Justice: Issues of Social Justice*, Vol. IV. New Delhi: Sage, 2009, p. 452.

31. Ibid., p. 452.

32. Sasanka Perera and Selvy Thiruchandran, *Stories of Survivors: Socio-political Contexts of Female Headed Households in Post-Terror Southern Sri Lanka*, Vol. I. New Delhi: Vikas Publishing House, 1999.

33. Darini Rajasingham-Senanayake, 'Post Victimisation: Cultural Transformation and Women's Empowerment in War and Displacement', in Selvy Thiruchandran (ed.), *Women, Narration and Nation: Collective Images and Multiple Identities*. New Delhi: S. Chand & Company Ltd, pp. 136–137.

34. Bolan Gangopadhyay, 'Reintegrating the Displaced, Refracturing the Domsestic: A Report on the Experiences at Uday Vila', in Pradip Bose

(ed.), *Refugees in West Bengal: Institutional Practices and Contested Identities*. Kolkata: Calcutta Research Group, 2000, pp. 98–105.

35. Manju Chattopadhyay, 'Refugee Women in Bengal'. *Refugee Watch* 10 & 11, 2000, pp. 45, 47.

36. Linda Bartolomei and Eileen Pittaway, 'From Rhetoric to Reality: Achieving Gender Equality for Refugee Women and Girls'. World Refugee Council Research Paper No. 3, August 2018, p. 3. Available at https://www.cigionline.org/sites/default/files/documents/WRC%20Research%20Paper%20no.3_0.pdf (accessed July 2024).

37. Ishita Chakravarty and Deepita Chakravarty, 'For Bed and Board Only: Children Domestic Workers in Post Partition Calcutta (1951–1981)'. *Modern Asian Studies* 47(2), 2013, p. 585.

38. Jasodhara Bagchi, 'Women Since Independence', pp. 42–43, and Bharati Ray, 'Women in Calcutta: The Years of Change', in Sukanta Chaudhuri (ed.), *Calcutta: The Living City*, Vol. II. Calcutta: Oxford University Press, 1995.

39. Gameela Samarasinghe, 'Stories of Coping', in Perera and Thiruchandran (eds), *Stories of Survivors*, p. 113.

40. Comment attributed to Elaben Bhatt of SEWA in Vasudha Dhagamwar, 'The Women in Gujarat's Camps–I'. *The Hindu*, 22 May 2002, p. 1.

41. Samarasinghe, 'Stories of Coping', p. 118.

42. Rajasingham-Senanayake, 'Post Victimisation', p. 143.

43. Paula Banerjee, 'Resisting Erasure: Women IDPs in South Asia', in Paula Banerjee, Sabyasachi Basu Raychowdhury, and Samir Das (eds), *Internal Displacement in South Asia: The Relevance of the UN Guiding Principles*. New Delhi: Sage, 2005.

44. Linda Bartolomei and Eileen Pittaway, 'Refugees, Race and Gender: The Multiple Discrimination Against Refugee Women'. *Refuge* 19(6), 2001, p. 23.

8

Asian Women Domestic Workers in the Gulf

Experiences from Kerala, Sri Lanka, and the Philippines

Ilina Sen

Introduction

This chapter focuses on the challenges faced by women domestic workers from three sending countries, and discusses the commonality and differences in their experience. Contrary to popular belief, women domestic workers and caregivers are often the main earning members of impoverished families in Kerala and Sri Lanka. Single Muslim women dominate the migrant streams from South Asia, although women from Hindu, Buddhist, and Christian communities migrate as well, breaking yet another myth about women's mobility for economic purposes. Domestic workers from Kerala and Sri Lanka are both documented and undocumented. The undocumented women workers from Kerala live and work in insecure conditions and are heavily dependent on a network of touts and corrupt officialdom, such as the infamous and unofficial 'Kasergode Embassy' (KE), who sometimes provides assistance at a price, and at all times, functions as a surveillance and regulatory agency over these women's lives. While working conditions differ between employment at Emirati households and expatriate South Asian ones, women workers, particularly the undocumented ones, live in perpetual fear of running foul of the criminal justice systems in the Gulf. In this situation, the touts of the KE, who are their exploiters, assume a double role as their helpers and protectors, thereby tightening their control over the women.

Among the sending countries, the Philippines is unique in running (since 2015) a sustained pre-migration training programme for unskilled women workers prior to departure, which includes components of legal literacy, skill development, financial accounting and savings systems, as well as re-integration issues in the family and community once they come back home. This offers them a certain level of formal protection during their sojourn in the Gulf. However, in view of the sheer volume of migrant workers, both male and female, in the major Gulf countries, there is in effect only minimal protection from home government consular services in ordinary situations. It is important that official agencies take cognizance of the phenomenon of migration of single women on the lowest rung of the job market in the Gulf, and of the extent and volume of the same. It is also incumbent upon the countries of origin and destination, along with multilateral organisations such as the International Labour Organization (ILO) and international bodies like UN Women, to collaborate in establishing legal frameworks, enforcement mechanisms, and welfare programmes aimed at protecting these women from exploitation, abuse, and trafficking.

Women's Solo Migration: Empowerment or Vulnerability?

The oil price hike of 1973 and the consequent earnings of large revenue had accelerated a process of industrialisation and social change in West Asian countries, necessitating the services of a lot of foreign workers. Large numbers of workers have been migrating to West Asia from India since then. Migration, which started with a few thousand per year during the mid-1970s, rapidly grew to an estimated 1.5 million Indian workers in the Gulf by the early 1990s.[1] By 2023, the number of Indian migrants in the Gulf had increased to over 9 million.[2] Similarly, migration from the

Philippines surged, with female migration increasing by 63 per cent between 1965 and 1990, and as of 2021, there were 2.2 million overseas Filipino workers (Philippine Statistics Authority, 2021).[3]

A general assumption is that Gulf migrants are mostly single men. However, as scholars like Nana Oishi (2002)[4] have pointed out, the feminisation of international labour migration is now a global trend. The percentage of women in the migrant population (both permanent immigrants and temporary migrants) has been increasing in the post-war period,[5] and now women comprise the majority of international migrants. Quoting Hania Zlotnik (1998),[6] Oishi estimates that the number of female migrants across the world has increased by 63 per cent—from 35 million to 57 million—between 1965 and 1990, an increase 8 per cent higher than that of male migrants. In the US, in 1998, 53.5 per cent of newly admitted immigrants were women.

Women are no longer just following their fathers or husbands—they migrate in their own capacities as workers. However, as the number of migrant women increased, the incidence of abuse and exploitation has also risen. Since most migrant women work at the bottom rung of the occupational hierarchy, they are extremely vulnerable. The vast majority of them work as housemaids, entertainers, nurses, and factory workers. Housemaids are especially vulnerable because they work in private homes where the authority can conduct very little inspection. Problems they face include sexual harassment, rape, non-payment or underpayment of wages, verbal/physical abuse, and so on.

Because of these growing problems, many international organisations have started addressing the issue of female migration. For instance, the UN Population Conference in Cairo, the UN Women's Conference in Beijing, the General Assembly, and other international conferences and meetings have been addressing the problems that migrant women are facing. The UN General Assembly adopted the Resolution on Violence against Migrant Women Workers in 1994. This Resolution was also adopted by the UN Commission on the Status of Women and the Commission on Human Rights, both of which have started taking initiatives to encourage member states to adopt and implement effective measures to protect migrant women. However, despite the growth of attention on one hand and the challenges and abuses that migrant women face during their emigration and employment on the other, there has been no systematic research to explain the mechanism and the patterns of international female migration.

Women's larger propensity to emigrate for low-skilled jobs is an indication of their comparatively greater 'agency', as in the Philippines and Sri Lanka. However, it can also be construed as a response to the desperate circumstances in which loss of rural livelihoods, poverty, conflict, and other variables may be pushing them. Thus, empowerment and vulnerability act as a double bind to push women to migrate in search of insecure but comparatively better paid jobs, which they can access in the Gulf. The respective importance of the 'push' and 'pull' factors may vary in individual or group decisions to migrate at any given point in time.

Female Migration into Gulf-based Housework from Kerala

As of 2023, the total number of Indian migrants in West Asia was estimated to be over 9 million, with more than 2.5 million coming from Kerala. Kerala now receives an annual remittance of approximately Rs 90,000 crore from Gulf nations, reflecting the growing dependence of its economy on Gulf migration.[7] Migration and the flow of remittances had resulted in unprecedented changes in Kerala's economy since the mid-1970s.[8] Extensive economic, social, and cultural changes have resulted from this process in the Kerala homeland, including a decrease in supply and an increase in the demand for unskilled workers, as well as social mobility among the families of migrant workers. There is by now sufficient evidence to indicate that the Gulf migration story is not a simple narrative. An entry in *Countercurrents* (2018)[9] indicates, on the basis of replies received to a Right to Information (RTI) query filed by Venkatesh Nayak, that 10 Indian workers die in the Gulf nations per day—for each $1 billion remitted, 117 deaths occur.

Between 2012 and mid-2018, more than 24,570 Indian workers died in six Gulf countries—Bahrain, Kuwait, Oman, Qatar, Saudi Arabia, and the United Arab Emirates (UAE).

One major problem in the existing literature on Kerala's (and more generally, South Asia's) Gulf migration is an aggregation of Gulf migrant experiences. This is born both of reliance on statistical data and survey work and the use of such generalising glosses as 'migrant' or 'Gulf'. It is important to read the nuances in the Gulf migration story. That women, especially single women, are significant actors in the migration story is generally not understood or acknowledged. Economic hardship, declining returns from agriculture, and desertion by male partners are among the reasons that have pushed women to enter the unskilled-job market in the Gulf as solo flyers, and in this lies their story of daring, overcoming odds, and at the same time being vulnerable and dependent on systemic forces that are at best semi-criminal in nature.

As Caroline and Filippo Osella (2008)[10] have pointed out on the basis of their oral history collection with migrant women from Kerala working in the Gulf,

> Women have an especially strong future orientation and a willingness to overlook many hardships in order to furnish their kids with a *chance*: sacrifice and struggle now for the sake of an imagined future. Women are not speaking of themselves having a comfortable old age if their children do well: the future being planned for is not their own, but is child-focused. As ... case studies ... suggest, for women, husband's career prospects and aging parents' expectations of support are secondary to the imperative of maximising children's life-chances. Indeed, there is a clear expectation ... that older generations must cede to younger and fit in with their needs. While fathers must balance their own career or lifestyle aspirations with consideration for their children, grandparents also have to make sacrifices.

Their findings also seem to indicate that many of the better educated Kerala migrants use the Gulf as a stage post en route to the UK or the USA, while those who are less qualified and have fewer options cling on to their Gulf locations.

An important piece of qualitative research by Bindhulakshmi P. (2018)[11] gives us rare insights into the world of undocumented women domestic workers from Kerala who are working in Qatar and the UAE. The Indian government forbids those with education below the Class 10 level from leaving the country without obtaining emigration clearance. Passports issued to such persons carry a clear ECR (emigration clearance required) stamp. However, the process of obtaining an ECR, which is supposed to follow statutory checks, is where the corruption begins. An emigration clearance is available at a price, and through touts, many of whom belong to the Muslim majority Kasergode district in north Kerala. An organised illegal network based in Kasergode is referred to in popular parlance as the 'Kasergode embassy'. Since Emirati and Qatari employers prefer Muslim workers, the KE plays an important facilitating role in matching employer and employee, and in greasing the official channels through which this can effectively be put in place. On arrival, the employee is supposed to deposit their passport with the employer for the duration of the contract. In case fraud is detected at any point, the passport is liable to be seized by the UAE administration. In such cases, as well as in cases of lost passports, the KE swings into action to organise a duplicate passport (sometimes of dubious authenticity) because without a passport, a migrant worker will never be able to leave the host country. In this way, the undocumented or semi-legal migrant worker becomes beholden to the KE, which exercises considerable power and authority over the worker. For women workers, the KE and its activities are a double-edged sword. On the one hand, the KE exercises power and authority over the workers, but on the other, they are also a small source of familiarity and security in a foreign land.

In general, Malayali domestic workers are employed in Emirati or in Indian expatriate households in the UAE. Conditions of work are a little better in Emirati households, and it is common for the worker to have a room to herself and better salaries and working conditions there. In Indian households, since most middle and upper-middle class Indians live in rented homes, the worker is generally expected to sleep in the living room after the family has finished its social/family activities for the day. She is also expected to rise early and vacate her sleeping space for the family as soon as possible. The lack of private space and time can be very difficult for a lonely worker, particularly where the bonding with the employer family is insufficient. Some undocumented workers prefer to live in shared rented spaces, arranged once again by the ever-obliging KE. Such workers have a better support structure among the peer group, and access to public spaces like parks and public transport. However, many such workers are more strongly in the clutches of the KE than those who live with their employers. Many women migrate through, and are supported in the Gulf by, kinship networks and/or protective men, who sometimes arrange for sexual labour for the women as an additional source of financial recompense, and are effectively pimps attached to the KE.

Sri Lankan Muslim Women as Domestic Workers in the Gulf

According to Sriyani Tidball (2011),[12] more than 1.7 million Sri Lankans worked abroad, and nearly 600,000 were domestic workers. In Saudi Arabia, the most common destination, they call Sri Lanka 'the country of housemaids'. Of the approximately 120,000 Sri Lankan women who leave each year for the Gulf, 15-20 per cent return prematurely, face abuse and non-payment of salary, or get drawn into illicit human trafficking schemes or prostitution.

Hundreds of domestic workers have become pregnant, often after rape, producing children who, until Sri Lanka's Constitution was recently amended, were stateless because their fathers were foreigners.[13] Saudi Arabia, Qatar, Kuwait, Lebanon, UAE, and Jordan were the major labour receiving countries, which have captured over 86 per cent of the Sri Lankan foreign workers. Their work contracts do not fall under labour laws but under the jurisdiction of immigration authorities. The number of workers who departed for foreign employment in 2009 was 247,119. Female participation was at 51.73 per cent of the total departures, and 89 per cent of the total number of female migrant workers who left Sri Lanka went as domestic helpers. According to data from the Sri Lanka Bureau of Foreign Employment, physical and sexual harassment of housemaids was common in all receiving countries, with Saudi Arabia topping the list of employer abuse reported.

Two of the most notorious cases of Sri Lankan domestic help abuse from Saudi Arabia are those of Aryabathi—who had 24 nails hammered into her hands and foot, as punishment for complaining that she was overworked—and Rizaana Nafeeq, aged 19—who was executed by beheading for allegedly murdering her employer's child in 2010. A vibrant international campaign for Rizaana's release failed to move the Saudi authorities, and her grieving employers refused to demand blood money from Rizaana's family, which apparently was the only way she could be let off. Rizaana maintained to the end that the child had choked on milk being drunk out of a bottle, and that the police had tortured her and made her sign papers in Arabic that she could not read.

The distress migration of Sri Lankan domestic helpers to the Gulf was a direct consequence of the ethnic cleansing carried out by the Liberation Tigers of Tamil Eelam (LTTE) in the early years of the 1990s.[14] There were simmering tensions between the LTTE leadership, who were mostly Hindu and Christian, and the Muslims of Killinochi, who were supposed to be of mixed Tamil, Sinhala, and 'Moorish' origin. The LTTE claimed that the Muslims were agents of the Sri Lankan state and the Indian Peace Keeping Forces. Massacres of Muslims in Batticaloa and Killinochi took place in 1990 and 1992, and those Muslims who were spared and had the means to leave the country, did so. Only the poorest were left, and Rizaana was the oldest child of a struggling fisherman with eight other children. It is fairly clear that she and her family accepted a tout's proposal to send her to Saudi as house help as a way out of a desperate financial situation. Her 'crime' two months into her three-year contract, and her unsuccessful entanglement with the Saudi legal system is a tragic reminder of the fate of hundreds of unfortunate migrant house helps in the Gulf.

There is also evidence from other locations about the abusive work and life conditions of Sri Lankan female domestic workers. Ray Jureidini and Nayla Moukarbel[15] document the work conditions of Sri Lankan women working as house help in Lebanon, and characterise their lives as 'contract slavery'. According to them, since the early 1990s, there has been a large influx of Sri Lankan women into Lebanon, serving primarily as domestic labour in private households. The Sri Lankan government, as with other countries, has actively encouraged the 'export' of domestic labour as it has become the largest single source of foreign revenue for the country. As they become part of the process of feminisation of international migration and trafficking in human labour, both the employment relations and social status of these women leave them extremely vulnerable to exploitation and abuse. The authors' analysis of 70 interviews with Sri Lankan women in Lebanon reveals the living conditions of these women, the treatment meted out to them by their employers, and the manner in which legal and administrative arrangements have facilitated the poor living and working conditions and entrapment which many of them encounter. The authors argue that these systemic issues contribute significantly to the vulnerability of Sri Lankan domestic workers, leaving them exposed to exploitation and abuse.

UN Concerns and the Philippines' Training and Legal Literacy for Domestic Workers

Within the UN system, the ILO and UN Women have long concerned themselves with the issues of migrant domestic workers. An ILO report from 2004[16] notes that migration is recognised as beneficial to both sending and receiving countries. Migration relieves unemployment pressures in countries of origin, and provides productive labour and an economic lifeline for millions of women and men. At the same time, remittances have a very positive impact on home economies, representing a significant source of external funding for many developing countries. In the receiving countries, migrant workers usually take on jobs that are not attractive to national workers, yet are in demand in the labour market. In addition, migration can be empowering in terms of enhancing self-esteem, and increasing the economic independence of migrant workers. However, migration has also permitted unscrupulous employers, recruitment agents, and others some practices that are considered abusive by international standards.

In general, abuse and labour exploitation in male-dominated sectors are well-documented and more visible since men usually work in groups in construction and agriculture. Abuse and exploitation of women migrant workers are less well-known since they are likely to occur at an earlier stage of the migration process or in more invisible situations. Such abuse can include the demand for higher payments by agencies, greater exposure to robbery, frequent violations of physical integrity (punishments, intimidation, ridicule, and humiliation), and sexual harassment.

Since women migrant workers often go into individualised and unregulated work environments (for example, domestic service), data on migrant women in invisible occupations like domestic work is not readily available. Despite the data challenges, it is known that the number of women migrating into Arab League states is increasing rapidly in recent years. In several countries, for example, women migrants represented almost 30 per cent of all inflows in 2000, compared to 8 per cent in the early 1980s.

Many domestic workers in four studies from the Arab region[17] complained of not having enough sleep and being 'on-call' all the time—many mentioned having to wake up during the night to take care of babies. The workload recorded by most of these domestic workers comprised: the general cleaning of the house, washing clothes, washing dishes, cooking, washing cars, ironing, looking after children, playing with them and putting them to bed, giving children or elderly persons a bath, taking children for a walk, assisting children to get ready for school and taking them to school, assisting children with their homework, taking care of elderly persons, helping carry the bags during shopping, accompanying the family during outings and helping in whatever is necessary, mending used clothes and sewing new clothes, and waking up during the night to take care of the sick and crying children or elderly persons.

In addition to these tasks, domestic workers mentioned that their employers expected them to work in their relatives or friends' homes, especially when they had visitors, without any extra payment. Other additional tasks performed by a small number of women migrant domestic workers included giving massages to their employers and hairdressing. Monthly off-duty days were either nil or one day per month at the discretion of the employers.

Although the South Asian countries are major sender states of female domestic help, it is the Philippines, and to some extent Malaysia and Indonesia, which have a better educated profile of expatriate workers being sent out, and which took action on some of the ILO's recommendations.[18] With the ratification of the ILO Domestic Workers Convention, 2011 (No. 189) and enactment of the Domestic Workers' Act (Republic Act 10361) by the Philippine government, the ILO continues to support the promotion of decent work for domestic workers through the Domestic Workers Empowerment Programme (DWEP), funded by the Japan Fund for Building Social Safety Nets in Asia and the Pacific. Collaboration between the ILO and tripartite constituents[19] and other social partners will utilise a training module focusing on the financial and skills development of domestic workers in the Philippines, while reinforcing self-value and empowerment throughout the training. The DWEP has been in place since 2013 and remains active. The initiative continues to be supported by partnerships between the ILO, trade unions, government institutions, and other stakeholders, ensuring ongoing training and support for domestic workers in the Philippines.

The concept of DWEP came from previous initiatives like the Community-Based Enterprise Development (C-BED) and Migrant Women Empowerment Programme (MWEP), which were developed by the ILO in an effort to make business development training an option in any community. Based on this experience, the project conducted stakeholder mapping and consultations among target implementing partners; designed, developed, and translated a training curriculum and toolkit for self-implementation by domestic workers; and supported domestic-worker associations, trade unions, and government institutions to conduct capacity building and training sessions.

Today, Filipinas who want to work overseas as foreign domestic workers must take a training course approved by the Technical Education Skills Development Authority (TESDA). This government unit oversees the country's different training centres, which provide these courses at an expected cost of between $58 and $144 (P2,000 to P5,000). Certificates are valid for five years. Without the course, the Philippine Embassy may not notarise helpers' contracts.

The idea behind the training is to upskill workers so that they can demand higher salaries than workers from other countries. Workers learn about workplace communication, professionalism, and health and safety practices. They also learn to clean the different rooms of a house, wash and iron, and how to prepare and serve food.

The demand for positions abroad is high, as finding employment in the Philippines—in many sectors—is becoming increasingly difficult. Domestic work, which does not require higher education, is widely seen as an accessible job for working-class Filipinas that pays substantially more abroad than the same job at home. Helpers will then need to undergo a performance assessment before receiving their certifications (unless they prove that they have years of experience). Once complete, they have to take this National Certificate to the Philippine Overseas Employment Administration (POEA), together with their work contracts. The certificate is needed for the POEA to issue the helpers' Overseas Employment Certificate (OEC), which is required to leave the country.

Although the training is supposed to protect domestic workers and upskill them, there are several reports of some training centres taking advantage of aspiring domestic helpers by charging them incredibly high training fees. These fees can be as high as P100,000. The centres often claim that these fees are needed to cover food and boarding expenses. Government advertisements and posters warn aspiring trainees to be aware that domestic workers should not pay more than P20,000 for everything, and also caution those undertaking a direct hire to assist domestic helpers by finding an ethical training centre: '[Agencies] know the women can easily be forced into paying that excessive fee—there's a long queue of applicants for [each] job'.

At an overseas academy, dozens of women can be seen hurriedly practising different household chores: tightly folding bed corners, cooking Chinese fried rice, setting tables with swan-shaped napkins, caring for small dogs in cages, and drying laundry on the roof. A large group huddled in a classroom peered at a whiteboard that read, 'Duvet—Crosswise, ¼ on spot, ¾ on top', along with a tiringly long list of other rules for making a bed.[20]

Thanks to the Philippine government's TESDA, which accredits scores of training centres to certify foreign domestic workers, women are pouring out of the country in search of work. Although Saudi Arabia and the UAE accept most overseas foreign workers from the Philippines, Hong Kong is also a popular destination, and as of 2023, approximately 197,817 Filipino domestic workers are registered in Hong Kong, a decrease from previous years due to factors such as the COVID-19 pandemic and travel restrictions. [21]

But a painful life often awaits many of them there. In Hong Kong, foreign domestic workers must live with their employers—often in notoriously tiny living quarters—to receive a visa and are not legally entitled to the minimum wage for domestic workers from Hong Kong. Mistreatment of domestic workers is rampant. Horror stories of psychological and physical abuse abound. It is common to hear of domestic workers being denied food and having to be on call 24 hours a day.

The Philippines has some 2.4 million workers abroad, and in recent years, the government has become increasingly systematic about accounting for their safety. A law passed[22] in May 2013 protects domestic workers 'against abuse, harassment, violence, economic exploitation, and performance of work that is hazardous to their physical and mental health'. Among its provisions are the regulations of private employment agencies as well as the requirement that all domestic workers heading overseas procure certificates from TESDA-accredited training schools.

Despite the good intentions of the Philippines state, the fact remains that some domestic workers will return to the Philippines without having made any money—and because common fees range from training school to paying the employment agency that brokers their contracts, their debt could be insurmountable before they even start work. The Philippines experiment is very new, and it is too early to figure out whether the desired results are being achieved under this scheme. The DWEP was successfully launched and, although its initial phase concluded in 2015, the training modules and toolkits developed continue to be used by trade unions and government institutions in the Philippines. This indicates a sustained commitment to empowering domestic workers, particularly in Southeast Asia. The programme's ongoing use reflects a level of commitment that might be more easily achievable in smaller nation-states with less hierarchical societies.[23]

Concluding Remarks

The above discussion reveals both the difficulties faced by female South Asian migrants engaged in domestic work in the Gulf region and the absence of systematic and consistent data on the volume of migration and issues that the workers might face. This problem is particularly acute in the case of undocumented and semi-legal workers. There is no monitoring authority either in the South Asian consular services in the Gulf countries or in the emigration or labour departments of any major state in the Gulf region in this regard. Qualitative data and a few highlighted cases indicate that abuse is common, yet women are condemned to leading atomised and isolated existences, and find whatever support systems they can on their own. It is in this context that they are forced to rely on semi-criminal groups like the KE—organisations which offer some protection and troubleshooting services to women at the same time as they control and exploit them.

In this context, the Southeast Asian states, especially the Philippines, have shown that it is possible to better equip aspiring female migrant domestic workers through compulsory training programmes that they must undertake prior to seeking emigration. While such programmes may increase the skill and confidence levels of individual women and improve their legal literacy, there is still no effective support structure at destination countries which can make a sustained difference for a significant number of women. Unless there is a political commitment to creating such structures in both sending and receiving countries, not much will change. This requires both a recognition and understanding of the dimensions of the problem, as well as serious work in lobbying and putting the basic infrastructure in place. One sees a long struggle ahead, but let that not deter us from making a beginning, however small, in the right direction.

Notes

1. B. A. Prakash, 'Gulf Migration and its Economic Impact: The Kerala Experience'. *Economic and Political Weekly* 33(50), 12 December 1998, pp. 3209-3213; see p. 3210.

2. Migration Data Portal, 2023. Available at https://www.migrationdataportal.org/regional-data-overview/migration-data-western-asia; https://psa.gov.ph/statistics/survey/labor-and-employment/survey-overseas-filipinos (accessed November 2024).

3. H. Zlotnik, 'International Migration 1965–96: An Overview'. *Population and Development Review* 24(3), 1998, pp. 429–468.

4. Nana Oishi, 'Gender and Migration: An Integrative Approach'. University of California at San Diego Working Paper 49, pp. 1–18. San Diego: The Center for Comparative Immigration Studies, University of California, 2002. Available at https://ccis.ucsd.edu/_files/wp49.pdf (accessed November 2024).

5. In this context, the phrase '*post-war period*' refers to the broader global changes that occurred after World War II and subsequent regional conflicts like the Vietnam War. More specifically, it includes the period after the 1973 oil crisis. See Oishi, 'Gender and Migration'.

6. Zlotnik, 'International Migration 1965–96'.

7. Migration Data Portal, 2023.

8. Prakash, 'Gulf migration and its economic impact'.

9. '10 Indian workers die in Gulf nations per day, for each $1 billion remitted 117 deaths occur'. *Counterview*, 6 November 2018.

10. Caroline Osella and Filippo Osella, 'Nuancing The Migrant Experience: Perspectives from Kerala, South India', in Susan Koshy and S. Radhakrishnan (eds), *Transnational South Asian: Making of a Neo Diaspora*. Delhi: Oxford University Press, 2008.

11. Bindhulakshmi P., 'Making Sense of Legality: Everyday Resistance and Survival Tactics by Undocumented Indian Female Workers in the United Arab Emirates', in Jorge Novak, Madhumati Dutta, and Peter Birke (eds), *Workers Movements and Strikes in the 21st Century: A Global Perspective*. London and New York: Rowman and Littlefield, 2018.

12. Sriyani Tidball, 'Migration of Sri Lankan Women as Housemaids to the Middle East'. Third Annual Interdisciplinary Conference on Human Trafficking, 2011.

13. This refers to the issue of statelessness in Sri Lanka, where children born to Sri Lankan mothers and foreign fathers were not automatically granted Sri Lankan citizenship. Sri Lanka addressed this issue through an amendment to its Constitution and citizenship laws. In 2016, the Citizenship (Amendment) Act No. 16 of 2003 was revised, allowing dual citizenship and making it easier for children born abroad or to foreign fathers to acquire Sri Lankan nationality. Prior to this amendment, citizenship was primarily determined by the nationality of the father, which left many children of migrant workers in the Gulf stateless.

14. Rajan Hoole, *Sri Lanka: The Arrogance of Power—Myths, Decadence and Murder*. Jaffna: University Teachers for Human Rights, 2001.

15. Ray Jureidini and Nayla Moukarbel, 'Female Sri Lankan Domestic Workers in Lebanon: A Case of "Contract Slavery"?' *Journal of Ethnic and Migration Studies* 30(4), July 2004, pp. 581–607.

16. Gloria Moreno-Fontes Chammartin, 'Women Migrant Workers' Protection in Arab League States', in Simel Esim and Monica Smith (eds), *Gender and Migration in Arab States: The Case of Domestic Workers*. Beirut: ILO Regional Office for Arab States, 2004.

17. The four studies referenced here are based on research conducted by the ILO on domestic workers in Bahrain, Kuwait, Lebanon, and the United Arab Emirates. These studies, authored by various researchers, including Sabika Al-Najjar, Martin Godfrey, Ray Jureidini, and Rima Sabban, were based on interviews with and questionnaires given

to domestic workers and their employers. The findings consistently highlighted the common issues faced by migrant domestic workers, such as long working hours, inadequate rest, and being on call round the clock. These studies reflect the challenging conditions under which many domestic workers in the Arab region operate, often without legal protections or adequate support.

18. These recommendations stem primarily from ILO Convention No. 189 on decent work for domestic workers. The Convention emphasises protections such as ensuring fair wages, reasonable working hours, rest periods, and social security benefits, as well as providing legal frameworks to protect domestic workers from abuse and exploitation. It also promotes access to training and skill development to improve their employability and economic independence. The Philippines, for example, has implemented these recommendations through the ratification of the convention and the passage of the Republic Act 10361 (Domestic Workers' Act), which enshrines these protections into law. Similarly, Malaysia and Indonesia have taken steps to improve conditions for their expatriate domestic workers by enhancing training programmes and implementing legal protections. Thus, these countries have developed a better profile of educated and protected expatriate workers compared to their South Asian counterparts.

19. The term '*tripartite constituents*' refers to the three main groups involved in labour-related decision-making processes under the ILO framework: governments, employers, and workers (represented by trade unions). These parties collaborate to address labour rights, policy formulation, and programmes, including those for domestic workers. See https://www.ilo.org/projects-and-partnerships/projects/domestic-workers-empowerment-programme-dwep (accessed November 2024).

20. Justin Heifetz, 'Inside the Dubious Schools Training Filipina Women for Domestic Work Overseas'. *Vice*, 10 April 2017. Available at https://www.vice.com/en/article/inside-the-dubious-schools-training-filipina-women-for-domestic-work-overseas-2/ (accessed November 2024).

21. Heifetz, 'Inside the Dubious Schools Training Filipina Women for Domestic Work Overseas'; J. Tobias, 'Hong Kong's pitch to OFWs: Fairness, good pay, clear protection from HK govt'. *Philstar Global*, 10 January 2023. Available at https://www.philstar.com/world/2023/01/20/2238241/hong-kongs-pitch-ofws-fairness-good-pay-clear-protection-hk-govt (accessed November 2024).

22. The law referred to is the Republic Act No. 10361, also known as the 'Domestic Workers Act' or 'Batas Kasambahay', passed in May 2013. This law provides comprehensive protection for domestic workers in the Philippines, covering areas such as abuse, harassment, economic exploitation, and hazardous work conditions. See https://www.dole.gov.ph/files/IRR%20of%20domestic%20workers%20act.pdf (accessed November 2024).

23. See https://www.ilo.org/projects-and-partnerships/projects/domestic-workers-empowerment-programme-dwep (accessed November 2024).

9

Refugee Economy
An Inside Realm of Global Capitalism

Byasdeb Dasgupta

Global capitalism, as it has evolved in the post-World War II era, always looks for cutting-edge competition in the market, and firms always seek sustainable ways to stay in the competition. This is more so under neoliberal globalisation all over the world, ever since the decade of the 1990s. Under neoliberalism, labour has become the risk-bearing factor in the global market—it bears all the risk of neoliberal capitalism, which is market driven, by becoming as cheap as possible over time. Further, to make labour cheap, there are various ploys instituted by neoliberal global capitalism within the market. One of the most successful means, as enunciated by neoliberal global capitalism in recent times, is the informalisation of the space of labour, which helps to make labour as cheap as possible. Moreover, refugee economy, or the influx of refugees at the heart of the market, helps to sustain this process of informalisation. Hence, refugee economy is not something 'abnormal' that is shaping contemporary global markets. Rather, it is something 'normal', occurring inside the very heart of global capitalism in modern days.

Immediately after World War II, global capitalism was facilitated by the direct intervention of the state. This was, however, not the case during the last three decades of the twentieth century, after the advent of neoliberalism all over the world. Neoliberalism is an ideology based upon the *laissez faire* concept of the market—the market under neoliberalism is at the centre of all economic activities. As such, the accumulation and circulation of capital take place through different markets. The market is, therefore, a panacea. In a neoliberal system, it is held that the market can cure all economic ills and bring in the much-coveted harmony into the system, which is essentially induced by global capitalism.

Gone are the days of the welfare state in the West. Now, neoliberalism demands that the market be given a free hand in all economic activities, while the state will remain as a minimal state and only facilitate the process. With welfarism waning in this age of neoliberalism, many social securities which used to be provided to the citizens of several welfare states in the 1950s, 1960s, and 1970s have also waned. So, what can one expect with regard to the protection of the refugees created since the 1990s with the dismantling of the erstwhile socialist block? At this stage, it is a difficult question to answer. Before we attempt to answer it, let us take a look at global capitalism, and then the refugee problem as they have evolved in the last 30 years of the twentieth century.

The immediate post-World War II era was quite anxious about the sustainability of capitalism as a worldwide system. This fear was more so because of the emergence of the socialist bloc as an alternative to capitalism. Keynesian policies, which warrant state intervention and state-based protection to capitalism and the markets, were adopted in the newly emergent welfare states of the West, and also in the countries newly liberated from colonial rule. State-based planning was given the task of reconstructing Europe and developing the newly emerged Third World countries. Thus, global capitalism remained dependent on state intervention and markets remained subservient to the state. This relationship was accepted all over the world, given the fear of socialism as an alternative social reality. However, by the end of the 1960s and the beginning of the 1970s, a crisis arose from within this capitalist system: it became apparent that Keynesianism was not working to solve the problem of rising unemployment and inflation. In mainstream macroeconomic theory, there is a trade-off between inflation and unemployment. From the late 1960s in the welfarist states, inflation and unemployment started surfacing together—a situation that came to be known as 'stagflation'. This was also a crisis in mainstream economic theory as, at the time, no mainstream solution could be garnered for it. As such, gradually all the countries of the West, which till then had adhered to welfarism, started shunning Keynesianism as a policy tool, which in turn gradually charted the path to neoliberalism.

Global capitalism received an immense boost with the advent of neoliberalism, although the period immediately after World War II was termed by some scholars as the golden days of capitalism. The West adopted neoliberal economic policies, rendering the state a mere facilitator of the market, and at the same time forced the Third World onto the path of neoliberalism. The primary features of neoliberalism are as follows:

(a) Market will replace the state as the most significant socio-economic institution in the functioning of capitalism—both locally and globally.

(b) Anything private—especially entrepreneurship—will be favoured in replacing public investment and the state-aided social security system. Private investment (implying investment by giant multinational corporations) will thus replace public investment. Even social sectors like health and education will be taken care of by private entrepreneurship and no longer by the state.

(c) Foreign capital or global capital will be the determining factor of economic growth and development, which, here, signifies large MNC-led industrialisation. This implies an increase in the degree of what is referred to as the primitive accumulation of capital, and the further creation of huge reserves of labour. Thus, labour of any sort becomes the risk-bearing factor for the ascent of (global) capital.

(d) The Free Market is idealised as the essence of the neoliberal doctrine, which states that free and perfect competition is theoretically set as the shape and structure of this market. Neoliberalism follows that the market is a level playing field, where harmony always prevails. It further holds that although governments may fail, the market never will. Thus, for this competition to take place, and for entrepreneurs to ensure their survival, cost-cutting became the strategy of every private entrepreneur (even in the public sector, where any remnant of it still prevails). Furthermore, in this practice, the onus falls upon labour. Thus was the notion of flexi labour conceived.

(e) The basic idea of labour flexibility rests upon four types of flexibilities—numerical flexibility (easy hire and fire and no voice representing the right of labour), wage flexibility (wages can be revised up and down and as and when required), functional flexibility (a labourer should possess multiple levels of skills, as opposed to the Fordist notion of specialisation), and temporal flexibility (also known as seasonal flexibility, this is the numerical flexibility over time).

Given the above features of neoliberal economic policies, since the 1980s, global capitalism has operated through various circuits of capital, both globally and locally. In doing so, it has contacted various types of class processes,[1] some of which are capitalist class processes while others are not, and still others that might have remained outside its scope. From the point of view of performance and the appropriation of surplus labour (which is a Marxian concept), one can distinguish between six different types of class processes as per Chakrabarti, et al. (2012):[2]

(i) Independent or self-appropriative class process;
(ii) Sole proprietorship, which may be a serf-based/feudal/capitalist class process that is essentially exploitative, where exploitation is as conceptualised by Marx;
(iii) Communitic class process–I, where one person performs the surplus labour, but the appropriation of that surplus is decided by the whole community jointly, including the performer of surplus labour;
(iv) Communitic class process–II, where the entire community performs the surplus labour, but its appropriation is decided by only one individual, who acts as a representative of that community;
(v) Capitalist class process, where a collective of labourers performs the surplus labour, for instance within a factory, but its appropriation is done by the owner or the share-holder capitalists (the latter resembles corporate capitalists);
(vi) Communistic class process, where the collective of labourers performs as well as appropriates surplus labour.

With global capitalism playing the hegemonic role in the socio-economic system all over the world, all these class processes may exist simultaneously. Moreover, a global capitalist enterprise or an MNC may have connections to these various class processes taken together.

As shown above, not all six class processes are exploitative. Marx defined exploitation as an economic category, and as the appropriation of surplus labour by the non-performer(s) of surplus labour. Note that under capitalism, surplus labour becomes surplus value through market exchange. The market plays its role under capitalism by commodifying every single object meant for economic exchange, including labour power. Class processes (i) Independent Class Process, (iii) Communitic I, (iv) Communitic II, and (vi) Communistic are non-exploitative. The remaining two (Class Process ii and v) are essentially exploitative. A capitalist class enterprise (including the global one) is essentially signified by class processes (ii) and/or (v) above. At the centre or the hub of a capitalist class enterprise (including the global capitalist enterprise), the class process has to be exploitative—otherwise the generation of surplus value and the accumulation of capital will not take place. However, as we have said above, in this age of competition based on cost-cutting among capitalist enterprises, the main target is to perpetually cheapen or devalue labour so as to intensify surplus generation and capital accumulation manifold. Thus, the networks or circuits of global capital are created by joining various types of class process-based enterprise with the main centre of the enterprise. In today's virtual world, maybe there is no centre! Yet, the circuits exist, connecting various capital and non-capital enterprises, including the independent class process-oriented enterprises, with the global capitalist enterprise. As a result, two things are justified, which we find in our concrete reality—(a) labour flexibility in the form of casualisation and contractualisation, and (b) outsourcing and sub-contracting. The network between different varieties of class enterprises (including the self-employed mode) by the global capitalist enterprise is built in order to cheapen and control labour as far as possible.

Within the global capitalist system, or rather, the global capitalist networks, there is a plethora of nodes of informal enterprises. In fact, if one critically assesses the existence of informal enterprises in the context of the global capitalist system, one may come across two different types of informal enterprises—one that is linked with the global capitalist chain and another that is not. We may call the first type Informal Sector I and the second type Informal Sector II.

If an informal enterprise (which may be a one-man show) is linked with the global capitalist chain, it does not mean that the class process within the enterprise will also be capitalist. However, they are essentially exploitative. So, Informal Sector I (even signifying a class process different from the capitalist class process) is very much imbedded within the global capitalist system. Informal Sector II (which mostly caters to the needs of the local economy) is outside the global capitalist chain, but is in some way related to the global capitalist system, by fulfilling some of the needs of the global capitalist economic system.

On the one hand, the processes of outsourcing and sub-contracting an informal enterprise in Informal Sector I lie within the global capitalist system. On the other hand, through market exchange, an informal enterprise in Informal Sector II is related or connected to the global capitalist system in this neoliberal age. Neoliberalism has, in fact, accepted the existence of informal enterprises and operates to provide social security to the workers in the informal sector, which gives it a façade of inclusive development.

Of late, one of the distinctive characteristics of the global capitalist system has been the process of informalisation. According to some scholars, some informal spaces belong to non-capital. However, despite this, the very space is hegemonised by global capital. One particular reason for this rapid growth of informalisation all over the world is to make way for cheap labour, in order to contain the labour cost of production or variable capital *a la* Marx. Another way of cheapening or devaluing productive labour[3] is to create a mass reserve army of labour as far as possible in the present socio-economic context. One way to achieve this is by generating an influx of refugees on some political pretext or other. While the capitalist system is global, the problem of refugee influx, at first instance, may look like a local problem for the host economy. However, particularly in the recent European context, we find that the refugee flows are cutting across international borders, sometimes calling for some sort of global protection system, but in vain.

While global capitalism is an economic issue, refugee influx is mostly viewed as a political issue. However, if one closely evaluates the global circuits of capital as well as the generation of refugee flows, one can see how both have political and economic underpinnings. On the one hand, global capitalism needs the political domination of a space to spread its circuits, including the webs of informal networks. On the other hand, the influx of refugees has a bearing on the host economy. A refugee is always envisaged as an anathema to the working population in the host economy, and a political atmosphere is built around that sentiment among local citizens. The rise of extreme populist rightist political parties in recent times in many parts of the world, particularly in Europe and the USA, is a great example of that. The slogan 'America is for the Americans' has of late gained popularity, standing against provisions of global protection to refugee groups.

The above political scenario is a ploy in the recent context of global capitalism, which is quite comfortable with these refugee flows as they serve as an expanding reserve army of labour. It then turns out to be increasingly easier to control and devalue productive labour in the various class processes mentioned above—the labour which procreates discretionary surplus in an economy. Such is the hegemonic role of global capital. We need to mention here that 'the origin of global capitalism', characterised by the term 'original', or what is popularly referred to as 'primitive accumulation', 'is a continual moment of creation-destruction-recreation of labour power through violence over the conditions of existence' of Third World societies.[4] The origin of the creation of refugees, to a certain extent, is interrelated to what is referred to above as original accumulation. If original accumulation is a continual process for global capitalism, so is the creation of refugees through political turmoil, war, and other reasons, since the continual generation of refugee flows signifies the displacement of local populations from their means of subsistence and from their land, without which original accumulation—or what David Harvey described as accumulation by dispossession—cannot take place.

As a consequence, refugee creation, which expands the global reserve army of labour, and original accumulation from where the refugees have been displaced or dislodged go hand-in-hand. In this context, the refugee, who is envisaged as an abnormal subject in the host economy and foreclosed in the discussion of global capitalism, is very much a *normal subject*, to be hegemonised by the global capitalist system. Global capitalism as a philosophical order forecloses what it finds abnormal from its own perspective. A refugee in the host economy is abnormal in the sense that they lack what a natural citizen in the host economy has a right to. As a result, any concern for the refugee population is framed outside the workings of the global capitalist chain. In the political sphere, it calls for special attention, including the question of statelessness of the refugee population in the host economy.

What happens, then, to the global protection of refugees from the perspective of global capitalism? As we have shown above, a refugee is very much an insider in the global capitalist system, due to two concerns: the continual process of original accumulation, and the absorption of the potential refugee labour force in the informal enterprises (be it in Informal Sector I or II). As a refugee lacks the basic rights of citizenship in the host economy, they are unable to become part of the formal space of the economy, which cannot absorb a stateless person by law. Thus, a refugee has no other option but to be absorbed in the informal space—most of the time at a monetary return or necessary labour value, which is comparatively much lower than that of a citizen in the host economy. Moreover, this absorption is not without violence—there is contest with the local working force, as well as within the refugees themselves. The productive labour of a refugee is much devalued, which in turn facilitates the cheapening of labour or variable capital. Since refugees (particularly the working population among the refugee community) lack most of the basic rights of a citizen in a modern nation-state, their capacity to represent themselves remains substantially weak. It helps the productive capitalists to control labour much more easily. As is well-known in the Marxian tradition, if the control of productive capital is greater, so too is the generation of both absolute and relative surplus from different exploitative class processes, as we have noted above. The informal labour space helps global capitalism to absorb the refugee population and thereby further devalue productive labour. This, once again, vindicates our claim that labour is the risk-bearing factor in neoliberalism, and so is the productive labour of a refugee in general. Hence, global protection for the refugee population is a far cry.

Let us understand the global protection of refugees as a form of social security for them. This social security may include income security, job security, workplace security, skill security, voice-representation security, and some financial security (other than income security). However, as shown below, this very idea of a global protection system for the refugee as a subject under global capitalism is a substantially contested issue. This can be explicated in terms of the Marxian concept of production and social surplus, as delineated below. In fact, in a society, the total surplus generated from various class processes is distributed as production surplus and social surplus.[5] We can write:

Total Surplus (TS) = Production Surplus (PS) + Social Surplus (SS)

On the one hand, production surplus here means subsumed class[6] payments to meet the conditions for the Fundamental Class Process, which consists of performance and the appropriation of surplus labour. On the other hand, social surplus is spent to meet various socially determined needs, which are in no way connected with these conditions. Socially determined needs may include poverty alleviation, environmental protection, addressing unemployment, the needs of the old, the children, and the physically handicapped, to name a few. They may also include the global or local protection of refugees. However, this last need is quite different from the other socially determined needs mentioned above, as they constitute particular needs of a society at a particular point in time, and may be referred to as developmental needs. However, the need for the global or local protection of refugees cannot be considered a developmental need. Further, there may arise a conflict between payments for the global/local protection of refugees and for different developmental needs.

In a political democracy, developmental needs have economic as well as political significance. Whether payments for the protection of refugees will be made from the social surplus or not depends to a great extent on the political climate in the host economy. Suppose social surplus, along with socially determined developmental needs, also includes the protection of refugees. Then, we can write:

$$\text{Total Surplus (TS)} = PS + SS = PS + (SS_D + SS_A + SS_P) + SS_R$$

Where PS = Production Surplus, SS = Social Surplus, SS_D = Payments for needs for the old, children, physically handicapped, etc., SS_A = payments for environmental protection, SSP = payments for the social need of poverty, and SS_R = payments for the protection of refugees.

It is clearly discernible that there is a contest between production surplus (PS) and social surplus (SS). In fact, SS = TS – PS, which implies that social surplus is the residual amount left from the total surplus (TS) after meeting class-based needs in terms of production surplus.

Production surplus and social surplus share an overdetermined and contradictory relation. If class needs are substantially pressing at any time in a society, it is expected that a large share of the total surplus generated in that society will be distributed as production surplus. Therefore, little is left for payments as social surplus. However, if political compulsion warrants meeting the socially determined development needs, it may then be expected that a greater share of total surplus will be distributed as social surplus. Further, there is a contest between social surplus as socially determined development needs and the global/local protection of refugees. In fact, we can write:

$$SS_R = SS - (SS_D + SS_A + SS_P)$$

Thus, the protection of refugees as social surplus payment is residual from the total social surplus, after meeting all the socially determined development needs. As we have noted above, the protection of refugees in the host economy always becomes a political question. Only if the political climate is favourable for the protection of refugees will such payments be made.

Returning to the question of the global protection of refugees, one may come across further complexities in the above distribution of social surplus for refugee protection. If we consider the total surplus globally generated at any point in time, its distribution between production and social surplus will also be global. For example, total surplus may be generated in country A, B, and C, whereas their distribution as social surplus (after meeting the class needs in the form of production surplus) might occur in country D, E, and F. Now, suppose country F is in need of refugee protection. Whether the global surplus will be distributed as social surplus for the protection of refugees will always be contingent upon the global political conditions and the international economic relations between, on the one hand, country A, B, and C (countries from where surplus is generated), and on the other hand, country F, where refugee inflows have taken place. As such, for the meaningful global protection of refugees, a global struggle for surplus for the needs of the refugees has to arise. Yet, this struggle is a political one.

Summing up the main arguments in this chapter, we can assert that refugee inflows and the global capitalist system are compatible with each other, both economically and politically, especially under neoliberalism. Refugees swell the ranks of the reserve army of labour (both productive and unproductive, in the Marxian sense). Generally, a refugee economy is built on the basis of the continual informalisation of the production space. Moreover, both refugee generation and original accumulation are overdetermined and are continual processes under global capitalism. Refugees are usually absorbed in informal enterprises—some in Informal Sector I (linked directly with the global capitalist chain) and some in Informal Sector II (not linked directly with the global capitalist chain, but perhaps hegemonised by global capitalism). In this sense, the refugee as a subject is very much an insider in global capitalism. However, when it comes to the protection of refugees in the host economy, it is visualised as a local problem. The distribution of part of the social surplus for refugee protection becomes a politically contingent issue.

Moreover, there are several layers of contest for the claim of social surplus for refugee protection. Foremost, there is contest between the class needs (production surplus) and socially determined development needs. Second, as far as the claims of social surplus are concerned, there is a political struggle between the claims of socially determined development needs and refugee needs. Note here that socially determined developmental needs are concerned with the citizens of the host country, whereas refugee protection is necessary for those who have mostly become stateless. Finally, the very idea of global protection for refugees is contingent upon global political needs, along with the economic needs of global capitalism.

NOTES

1. Class is a process of performance, appropriation, distribution, and receipt of surplus labour. Performance and appropriation of surplus labour can be dubbed as Fundamental Class Process, and the distribution and receipt of surplus labour as Subsumed Class Process. Both Fundamental and Subsumed class processes mutually constitute each other or are overdetermined, where overdetermination is an Althusarian concept. See Stephen Resnick and Richard Wolff, *Knowledge and Class: A Marxian Critique of Political Economy*. Chicago: University of Chicago Press, 1989.

2. Anjan Chakrabarti, Anup Dhar, and Stephen Cullenberg. *World of the Third and Global Capitalism*. New Delhi: Worldview Press, 2012.

3. By productive labour, we mean labour which performs surplus labour in any class process. We are not using the term 'productive labour' as Adam Smith used it; rather, we use it following its Marxian connotation.

4. Anjan Chakrabarti, Anup Dhar, and Byasdeb Dasgupta, *The Indian Economy in Transition: Globalisation, Capitalism and Development*. New Delhi: Cambridge University Press, 2015, p. 65.

5. Ibid., pp. 297–298.

6. Subsumed class process consists of distribution and receipt of surplus labour.

Notes on the Contributors

Paula Banerjee is the IDRC Endowed Chair on Gender and Forced Displacement and Director, Centre on Gender and Forced Displacement in the Department of Gender and Development Studies, Department of Development and Sustainability, School of Environment, Resources and Development, Asian Institute of Technology, Thailand. She is former Vice-Chancellor of Sanskrit College and University and the former President of International Association for Studies in Forced Migration. She is particularly interested in the human rights of migrants and refugees and is also actively involved in the gender rights movement. Her recent publications include *The Long 2020* (2024); *Gender, Identity and Migration* (2022); *Indian Migrant Workers and the Pandemic* (2021), and *Statelessness in South Asia* (2016). She is the editor of *Refugee Watch* and a member and former Director of Mahanirban Calcutta Research Group.

Sabyasachi Basu Ray Chaudhury is a former Vice-Chancellor and Professor at the Department of Political Science, Rabindra Bharati University, Kolkata. His areas of research interest include global politics, South Asian politics, and refugees, migration, democracy, and human rights in the Global South. His publications include *The Rohingya in South Asia: People without a State* (2018), and *Sustainability of Rights after Globalisation* (2012).

Shibashis Chatterjee is Professor of International Relations at Jadavpur University, Kolkata. His scholarship spans international political theory, postcolonial thought, and South Asian geopolitics. He explores questions of sovereignty, democracy, and global ethics through grounded, critical perspectives. He also plays a key role in mentoring emerging scholars and strengthening South Asian contributions to global political discourse.

Byasdeb Dasgupta is Director and Professor of Economics at the Institute of Development Studies Kolkata (IDSK). He is known for his deep research on labour, political economy, and Marxist economics. Among his notable published works are *Unfreedom and Waged Work: Labour in India's Manufacturing Industry* (2009); and *The Indian Economy in Transition: Globalization, Capitalism and Development* (co-authored, 2015).

Bandana Purkayastha is Board of Trustees Distinguished Professor of Sociology and Asian and Asian American Studies at the University of Connecticut, where she is also Associate Dean for Social Sciences. She is also is currently Vice-President of National Associations at the International Sociological Association (2023–2027). Her research spans intersectionality, migration, gender, and human rights, with a sustained focus on Global South feminist frameworks.

Federico Rahola is Associate Professor of Sociology of Cultural Processes at the University of Genoa. His research focuses on border regimes, urban marginality, and the spatial politics of exclusion in contemporary Europe. Engaging with critical and postcolonial theory, he investigates how detention, migration, and governance intersect within neoliberal and securitised frameworks.

Ilina Sen was a human rights, trade union, and feminist activist, as well as a teacher and author associated with the women's movement in India. She is known for her deep involvement in trade-union activities in Chhattisgarh. She is also remembered for her work on Adivasi ecologies for the NGO Rupantar, which became a role model of alternative healthcare in remote areas. Her books include *A Political Memoir and Sukhvasin: The Migrant Woman of Chhattisgarh*. She was also President of the Indian Association of Women's Studies. She passed away in 2020 leaving behind an indelible mark in the topography of feminist activism in India.

Anita Sengupta is Director at Asia in Global Affairs, Kolkata, and a specialist in Eurasian studies. She was formerly a Fellow at the Maulana Abul Kalam Azad Institute of Asian Studies and served as Director of the Calcutta Research Group. Her research spans identity politics, borders, migration, and critical geopolitics, with a focus on Central Asia and Turkey.

Priya Singh is an IDRC Postdoctoral Researcher at the Centre on Gender and Forced Displacement, Asian Institute of Technology, Bangkok, and Associate Director at Asia in Global Affairs, Kolkata. Her research explores issues of nationalism, identity, gender, and marginality in Israel in particular, and the larger West Asian canvas. She has also been Fellow at the Maulana Abul Kalam Azad Institute of Asian Studies, Kolkata.

Index